NEXT YEAR IN AMERICA

A Family History of Eastern European Jews
in the Old and New Worlds

TAYLOR SHIROFF

Next Year in America

Copyright © 2024 by Taylor Shiroff
Tasfil Publishing LLC
Voorhees, New Jersey
All rights reserved.

No part of this book may be used or reproduced in any manner whatsoever without written permission except in the case of brief quotations embodied in critical articles, reviews, or books. For information, address Tasfil Publishing at info@tasfil.com.

Rights permissions for all quoted material have been applied for cited work that was not deemed "fair use."

Tasfil books may be purchased for educational, business, or sales promotional use. For information, please send an email with "Special Markets Department" in the subject line to info@tasfil.com

Permission is granted to use quotes from *World of Our Fathers* and *How We Lived* by Nina Howe, Literary Executor for the Estate of Irving Howe

Permissions are ongoing.

Library of Congress Control Number: 2024905724

Paperback ISBN 978-1-7354066-4-0
Hardback ISBN 978-1-964014-06-7
Ebook ISBN 978-1-964014-07-4

To Grandmom and Poppop

Contents

Introduction 1

Part I: Russia as Another Egypt 19

1. The Pale of Settlement 21
2. Jewish Poland 41
3. Jewish Ukraine 65
4. Beyond the Pale 93
5. How They Left—And Why 113
6. A Lost World 145

Part II: America as a New Jerusalem 161

7. Arrival in America 165
8. The American Dream 195
9. The Trenton Crockery Company 221
10. Amerikane Kinder 259
11. Into Our World 293
12. Afterword 323

Acknowledgments 333

About the Author 337

Notes and References 339

INTRODUCTION

◆────────◆

When I was younger, my family would cross the Delaware River from New Jersey into Pennsylvania to spend Sunday afternoons with my father's grandfather—the only one of his grandparents still alive when I was born.* We'd have lunch and then take Great-Poppop, as my sister and I called him, around town running errands. Frequently, that involved picking up his favorite garlic-turkey lunch meat and a visit to his barber, though he had only a handful of hair by the time I knew him.

During lunch, my sister and I would fill Great-Poppop in on the latest adventures of our young lives and show him any new treasures we may have acquired. I particularly remember how eager we were to show him the iPod Touches we received as Hannukah gifts in 2008—what would he make of a handheld, touch-screen computer that fit in our pockets? To show off the kinds of things such a device could do, the early math geek in me asked Great-Poppop what year he was born so that I could use the iPod's calculator app to figure out how many days old he was.

Today, over a decade later, I can almost perfectly recall the scene: the five of us sitting at a table in the back room of the Tiffany Diner on

---

* This book is about my father's family—I barely consciously knew my mother's parents. All grandparents, great-grandparents, etc. in this book are all from my father's side.

Roosevelt Boulevard in Northeast Philadelphia. I can vividly recall the simultaneous feelings of confusion, shock, amazement, curiosity, and appreciation that struck me when my calculator told me just how many days my great-grandfather had been alive. I couldn't quite believe it, nor could I understand it. I knew he was very, very old—and indeed, at ninety-two, he was—but I just couldn't imagine what it was like to have been alive for that long: all the people he knew, all the changes in the world he'd witnessed, all the events in his own life. So I asked him to tell me about his life as a little boy.

He did, and he went one better: he told us the story of how his parents came all the way from Ukraine to the United States, how his mother came first, how she earned enough money to bring "her boyfriend" over, how they finally married, and how his father took his mother's last name because she paid for his passage.

I remember looking at a world map when we returned home that day and locating Kyiv, where my great-grandfather told me his parents were from (although as we will see in Chapter 3, this wasn't quite right). I can very clearly recall the sense of amazement and wonder I felt (and still feel) at the magnitude of their roughly five thousand-mile journey. In school, I had learned about how the British, French, and Spanish crossed the Atlantic Ocean to colonize the Americas, but the story my great-grandfather told me seemed like a far more miraculous journey. How did his parents get all the way from Kyiv (or, more accurately, Chernihiv) to Philadelphia?

Over many dozens of visits in the subsequent couple of years, I also became fascinated by the enormous cultural and societal changes Great-Poppop had lived through, not only as an eyewitness but as a participant. There he was, a child of immigrants who greatly preferred Yiddish over their minimal English, a man who was born when horses and buggies were still a common mode of transportation, talking to me, a kid with a tiny computer in his hand, a kid who lived in a house in the suburbs—

a concept that only came to prominence about midway through Great-Poppop's life.

The dichotomy of my life compared to his is something that continues to amaze me. And I still find it hard to understand how he and much of his generation managed to so seamlessly settle in as ordinary Americans, despite being raised in a world that would feel very foreign to us today. Indeed, as with many of his contemporaries, Great-Poppop's own parents literally *were* foreign: they spent their entire childhoods and early adulthoods in Ukraine. How was it that (to me, at least) he seemed just as American as anyone else?

I still don't have the answer to that question. And at the time, I wasn't quite able to form it to ask. I *was* able to ask about his family and why his parents came to America, but my great-grandfather didn't always know the answers to my questions, and many times he simply said, "I don't know." Whether he had ever known, or if he had simply forgotten over the span of his long life, I'll never know. What became clear, however, was that a lot of information had been lost.

After a few more years of weekly visits, my great-grandfather passed away in 2013, at the age of ninety-six. He left, taking with him the last direct viewpoint straight into the world of the immigrant generation that I had access to. So many of my questions could now never be answered, at least not by someone who had seen and lived in that world themselves.

Later, when I asked his daughter—my grandmother—some of those questions, I found she knew little more than I did. What my grandmother *does* recall is something that proved common across many children of Jewish immigrants: those conversations, especially the ones regarding anything before the move to the United States, were exclusive to the older generations and almost exclusively conducted in Yiddish. It was believed the younger ones either did not need to hear or did not need to know. The result, unfortunately, is that *a lot of information has been lost.*

Of course, my grandparents and their siblings can still vividly describe what their parents were like in great detail, as well as many other family members—aunts, uncles, cousins, grandparents. Beyond the generation that they knew personally, however, much of even the most basic information, once again, *has been lost.*

Yet the same way in which you and I could probably go on endlessly describing our parents or grandparents, so, too, one must imagine, could my great-great-grandparents go on about their parents and grandparents. These were people they knew, people they spent the first two decades of their lives with, people as warm, real, and alive as we are today. And indeed, as I began researching my ancestors, I soon realized that those people lived incredible lives. I mean truly incredible—unbelievable.

Whether in Eastern Europe, where our story begins, or in America, where it ends, they endured and persevered through unimaginably difficult circumstances; they managed to thrive under cruelty and oppression; they had the remarkable courage to adventure to America and an impressive drive to ensure their success here.

But what makes their story so incredulous is not my ancestors' great historical significance, at least to anyone other than their descendants. After all, their names do not appear in history textbooks, nor do their hometowns in either the United States or Europe remember them. What makes them so special is the way their stories belong to an even bigger narrative, which is why I wrote this book.

The Exodus No One Talks About

The near-complete absence of any memoirs, mementos, or stories left behind by my ancestors long filled me with more questions, piling on top of the ones I had been wondering about since that eye-opening math exercise with Great-Poppop. When I began searching for answers—originally with a far simpler goal of writing a shorter and more casual personal history just for my own family—I found that my ancestors' stories were part of a much, much bigger narrative.

Next Year in America

My ancestors were among the roughly two million Jews who, between 1880 and 1924, left the Russian Empire and its poverty and persecution behind in favor of immigrating to the United States.[1] Even as an avid reader of history, I hardly knew anything about this period of immigration until I began my research. Before long, I realized I was far from the only one: for many reasons, the story of the Eastern European Jews' immigration to the United States is unfamiliar to most people today. With this in mind, as I continued my research, I felt increasingly compelled by what I found not only to recover my family's story as best as I could, but to try to tell the fuller, more complete narrative. This book is an attempt to tell that fascinating and compelling story: to understand why that two million came, what happened when they arrived, and how their children eventually assimilated in America.

Rather than attempting to tell this story through the overall experiences of Jewish immigrants as a collective group, I have chosen to tell it at the individual level as much as I can. As I see it, there are many advantages to doing so. Tracing the story of an individual person or family from their roots in Eastern Europe to their new home in America offers us a glimpse into the process of cultural change, assimilation, and transformation of self-identity. It allows us to understand what shaped personalities, what made people behave a certain way or do certain things. Focusing on the individual also naturally makes the story more personal and relatable. When we only know the aggregate, we often can only afford to put names on the most special or important characters: political leaders, religious authorities, cultural luminaries. The reality, though, is that most of our ancestors were not in that group—and thus they are effectively written out of most histories. How could we ever hope to know or understand who they were without shifting our focus to ordinary individuals?

The people and personalities in this book were the most natural group for me to choose: my own ancestors. Allow me to emphasize from the very start that this choice is not because my ancestors were particularly special or more important than anyone else's, and it does not mean that the story told here only pertains to my family. Of course, my ancestors had their unique quirks—plenty of them, in fact—but you will find none of their names in any other book. Most were born and raised in towns that I anticipate are entirely unfamiliar to most readers, with the sole exceptions of Kyiv and perhaps Chernihiv. As individual as each of their hometowns was, however, for the most part, they were not all too different. If you are of similar Eastern European Jewish ancestry, your ancestors may very well have been born in different towns in different regions, but their lives and experiences would have had much in common with those of my ancestors. This is entirely normal: it reflects the fact that our ancestors were typical, ordinary people.

That normalcy, that sense of being ordinary, is evident in the second half of the book, where the setting shifts to America. While one of my ancestors gets an entire chapter dedicated to the miraculous rise (and tragic fall) of his own business (a hardly uncommon story in early twentieth-century urban America), most of my other ancestors spent their lives in factories, tailoring and dressmaking shops, and even shipyards. Some moved up in the world relatively quickly, but many did not. If you heard anything about the immigrant experience from your own family, this all might sound familiar. So with my ancestors as our guides, we will explore both sides of the immigrant experience—in the Old World and in the New—through their lives.

As hinted at in this section's name, this period of mass immigration of Eastern European Jews to the United States is one that, given its scale, feels somewhat underdiscussed and sometimes even forgotten. One reason for this is that many first-generation immigrants were reluctant to talk to their children about their lives and families in the Old World. Additionally, and often relatedly, many second-generation immigrants preferred not to tell their children much about their upbringing in the early immigrant neighborhoods, especially if they felt they had "made it out." Naturally, but tragically, that has allowed many families' personal histories to slowly fade and disappear from their consciousness as generations came and went. I'll have more to say about this theme later, but again, I imagine that many readers (especially those of similar ancestry) can relate to the experience of their parents or grandparents never talking about their families or doing so only with great reluctance. Almost every person I spoke with while putting this book together, some related to me and others not, could recall asking their parents about their family and getting a response of "Why does it matter?" or "Why do you care?"

With popular awareness fading and with the immigrant generation now all but gone, we are left with only history as our guide. Unfortunately, but not always for any fault of its own, I have often found the most accessible writing about this era to feel incomplete, to paint with very broad strokes, and to focus on the well-known characters— people who often had limited commonalities with my ancestors or yours. For example, it is easy to say something like "two and a half million Jews came to the United States between 1880 and 1924" without stopping to think about what that sentence actually means. "Two and a half million" obscures anything about what these people were like, their families, their hometowns, their lines of work, and so on. "Jews" is to say nothing of the diversity within the Jewish religion in the Old World and even less about the experience of being Jewish in the New World. "Came to" provides no mental picture of what the process of immigration looked like—*how*, exactly, did my great-grandfather's parents get from the middle of Ukraine to Philadelphia in the first decade of the twentieth century? "To the United States" omits the other countries some Jews immigrated to while also saying nothing about why most came to the United States. "Between 1880 and 1924" attempts to get away without justifying *why* they came within these bounds and why they did not come before or after.

This book is an attempt to answer all these questions—and plenty more—from an ordinary individual's perspective. I have done my best to avoid vagueness and painting with broad strokes; where I have resorted to generalities, it is either because the reality was truly homogenous or because my research hit a dead end. Similarly, this book cannot possibly cover every aspect of the Jewish immigrant experience. While my ancestors so helpfully lived lives that will introduce us to most of what we need to know to understand their world, some parts will be missing. As such, this book occasionally spends little time discussing certain subjects that tend to come up in research on this era and omits others entirely. This is not because I find them uninteresting or unimportant; sometimes it is because I did not find them at all!

Many of the topics readers who are well versed in these fields might be surprised to find excluded or only briefly touched on were either irrelevant or relatively unimportant to the story at hand. A reader seeking a detailed glimpse into Philadelphia's unions and their Jewish members, for example, will be disappointed to find that I have little to say about them (while many of my ancestors might very well have been interested in union politics, I knew of no direct or serious involvement). Scholars of Poland's Jewish history may be surprised that I say little of Jewish life in Poland's bigger towns and cities (in which not one of my ancestors going back centuries lived). And Jewish American history scholars may be alarmed that I say relatively little about antisemitism in interwar America—regarding the quotas for Jewish students at Ivy League schools, for example—or that I have often simplified my discussion of Judaism's continuing evolution in America. (The first of my ancestors to obtain a college degree was my grandfather, who attended Temple University in the 1960s, and none of my ancestors were at the forefront of the debates within twentieth-century American Judaism.)

These criticisms and complaints may well be valid, but again, I am interested in the ordinary individual's experience. The average Jewish immigrant was more likely to be listening to a labor activist's speeches than to be the orator themselves; they were almost certainly in the

United States by the First World War's outbreak, and they had little influence or say in religious matters, even if their behavior helped motivate them. And, of course, given that I use the experiences of my own ancestors to guide the narrative, I am most immediately interested in the things that mattered in their lives, the things that made them who they were.

Let me use this opportunity to inform you that since this book begins in Europe and moves to America as the Eastern European Jews did between 1880 and 1924, very little is said about the Holocaust. In absolutely no way should the reader let this diminish the historical importance and relevance of the Holocaust, which remains immensely important and uncomfortably relevant to this day. I am—and my immediate ancestors were—incredibly lucky for the Holocaust to be largely absent from the main story told here. That being said, my ancestors had cousins, aunts, uncles, and presumably parents who were murdered by the Nazis; some are known to me, but certainly many, many more remain unknown. They deserve to be remembered, which is why Chapter 6 closes the first half of this book with the tragic history of Eastern European Jews between 1918 and 1945. However, I realize I could never hope to appropriately cover such a period—which includes the Holocaust as well as numerous other terribly violent programs targeting Jews and other minority groups—in only one chapter. While this book's purpose, topic, and scope do not allow for a complete history of the Holocaust or much discussion of its ongoing significance in Jewish life, there is no shortage of accessible materials on the Holocaust, and I encourage the reader to read them.

A History, a Story, or Something Else?

I have never been quite sure how to describe this book. Because I am telling this story through the people and personalities of my ancestors as much as I can, it is admittedly more personal than most works of history. Indeed, I wouldn't necessarily even classify this as a work of history. Trust me: this book contains plenty of history, the vast majority of which pertains not only to my ancestors but to the many millions of people whose ancestors were hanging out in Eastern Europe between the seventeenth and twentieth centuries, Jewish and gentile alike.

But while this text contains more than a fair amount of history, its subject of focus is different from those typically studied by historians. While historical works are traditionally concerned with larger or broader groups of people (i.e., nations, states, armies, governments, religions, etc.), this book uses individual people as its subjects. On that account, it might be closer to a biography or a biographical history. A biography, however, tends to center around one person or family. But given that the individuals of concern here are my ancestors, one could technically call it genealogy. While this book would not have been possible without intense genealogical research, I purposefully avoided writing a genealogy, as a genealogy would not have been as relevant to others who don't share ancestors with me. I may have started the research that turned into this book because I wanted to know how I got here, but I imagine few readers are reading this because they care about *me*—they are far more interested, I would hope, in the overall story that I tell. I will weave my limited personal experiences, conversations, and recollections into the latter chapters, but this is still not a story about myself.

I see this book as telling a story rather than being a history. This might be partially a matter of semantics, but I think there is a meaningful difference between the two. History drives this story, of course, but it does so by providing context for my ancestors' biographies. But their biographies are not only interesting in and of themselves; the way their lives evolve and change over time is an important part of the story as a whole.

The story I tell aims to answer questions about Eastern European Jews in the United States: why did they come here? Where did they come from? And how did so many assimilate in so little time? History alone cannot provide relatable, individualized, and personable answers to these questions. A pure biography would leave out too much of the broader historical context. A genealogy would focus too narrowly on my lineage and be difficult to generalize.

For these reasons, I have tried to write a "family history." In some sense, it is a collective biography—but of a family (indeed, many families) rather than any random group of people. Moreover, the collection is relatively small, allowing a focus on individual lives and personalities. By still being some part history, it retains a focus on time and space. I try to answer questions about causation, which naturally requires exploring the contexts in which these people lived. With families and their members as the subjects, considering history also naturally raises questions about change between—or sometimes even within—generations.

The end result, I hope, is for the experiences of Jewish immigrants from Eastern Europe to be better known and understood at a deeper, more personal level. While this book is most immediately about my ancestors, the reader should not forget the bigger picture. If they, too, are descendants of Eastern European Jews who came to the United States in the nineteenth and twentieth centuries, the reader can often swap out the names and places throughout this book for those of their own ancestors. But even readers who share none of these origins at all, even those without any Eastern European or Jewish blood whatsoever, can get something out of this too. The immigrant experience was far from uniquely Jewish. While the Jewish experience did have distinctive differences from the experiences of other contemporary ethnic groups, it still maintained much in common with the largest and most well known of those who came to the United States during the same time frame, especially the Irish and Italians. Given America's status as a "nation of immigrants," understanding the causes, experiences, and legacies of immigration is key to understanding America itself. Thankfully, the varying experiences of my ancestors can provide some insight to help that understanding.

Again, while I have written a family history based upon my own ancestors, this is for no reason other than because they were the most logical people to choose and because they are reasonably representative of the vast majority of their peers. Anybody could have written this book, and we would all benefit from more works like it.

Sources, Spelling, and Other Notes

The job of a historian is to detangle miniscule details from the complex knot of human civilization and sew them together into something coherent. This book is a guided tour down a few threads of that knot, stopping or skipping whenever needed. I should say that I am no professional historian by any means; indeed, a "real" historian might quite fairly say that I am unqualified to write this sort of book. While I am a professional researcher in another social science, I have hardly any formal training in historiography beyond a lifetime of passion for the subject and a few upper-level electives in college.

To reiterate what is hopefully clear by now, this book is not meant to be an exhaustive review of the history of Jews in Eastern Europe or in the United States, and it isn't. As a non-historian, I have relied greatly on a number of historical and sociological works. In fact, this book was only made possible thanks to the many outstanding resources created by those more properly qualified to write them. I cannot possibly mention every resource cited here—more details for all works cited can be found in the bibliography—but a few deserve specific praise.

First and foremost, I owe a particularly large debt to Irving Howe, whose monumental book *World of Our Fathers* stands out within this literature for a reason. Likewise, his work with Kenneth Libo, *How We Lived*, is an invaluable collection of contemporary primary sources; I will reference, borrow from, and quote from both texts generously. Stephen Birmingham's classic *The Rest of Us* is perhaps the book most similar to this one and offers a wonderful template for human-driven storytelling. My biggest criticism of Howe, Libo, and Birmingham, which in no way invalidates their work, is their near-exclusive focus on New York City.[*] For that reason I had to turn to Harry Boonin, Murray Friedman, and Allen Meyers. Boonin's lifetime of service to the history of Philadelphia's Jews has yielded a number of invaluable works, among them *The Jewish quarter of Philadelphia*, perhaps the greatest overview of Philadelphia Jewish history. Friedman's work proved equally invaluable to this project—particularly *Jewish Life in Philadelphia*, a volume he edited. Meyers's documentary books offer glimpses into the long-lost world of Philadelphia's Jewish quarter as well as North, Northeast, and West Philadelphia.

I also owe an immense debt of gratitude to those who published their own memoirs (all of whom are now no longer with us) as well as other published collections of memoirs and primary source materials. My ancestors left behind no memoirs, no journals, no diaries—essentially no artifacts preserving their experience, aside from a few precious photos. Meanwhile, despite its near-singular focus on New York, Irving Howe and Kenneth Libo's *How We Lived* is an amazing collection of contemporary newspaper articles, memoirs, and snippets of fiction that paint a complete picture of the early years of Jewish immigrants in America. Neil and Ruth Cowan's collection of interviews with first- and second-generation Jewish immigrants on just about every topic imaginable, *Our Parents' Lives*, grants us the answers to questions we may have never been able to ask. Mary Antin's memoir, *The Promised Land*, inspired not only the title of this book but perhaps the idea to even write it in the first place. As fascinating as her memoir is, it is worth reading just to experience Antin's gift for poetic prose. Last but not least, I could not have written Chapter 5 or 6 without YIVO's priceless collection of

---

[*] Boston and Philadelphia do not even appear in the index of *World of Our Fathers*, and Chicago gets one indirect mention. The final two pages of *How We Lived* are the only ones dedicated to other cities but primarily discuss moving out into the suburbs. *The Rest of Us* is explicitly about New York, though it occasionally mentions other cities.

the memoirs of Jewish immigrants, *My Future Is in America*.

Far too many works on Russian, Polish, and Ukrainian history—add to that works on the history of the Jews in each of these places—are cited for me to fairly pick out the quintessential among them, but nonetheless I must express gratitude for a few that I could not have written this book without. On Jewish life in Eastern Europe, in no particular order and with many important omissions: Yohanan Petrovsky-Shtern's *The Golden Age Shtetl*, Nicholas Riasanovsky and Mark Steinberg's *A History of Russia*, Orlando Figes' *The Story of Russia*, Serhii Plokhy's *The Gates of Europe*, Norman Davies' *God's Playground*, Antony Polonsky's *The Jews in Poland and Russia*, and Israel Bartar's *The Jews of Eastern Europe 1772-1881*. On Jewish life in the United States, with the same disclaimers: Jonathan Sarna's *American Judaism*, Jenna Weissman Joselit's *The Wonders of America*, Andrew Heinze's *Adapting to Abundance*, Susan Glenn's *Daughter of the Shtetl*, Eli Lederhendler's *Jewish Immigrants and American Capitalism*, and Sydney Weinberg's *The World of Our Mothers*, the much-needed female-focused counterpart to Irving Howe's *The World of Our Fathers*.

I also benefited greatly from a vast collection of online historical resources, including to the *Internet Encyclopedia of Ukraine*, the *YIVO Encyclopedia of Jews in Eastern Europe*, the Polin Museum of the History of Polish Jews' *Virtual Shtetl*, the *Jewish Virtual Library*, and a wide variety of records ranging from steamship ticket purchase records to Ukrainian tax records made available online and indexed by JewishGen. I cannot thank the publishers of these materials enough for making them so easily accessible online. It is all but impossible to understate the wonders that JewishGen has done for Jewish genealogy.

I especially want to express my endless thanks and gratitude to JRI-Poland, which has made an unimaginable number of records from Polish synagogues freely available online. As the reader will see, Chapter 2 of this book would have been entirely impossible without these records. JRI-Poland is a truly invaluable resource for those interested in Polish Jewish genealogy, and I am greatly indebted to the tireless work of their dedicated volunteers. I particularly want to thank Jean-Pierre Stroweis, who (among many other things) manages Staszów's records and generously assisted me in finding the full form of two very important records, even though it took sending somebody to a Polish archive to rescan them—just for me!

I explicitly cite every direct quote, and I have attempted to cite every number and statistic provided within the text. Most facts within the text are also cited, but some are not. That may be the case for several reasons. I have attempted to minimize the number of citations, which often means only one citation is left at the end of a paragraph. I also tend not to cite very broad or general historical facts; I ask the reader to consult the bibliography for the sources for those. Perhaps most prominently, I do not explicitly cite a wide variety of genealogical records. If I had done so, there would likely be well over one hundred citations by the end of Chapter 3, and later in the book, my frequent use of the United States Census quite possibly would have driven us to over five hundred endnotes. Similarly, there are two decades' worth of Philadelphia city directories that I do not cite for the same reason. I feel comfortable omitting in-text citations for these records as they pertain exclusively to my ancestors, but as many of these records as possible can be found in the genealogical bibliography.

While spelling, geography, and terminology might seem irrelevant, uninteresting, or unimportant, discussing them is a necessity when talking about Eastern Europe. I use current spellings of places rather than their historical (often Russian) or Yiddish names: Kyiv rather than Kiev, Odesa rather than Odessa, Berdychiv rather than Berdichev. As those three examples suggest, this is most relevant when talking about Ukraine. While Yiddish has helped (for no fault of its own) to preserve the Russian names for these places in the Jewish mind, Russia's imperialist war in Ukraine, still ongoing at the time of this writing, is a reminder of how important it is to refer to these places by their correct Ukrainian names. On a related note, I set places in their modern-day countries; in a historical narrative, though, I will often use the contemporaneous countries for clarity. For example, in the context of Chapter 3, Chernihiv is a Ukrainian city in the Russian Empire, even though the chapter's title is "Ukraine." Everything should be clear from context.

Similarly, phrases like "the Russian government" refer to the collective government of the Russian Empire: the tsar, his ministers, etc. I have tried to avoid it, but for clarity or grammatical reasons I occasionally refer to the Russian Empire as just "Russia." Except when stated otherwise, "Russia" should be understood to refer to the Russian Empire and not present-day Russia. This is an important distinction: while "Ukraine was part of Russia" is an acceptable statement if "Russia" refers to the Russian Empire, it quickly turns into Putin's hypernationalist propaganda when "Russia" is interpreted as the modern-day nation state or as a historical or ethnic Russian nation.

I thought long and hard about how to refer to the Jews living within the Russian Empire after 1771. The majority of Jews who immigrated to the United States referred to their former homeland as Russia rather than the more exact region in which they were born. Jews from Poland are one major exception: most referred to themselves as being from "Russia-Poland" or some variant thereof, or sometimes even just "Poland." Of course, none of this is necessarily surprising—Poland, Ukraine, Lithuania, Belarus, etc. were all part of the Russian Empire's lands in one way or another, some with varying degrees of autonomy. But it does make referring to the Jews living in these places somewhat complicated. Were they Russian Jews? If so, were they Russian Jews living in Poland or Ukraine? If they were Polish or Ukrainian Jews instead, why didn't they more consistently refer to themselves that way?

In thinking through these questions, it is important to remember that most Jews saw their "official nationality" as a far less important descriptor than just being "Jewish." That is, the vast majority of Jews living in Ukraine would have considered themselves as something like

"Jews living in Russia around a bunch of Ukrainians," and similarly for Jews living in Poland. They weren't themselves ethnically Ukrainian or Polish, nor were they Russian—they were simply Jews living within Russian borders around different Slavic ethnicities. Indeed, there was no independent Ukrainian state at the time—it would not have made any sense for a nineteenth-century Jew living within Ukraine's modern-day borders to refer to themselves as a Ukrainian.

One way to settle this is to simply refer to these Jews as *Eastern European Jews*, a term that I use widely throughout this book. I don't think this is the best description, as it lumps together Jews spread across a huge geographical area (which itself doesn't necessarily have obvious boundaries) with possibly very different qualities and experiences. It is nonetheless convenient. Here, I use it as a shortcut for saying "Jews from the Russian Empire who were living in Russia, Ukraine, Poland, Belarus, Romania, and Moldova" (which is a bit of a mouthful). When necessary, though, I refer to Jews living in Poland and Ukraine as Polish Jews and Ukrainian Jews, respectively, while I refer to all Jews living in the Russian Empire as Russian Jews.

Remember, however, that almost none of them were any bit ethnically Polish or Ukrainian, and they certainly were not ethnic Russians. This also does not necessarily imply any national allegiance. For example, few Jews living in Ukraine had any interest in Ukrainian nationalism until very late in the nineteenth century, for reasons we'll come to understand in Chapter 3. These terms only describe their place of birth or residence, not their nationality.

While writing this book, I often reflected on a quote by an author who had essentially no overlap whatsoever with my research but is a favorite of mine nonetheless. "I always write about Dublin," James Joyce wrote, "because if I can get to the heart of Dublin I can get to the heart of all the cities of the world. In the particular is contained the universal."

TAYLOR SHIROFF

If I am successful, this book will tell the universal story of the migration of the Jews of Eastern Europe to the United States through the particular stories of a few who made the journey: my ancestors.

Part I
RUSSIA AS ANOTHER EGYPT

The Passover season, when we celebrated our deliverance from the land of Egypt, and felt so glad and thankful, as if it had just happened, was the time our Gentile neighbors chose to remind us that Russia was another Egypt.[2]

~ Mary Antin

Chapter 1
THE PALE OF SETTLEMENT

The year 1881 marks a turning point in the history of the Jews as decisive as that of 70 A.D., when Titus's legion burned the Temple at Jerusalem, or 1492, when Ferdinand and Isabella decreed the expulsion from Spain.[3]
~ Irving Howe

To fully appreciate this story of Jewish immigration and assimilation, one must know from whence they came—and why they left. To that end, the first half of this book explores the world of eighteenth- and nineteenth-century Eastern Europe, with a focus on the Jewish experience. We begin our adventure in this chapter by introducing the time, place, and setting that form the backdrop of subsequent chapters, which will zoom into specific regions and specific times. We will get a sense of what life was like for my ancestors and their contemporaries, as well as what they were up against on a daily basis. We will see along the way how closely linked the Jewish experience was to many of the significant events that shaped much of the last several centuries of Eastern European history, some of which continue to be of great consequence today.

Just over a century ago, the Russian Empire was home to over five million Jews—more than half of the world's total at the time, and more than any other nation.[4] Practically all these five million lived in a region now split across Belarus, Poland, and Ukraine, where today, approximately just four hundred thousand Jews live. That extraordinary population collapse can almost entirely be explained by two events. The most recent was when roughly six million Jews, two-thirds of them from Eastern Europe, perished in the Holocaust.[5]

Before the Holocaust, however, was the mass migration of approximately two and a half million Jews—about one-third of all those in Eastern Europe—out of the Russian Empire between 1880 and 1925. The vast majority of them—over two million—came to the United States, while the rest dispersed throughout Western Europe.

To get a sense of how large that migration was, consider this: the Jewish population in the Russian Empire doubled between 1850 and 1897, as it did every fifty years prior to the twentieth century. The number reached a peak when the 1897 Census counted 5.5 million in the Empire. Yet due to the migration, that 5.5 million was essentially unchanged by 1933. Indeed, there were many million fewer Jews in Eastern Europe before the Second World War than there would have been had the trend for the population to double every half-century held up into the 1900s.[6]

The question, then, is why did they leave? What happened toward the late 1800s that spurred the exodus out of Russia? Later chapters will discuss the answer to that in fuller detail, but for now, in short, one can simply say that Jewish life in the Russian Empire had become intolerable by the closing quarter of the nineteenth century. However, although the deterioration in the quality of Jewish life was not sudden and should have been anything but an unexpected outcome, it was not necessarily inevitable. Rather, it resulted from a century's worth of terrible, inhumane, and reckless policymaking—mostly by choice—in the Russian Empire.

The Jews of Eastern Europe

Before the next two chapters fill in the histories of Poland and Ukraine with a little more color, let us first draw an outline of the history of Jews in Eastern Europe as briefly as we can. Without this historical backdrop, we cannot truly understand or appreciate the decisions of my ancestors—and millions of others—to leave and make a new home in the United States. After all, they weren't just leaving the Russian Empire; they were abandoning the lands that had been their home for nearly a thousand years.

Any attempt to tell the story of Eastern European Jews from the very beginning is immediately complicated at the first step: oddly enough, the process of Jewish migration into Eastern Europe has been all but entirely obscured by time. Even dating their arrival in Eastern Europe is difficult. We only know from a few lucky records that have survived to the present day that there was a Jewish community in Ukraine by no later than the tenth century, while archeological evidence such as the incredible discovery of a Jewish tombstone belonging to "David, son of Sar Shalom," who died on August 4, 1203, in Wrocław, Poland, tells us that Jews were living in Poland by the thirteenth century (and likely much earlier).[7]

The lack of a more precise history has left plenty of room for legends. The most popular tells us, with debated historicity, that the Khazars, who ruled over much of modern-day Ukraine over a thousand years ago, converted to Judaism in the eighth or ninth century and that Eastern European Jews have their origins in those who fled from the Khazar state as it collapsed in the following centuries. While the first part of the legend has a real chance of veracity, the second part—which has been used and abused by Zionists, anti-Zionists, Jews, and antisemites alike to support all kinds of myths—is almost certainly false.[8]

While it is difficult to say exactly when Jews first arrived in Eastern Europe, it is relatively easier to imagine what forces pushed them there, physically or figuratively. While Jews scattered far and wide in the wake of the destruction of the Second Temple in 70 CE, an event traditionally pointed to as the start of the Jewish Diaspora, this was certainly not the first time Jews had wandered beyond Israel and its immediate surroundings. Jews had first began traveling and then settling throughout much of the Mediterranean at least a few hundred centuries earlier, quite often owing to their work as merchants. In fact, it was all but certainly these mercantile interests that first brought the Jews to Eastern Europe. But by the end of the first millennium—at which point the Khazars were gone and Poland was first becoming a coherent state—the primary reasons for heading into Eastern Europe were the typical motivators of Jewish migration: expulsions and violence.

After a brief era of varying degrees of tolerance in a few Western European kingdoms, the tide had turned by the thirteenth century, at which point Jews soon became welcome to live in the realms of precariously few European monarchs. Especially after the once-tolerant Spanish and Portuguese rulers banished Jews from their kingdoms at the very end of the fifteenth century, Jews had little choice but to move east across Europe—or across the Atlantic Ocean to the Americas, as a small number of Sephardic Jews did.[9]

At the same time, Protestantism and the onset of the Reformation and the Counter-Reformation that followed reenergized anti-Judaic sentiment, particularly in Germany, making Europe an increasingly unsafe place for Jews to live. It turned out to be unsafe in another way too: plague. While the Black Death ravaged through Central and Western Europe in the fourteenth century, it left Poland relatively untouched. The devastation wrought by the plague—or just the fear of it—motivated many German Jews to flee further east, which brought them to Poland.[10]

It is important to note, however, that it was not only bad things that brought Jews to Eastern Europe. By 1264, the Jews of Krakow had been granted a charter guaranteeing them the right to travel, worship, and trade without interference, an exceptional contract that became the standard throughout much of Poland until the late eighteenth century. In fact, while the Spanish and Portuguese were focused on expelling Jews from their lands, Polish King Sigismund I openly encouraged them to immigrate to his country. Having already expanded and standardized the rights given to the Jews of Krakow two and a half centuries earlier, he guaranteed their right to settle where they wished, granted them significant autonomy, and even allowed them to handle the collection of their share of the tax burden themselves. While some towns continued to disallow Jewish residency, Jews were often permitted to establish their own towns, giving them an important role in settling dozens, perhaps hundreds, of towns across what is now Poland, Ukraine, and Belarus. This opportunity led to far more and far better economic opportunities for Jews in Poland than just about anywhere else in Europe at the time. Before long, Jews played a significant role in the Polish economy as merchants, traders, farmers, foresters and—last but certainly not least— in the production and trade of alcohol.[11]

The external factors pushing them to the east along with the relative freedom and better economic opportunities found in Poland soon made Poland home to one of the largest Jewish populations in the world. Jews went from making up less than 0.5 percent of Poland's population in 1500 to about 3 percent in 1672 and 5.5 percent in 1765. By that time, just about half lived in modern-day Ukraine, a quarter in Lithuania and Belarus, and the remaining quarter in central and western Poland.[12]

Wait a minute—how did we get from talking about Poland to Ukraine, Lithuania, and Belarus? The Europe of this period looked quite different from the Europe we know today. One of the most significant differences, both geographically and historically, was the existence of a very prominent and powerful kingdom: the Polish-Lithuanian Commonwealth. The Commonwealth was the largest country in Europe at the time: at its peak, it included nearly all of modern-day Poland, Lithuania, Belarus, and Ukraine. Most of the Commonwealth's Jews lived in what is today Poland and Western Ukraine—a consequence of Lithuania's expulsion of its Jews in 1495 as well as the traumatically violent history of Jewish life in Southeastern Ukraine, a story we'll get to in Chapter 3.

While Jewish life began to flourish in the Polish-Lithuanian

Commonwealth, it hardly existed whatsoever in its soon-to-be archnemesis: Russia. Russia, which was first born as Muscovy before becoming the Tsardom of Russia and later rebranded as the Russian Empire in 1721, had a very different history. Between its violent, remote, and turbulent rise to power and its relative youth, Russia barely had any Jewish population at all. In fact, in all likelihood, Moscow might not have even been settled by the time Kyiv had become home to its own Jewish community in the tenth or eleventh century. But as the Russian state grew over time, some Jews nonetheless found themselves within its borders, where they were subjected to persecution and frequent violence until they were ultimately banished from the Russian Empire in 1727 and then again in 1742 (the first time did not work so well). Between these banishments and the Russian Empire's continued expansion into what is now eastern Ukraine, the Jews who lived in Russia, or who lived too close to it for comfort, fled across the border to the Polish-Lithuanian Commonwealth, whether by choice or by force.[13]

It was around this time, however, that the glory days of Poland-Lithuania came to an end. By the mid-eighteenth century, the once-mighty Commonwealth had fallen into alternating periods of "anarchy tempered by civil war," as one observer put it. The three dominant Central and Eastern European powers at the time—Austria, Prussia, and the Russian Empire—decided to intervene. In 1772 and 1793, they carved away at its territory, dividing it between themselves, until the Third Partition finally left nothing behind and eliminated the Polish and Lithuanian sovereign states in 1795. Quite importantly, in many ways and for many people, the peoples of Poland, Belarus, Lithuania, Ukraine, and many surrounding regions had to wait well over a century to reemerge as truly independent nations.[14]

The Russian Empire and Pale of Settlement

Over the course of the Three Partitions, the Russian Empire's borders expanded to include the majority of Ukraine (they had already acquired a good chunk of eastern Ukraine, including Kyiv, in 1667), along with a considerable portion of Poland, which the Empire would more completely absorb later in 1830. With borders that now extended through much of modern-day Poland and Ukraine, the Empire also had roughly six million new inhabitants—perhaps as many as a million of whom were Jewish. With all these new lands and subjects came a number of new headaches. Of particular interest to us is one issue the Russians spent the remainder of the Empire's history catastrophically stumbling around trying—and failing—to answer: what would it do with the Jews who now lived within the Empire?[15]

The Pale of Settlement circa 1855.[16]

This was not the first time the Russian Empire had faced such a question, but this time was very different. The Empire had just annexed lands that were home to about four-fifths of the world's Jews—expulsions like the ones they tried in 1727 and 1742 were not going to be possible. New ideas were needed. As the eighteenth century came to an end, Tsarina Catherine the Great attempted to spell out a new approach toward the Jews:

> Her Majesty's love of humanism makes it impossible to exclude [the Jews] from the universal future commonwealth under Her blessed rule, while the Jews in turn as loyal subjects will dwell with appropriate humility and engage in trade and industry according to their skills.[17]

This did not, in fact, turn out to be as "impossible" as Catherine claimed. But why were the Jews even seen as such a problem in the first place?

To be sure, no answer to this question could be complete without noting that much of the problem was with the Jewish religion. Some caution is needed here. While today we might be tempted to call this antisemitism, the Empire's aversion to Jews is better described as anti-Judaism: their problem was on the basis of religion and generally not race or ethnicity. That kind of racially motivated thinking that fueled Hitler's ideology and the rise of Nazi Germany did not yet exist and wouldn't until the late nineteenth century (the word "antisemitism" was only coined in 1879). Russia's persecution, discrimination, and oppression of its Jewish communities were not on the basis that the Jews were an inferior race and had to be removed from society; in fact, as we will see, for some time Russia attempted to bring Jews into Russian life and society (just with some very steep rules and regulations, of course). Instead, Russia's main problem with its newfound Jewish population was that the Jews practiced an "inferior" religion, one that proudly denied not just the Russian Orthodox Church but also Christianity as a whole. Only by understanding this can we understand why, despite its hatred of the Jews, Russia nonetheless sought to baptize as many as it could and bring them into Russian life.[18]

Aside from religion, the Russian Empire also had a more fundamental problem: it struggled to figure out what to do with non-Russians within its borders. That was a particularly pressing issue for the Empire, as its leaders and intellectuals often saw non-Russians as a threat to Russian life, society, and nationality. The unique and often bizarre history of the region aside, one of the most important reasons this was the case even as many of Russia's western neighbors were opening up their societies (at least relatively) has to do with Russia's belated maturation into an early modern state.

It might seem strange at first that in the case of the Jews, for example, Russia pursued such a harsh and illiberal ideology just as Jewish emancipation arrived in many of its western neighbors. But the possibility of Jewish emancipation was in no small part due to the development of a stratified and hierarchical social system in much of Central and Western Europe. States such as pre-partition Poland became used to multiple distinct, semi-autonomous bodies making up the state and society at large: the nobility could do their thing, as could the church, and, particularly in Poland, so could the Jews. The Jews had their own local self-government, complete with their own leaders, lawmakers and law enforcement, and even judges, which seemed to make sense to all parties involved.[19]

While this might seem striking, it wasn't too different from how the nobility had their own estates or how the Catholic Church has its own canon law, independent of local civil law. But while Russia's western neighbors had managed to wrap their minds around the possibility of this sort of thing by the late eighteenth century, Russia was only then starting to imagine how such an arrangement could ever work. After all, so far in Russia the Church *was* the state, and indeed the tsar was really the state (and the Church, too, for that matter). So, then, what could the Jews be? How would they be a part of the Russian Empire as a distinct group with little in common with their neighbors?[20]

The Empire would struggle to come up with a consistent, coherent, and practical answer to this question for the rest of its life. As the Empire developed and expanded in the seventeenth and eighteenth centuries, successive Russian tsars developed a certain idea about what it meant to be a good and proper subject of the Empire, as well as what should characterize the Empire itself. In 1833, one of Tsar Nicholas I's closest advisors, Sergei Uvarov, put forth a three-part ideology soon adopted by the tsar: autocracy, orthodoxy, and nationality. The Empire and its subjects were to be wholly obedient to the tsar; they were to be Russian Orthodox Christians and as ethnically, culturally, and socially Russian as possible. In this regard, the Jews were not the only group that posed a challenge; the Empire had a problem with every nationality dwelling within its borders, from the Ukrainians, Poles, and Belarussians to the Armenians, Georgians, and Tatars. At one point or another, each group (and many others) experienced the suppression of their language, culture, and nationality.[21]

Jews, however, presented some unique challenges to the Russian state. Not only were they not Russian, but neither were they Slavic—and they took pride in their separateness and distinctness. As shtetl historian Yaffa Eliach put it:

> As a non-Christian group, numbering in the millions, with its own distinct cultural identity, traditions, beliefs, loyalties, and institutions of self-government, the Jews constituted a challenge to an absolutist regime determined to exercise control over every aspect of its citizens' lives.[22]

Moreover, while the vast majority of Ukrainians, Poles, and Belarussians at least practiced some variety of Christianity, the Jews emphatically denied that religion. Consequently, they were associated with a number of popular legends, some of which held that they regularly took part in a variety of Satanic rituals or engaged in child sacrifice, and the charge of being "Christ killers" was popular. It did not help that many Jews were skilled and experienced artisans and merchants who could, and often did, outcompete their Russian counterparts, and some Jews even came to own land and property. Hence the Empire was concerned that Jews might continue to provide economic benefits to the Polish nobility (who, bizarrely, still owned many of the towns and shtetls where Jews resided), as they had done for centuries, all the while "contaminating" Russian society with Judaism. The Russian peasants hated the fact that Jews owned many of the region's taverns and were outraged by the idea of Jewish landlords—and don't even get them started on the fact that the Jews seemed to get along well with the mostly Catholic Polish nobility, who the Orthodox Russian peasants sometimes hated even more than the Jews.[23]

With far too many Jews to expel but plenty of evidence attesting to their economic benefits, Catherine the Great and her advisors came up with a new idea: the Pale of Settlement. With "pale" from the Latin *palus* ("stake" or "territory"), it was an accurate name: for nearly a century and a half after its creation in 1791, the Pale of Settlement, which included much of modern-day Poland, Belarus, and Ukraine, was the only area where Jews could legally settle. The Pale was hardly just about residency, however. After all, the Russian Empire was not only interested in confining its Jews to one place, and it certainly had no interest in leaving them alone. The intention was to turn them into Russians, preferably Orthodox Christian Russians, who would contribute to the Russian economy and become loyal subjects of the tsar. They did not want Jewish Russians or Russian Jews; they wanted Russian Russians.[24]

Life in the Pale of Settlement

Of course, the Russian Empire's hopes to Russify and baptize its approximately one million Jews were hardly ever fulfilled. From the

Pale's creation in 1791 through its demise alongside the Empire in the Russian Revolution over a century later, the Empire tirelessly imposed restrictions, mandates, and prohibitions of every kind in an attempt to Russify its Jews.* The details changed as tsars came and went, which meant rules and restrictions constantly evolved—hence the rabbi's otherwise bizarre prayer in the opening of *Fiddler on the Roof:* "God bless and keep the Czar." Better the devil you know than the devil you don't.

Nothing was a settled matter. While the Pale was the only part of the Russian Empire in which Jews *could* live, it was not a place in which Jews had the *right* to live. Towns within its borders were free to expel some or all of their Jews, just as they were free to prohibit their residency whatsoever. Indeed, despite Catherine's words quoted above, the Pale made no promise of a peaceful and undisturbed life. Restrictive regulations that specifically targeted Jews piled up to such great heights as the nineteenth century went on that it became all but impossible to know what all the rules even were. And though somewhat infrequent at first, Jews were certainly not guaranteed protection from violence.

To understand how all this could be possible in the region of the Empire specifically set aside for Jewish residency, it is important to keep in mind that the Pale was anything but exclusively Jewish. Jews often formed majorities in many of the Pale's rural towns, but a far larger number of the general population were Christians of one kind or another.[25]

At first, the Empire's main concern was to assert itself over any remaining Polish influence in its new (and formerly Polish) territories. As it worked to replace Polish culture, religion, and language with Russian counterparts, it also sought to establish allegiance to the tsar. That meant removing any loyalty to Polish institutions that persisted—

---

* It should, of course, be noted that similar policies were imposed on just about every other minority group in the Russian Empire, from the Indigenous peoples of Siberia to the Ukrainians.

particularly the Polish nobility, who continued to own many towns. As long-time beneficiaries of Polish tolerance, the Jews suffered greatly as a result.

To undermine the wealth and power of the Polish nobility, Russians progressively banned Jews from working in the professions that had created so much wealth for the nobles in the first place. To a similar end, they often limited how many Jews could live in a certain town or how many could work in the permitted professions. In what is perhaps reminiscent of some of the misguided recent discourse around immigration policy in the United States, the Empire was worried that the Jews would dominate Russians in the marketplace, bring down their wages, and eventually destroy their jobs—all while benefiting a foreign nation, Poland. By banning the trade of products made by the talented Jewish artisans and craftsmen of the Pale, ranging from jewelry and wine to fans and tobacco pipes, the Empire could also starve the rich Polish nobility who still lived within the Pale of their appetite for luxury goods. The import of early manufacturing and industrial equipment was also entirely banned; this way, the Empire thought, Russia would be forced to develop its own manufacturing facilities and become self-reliant. And in a confused approach to somehow pressure Jews to convert to the religion of a tsar who sought to ensure their poverty as a means to crush the Poles, Jews had their rights stripped to those held by foreigners, were forced to pay considerably burdensome taxes, and were often subjected to ritualized humiliation.[26]

Then, in 1827, Tsar Nicholas I had what he thought was a great idea; in Jewish memory, however, it left a traumatic wound. Nicholas understood that the Jews might be naturally inclined to support the Polish nobility, who, after all, had allowed them many freedoms. But he was also aware of many Jews' genuine and perhaps even patriotic support of the Empire during the Napoleonic Wars (in Ukraine, at least) and thought that, with a little nudging, Jews would willingly and completely turn themselves into Russians. Indeed, Nicholas's own ministers thought—and expected—that before long, Jews would "move toward useful occupations," "submit themselves to the civil laws," and "defend the motherland."[27] Thus came Nicholas's "great" idea: force Jews to serve in the Russian Army by conscription, which was known as the cantonist system. In his mind, the military experience would baptize Jews into Russianness—at least figuratively, but he also hoped literally—and instill an allegiance to the tsar and a sense of Russian patriotism. Interestingly, Nicholas did not force Poles into conscription; he explicitly forbade it—but not to keep Poles safe or to give them a break. He excluded them specifically because he felt could not trust them. While the Jews demonstrated that they could be loyal to the Empire, the tsar hardly believed the Polish could ever be.[28]

Conscription was nothing new in Russia in 1827, and avoiding it had historically been as easy as paying a fee. But Nicholas took away that option—there was no way out now. Understandably, however, Jews had little interest in fighting in the Russian Army and resisted conscription as much as they could. Their resistance became so strong that each community in the Pale had to be assigned an official to serve as what was essentially the town's chief kidnapper, who would ensure that one way or another, Jewish men (boys) would be sent to the army. Their victims, often poor or otherwise vulnerable children as young as twelve, were torn from their families and sent to training camps far beyond the Pale, both literally and figuratively, where they were treated brutally, cruelly taunted into baptism, and all but forbidden from practicing even the most essential tenets of the Jewish faith. Those who resisted were deprived of food, sleep, and shelter; many were beaten. One (likely apocryphal) story tells of a conscript who drowned himself out of protest in front of Tsar Nicholas during an official visit. And the training was just the beginning of it all: after six years, conscripts would begin twenty-five years of military service, where they were treated hardly any better than in the training camps. Not until 1856 did the laws ease up, at which point somewhere between twenty-five and forty thousand Jews had been conscripted and Russia's Jews had lost any fragment of remaining trust or allegiance to the tsar.[29]

As it became more and more evident that Russia's Jews had very little interest in or care for autocracy, orthodoxy, or Russian nationality, the Empire became less tolerant, increasingly harsh, and ever more impatient for their assimilation. At the same time, the Empire also adopted a somewhat contradictory stance that the Jews could never be assimilated, and perhaps even that they shouldn't be—Russians and Jews should simply not mix. On top of all this, two Polish uprisings in 1830 and 1863 and the wave of revolutions across Europe in 1848 had deeply spooked the tsar, who was always terrified of revolution, most of all in Poland. So the Empire intensified its efforts to assimilate its minority groups—including but not limited to the Poles, Ukrainians, and Jews—by increasingly unpleasant means.

The Jews bore the brunt of the Empire's iron-fist strategy. By the end of the nineteenth century, some 1,400 statutes and regulations controlled nearly every aspect of Jewish life. Punitive tax burdens reappeared; new restrictions were placed on occupations and places of residency; the right to own land was, in many cases, taken away; quotas were implemented to limit the number of Jews who could enroll in higher-level education; and, to cut the list short, the ability to serve in some government roles was taken away. Needless to say, this strategy—which ultimately amounted to enforcing the placement of Jews at the lowest level of Russian society—did little to Russify them or build any allegiance to Russia within them, but it did do wonders to dramatically worsen the quality of Jewish life in the Pale.[30]

Although the conditions of the Pale made for a terrible way of life, after several millennia of experience with that kind of thing, Russia's Jews settled in and made do—for the time being, at least. Unsurprisingly, very few—no more than 5 percent—lived outside the Pale (those who did were often in cold and inhospitable rural colonies in Siberia, where they had been allowed the "privilege" to settle in return for service and suffering in the Russian Army). At the same time, Jews quite often remained at least somewhat unwelcome in the bigger cities within the Pale; for that reason, at best they made up only a third of the populations of Kyiv, Warsaw, and Odesa. But the Empire had also banned Jews from farming and agriculture for the most part, so owning and working land in the rural countryside was not an option either.[31]

With nowhere else to go, most Jews within the Pale simply stayed put. After all, many were in towns still owned and managed by the Polish nobility, where life hadn't been too bad and where one could at least make a living. Of course, the terms had now changed. But again, with few choices as to where to go, most opted to settle in. Moreover, in many of these typically small towns of a few thousand residents (though some had tens of thousands), they were often the majority. A particularly vivid recollection sets the scene:

> A jumble of wooden houses clustered higgledy-piggledy about a market-place...as crowded as a slum. [The streets] are as tortuous as a Talmudic argument. They are bent into question marks and folded into parentheses. They run into culs-de-sac like a theory arrested by a fact; they ooze off into lanes, alleys, back yards...[at the center is] the market-place, with its shops, booths, tables, stands, butchers' blocks. Hither come daily, except during the winter, the peasants and peasant women from many miles around, bring their live-stock and vegetables, their fish and hides, their wagonloads of grain, melons, parsley, radishes, and garlic...the tumult of the market-place...is one of the wonders of the world.[32]

Over time, these towns came to have something of a specifically Jewish character to them: they weren't just towns; they were *shtetls*. To be clear, it wasn't that any Jewish-majority town was automatically a shtetl, nor did shtetl status require a Jewish majority in the first place. A shtetl was home to a complete, close-knit, and vibrant Jewish community where Jewish life could thrive even under Russian rule. To be sure, the poverty, second-class citizenship, and despair that we think about when we imagine life in the shtetl was very real, but as economically, legally, and socially dark, desolate, and destitute as life within the Pale could be, its Jewish communities persevered.

In the shtetls, one could find a rich and thriving Jewish culture, religion, and tradition. At its best, the shtetl was not merely the center of family and religious life—it was the center of the universe, essentially, for its inhabitants. Its wealth of Jewish culture and religion meant that "Jews did not need to walk miles in the dirt behind a wagon carrying a coffin to a distant town cemetery," nor did they "need to go to a bigger city to hear the Purim story of the blessed Mordekhai and the cursed Haman."[33] This was what made a shtetl something other than just an ordinary town.[34]

Jewish children, including some girls, had access to a wealth of traditional Jewish knowledge in the shtetls. In their schools, the *heders* and *yeshivahs*, children studied everything from the Torah and the Talmud to more niche texts on Jewish morality, philosophy, and law. The proliferation of Jewish schools meant about two-thirds of male Russian Jews could read and write in 1897, when only about one-third of non-Jewish Russian males could.[35]

The family structure was generally matriarchal: the husband may have been the head of the household, but the wife was its chief of staff. Women were "strong, powerful, shrewd, corpulent, imposing, and vociferous" and often dominant in the household, where they primarily, though not exclusively, raised the children, kept the house in good and clean shape, and cooked.[36] Somehow, between reciting prayers beneath amulets hung from the wall to protect newborn infants from evil spirits and arranging marriages for their older children, many women also worked, traded, and retailed to bring in extra income; some learned to speak and even read foreign languages.[37]

The inescapable reality of daily life in the Pale, however, meant that it was never really home. The harshness outside the warmth of the Jewish community reinforced its role as just another stop along the Diaspora, one where the Passover seder-concluding phrase "next year in Jerusalem" was evermore a genuine prayer of aspiration. At best, the quality of life for Jews remained the same; more often, it fell and continued to fall, leaving deep, widespread poverty in its place. Even the schools were reduced to "filthy rooms," as one 1894 report testified, "crowded from nine in the morning until nine in the evening with pale, starved children."[38] Poverty was all but ensured, and disease and sickness became default features of childhood:

> The interior side of the wall [of our house] facing the street was damp and often dirty, so the children would indeed get sick. My brother and I would go from one illness to the next, scarlet fever, diphtheria, not to mention all the other childhood illnesses. I recall that my mother would leave my brother sick in bed [and go to see the Rabbi]. When she came back, she would say that the rebbe had given her an amulet and promised to pray to God himself. Nevertheless, he told her to call the doctor.[39]

Not even industrialization, which finally appeared in Russia in the nineteenth century, would save the shtetl, as the livelihoods of so many of its Jewish inhabitants depended on the shtetl marketplace and the artisan- and craftsman-made goods sold there. Only a railroad could change this—but even if a shtetl was lucky enough to receive a railroad, many inhabitants used it to leave the shtetl behind for good rather than for any economic benefit. Likewise, the long-overdue abolition of serfdom in 1861, a liberal reform, also helped to bring about the shtetl's decline, as it led to the mass relocation of Ukrainian and Polish peasants into the shtetls, where they created even more overcrowding and economic competition. And, of course, the institution of a state monopoly on liquor production took away what had become one of the few decent industries available for Jews, in which many had participated.[40]

In addition to economic deprivation and religious oppression, violence against Jews became another stable feature of shtetl life, particularly after 1881. Tsar Alexander II was assassinated in March of that year; naturally, the Jews were blamed. Violent antisemitic riots broke out throughout much of the Pale, devastating Jewish communities and killing an unimaginable number of people. Sometimes it was organized violence and destruction carried out as a group—as in a pogrom—while other times it could be more sporadic and arbitrary. One Ukrainian Jew who later came to America recalled a soldier breaking into her family's home, which included a room rented out to a tenant, at nine o'clock some Monday morning. "The soldier [asked] me whether I was Christian or Jewish. I replied that I was a Christian and was the tenant's daughter." The tenant denied this, which further egged on the soldier, who then:

> Demanded that I make the sign of the cross, saying that he would release me if I were a Christian child but would kill me if I were Jewish. In terror, I kissed his hand and called him "brother" and begged him to release me, but the soldier replied using the Russian slang term "that a goose and a pig have no relationship!"[41]

Pogroms could break out seemingly at any moment, especially in moments of political turmoil or vulnerability; they were terrifying counterexamples to the supposed wisdom of crowds.[42] In addition to the destruction of homes, businesses, and human lives, they posed an additional danger to women: one Jewish immigrant recalled how "they used to rape girls, and my mother decided they should send me [to America]...in those days, they were afraid for girls." She then summed up the situation of the Pale's millions of Jews so accurately: "It was dangerous just to be."[43]

And so, by the end of the nineteenth century, Russia's Jews—dehumanized, hungry, tired, and poor—had understandably reached a breaking point. As a result of Russia's inability to recognize the potential of the Jews to supercharge its slow and belated modernization and industrialization processes or even just to recognize them as human beings worthy of respect and basic rights, Russia came out of the nineteenth century shouting of the Jews' intent to bring on socialism, obliterate Christianity, and destroy the Empire. Entirely by choice, Russia proved decidedly unable to reap the benefits of hosting such a sizable Jewish population. This would forever remain a lost opportunity passed up by the Russian Empire, which took the Pale of Settlement to its grave.[44]

> *The shtetl would not exist without its Jews—trading, producing, and exchanging whatever could be exchanged, traded or produced. The shtetl for us is a place, but perhaps we need to reconceptualize it also as an action, a whir of activity. After all, it was this activity that shaped the shtetl's unique golden age and its suppression that triggered the shtetl's demise. Had Russia come to grips with the shtetls' character and activity, its relations with its Jews would have taken a different path. This did not happen.*[45]
> ~Yohanan Petrovsky-Shtern

Now, having completed our introduction to nineteenth-century Russia, its history, and its personality, let us take a closer look within the Pale of Settlement itself and finally get to the true heart of this book by meeting some people who lived there.

Chapter 2
JEWISH POLAND

―――――◆―――――

Zionist melodies, Hasidic melodies, and revolutionary songs mingled in the air, creating a harmonious symphony of a hopeful youth longing for redemption. Some sought to join up with their Creator. Some dreamed of the land of their forefathers, where they would build a new life for their people, and some hoped to bring redemption for all mankind.[46]
~ Staszówer Moshe Rotenberg

By the time of the Partitions of Poland and the creation of the Pale of Settlement at the end of the 1700s, Russia had spent nearly a century developing a vile, harshly anti-Polish national spirit fueled by Poland's Catholicism, relative economic advantage, and backing of the French Revolution (and, later, Napoleon). Ironically for the increasingly antisemitic and hypernationalist Russians, a critical source of Poland's economic power had been its Jewish population. Many Jews in Poland had become well-traveled merchants and skilled artisans; however, they were all but banned from living in the Russian Empire until the Pale's creation.

Prior to the Partitions, many of Poland's Jews lived in small towns owned by rich Polish magnates, who typically extended a volatile and unpredictable tolerance toward their Jewish residents in return for their economic benefits. Over the eighteenth century, the Russian Empire slowly put the private ownership of these towns to an end, effectively trading their treasuries' wealth for control over the often remote and small towns. This process took different forms in different places: whereas it almost came as a welcome relief to the Jews of modern-day Ukraine, the Jews of Poland experienced a harsher and crueler rule, perhaps because Russia hated the Jews as much as it hated the Poles.[47]

Southern Poland: Staszów

The history of Staszów, one of my ancestral hometowns, provides a glimpse into an archetypal Polish shtetl and its experience with the new Russian authority. A small countryside town between Krakow and Lublin, Staszów was first settled in the thirteenth century. Its first Jews moved in about 300 years later in the early sixteenth century but soon ran into trouble when they were banished—and some executed—in 1610. They could not, and did not, return until 1690.[48]

Shortly after their return, Jews were given full privileges of the city by the town's Polish owners in 1718, which allowed them many highly valued privileges. They could maintain a synagogue and cemetery without church interference, for example. They could work freely as artisans, merchants, brewers, bakers, and butchers without needing to contribute to greedy guilds. They could be tried under the same laws in the same courts as Christians. Even better, they paid relatively fair taxes.

By the mid-eighteenth century, roughly 700 Jews lived in about seventy homes in Staszów, where they made up about half of the town's population; by the end of the century, many lived in the center of town, often above their self-owned businesses. Some Jews, including several women, were able to earn a relatively good living by working in early weaving factories, which opened around the turn of the nineteenth century.[49]

Whatever social and economic development was underway in Staszów by the end of the eighteenth century, however, the Third Partition of Poland in 1795 effectively put an end to it. When the Russians, Prussians, and Austrians concluded their tense negotiations over how to split up Poland's remains, it was decided that Austria would complete its absorption of Galicia, the region of southeastern Poland, so Staszów entered the Austrian Empire.

Staszów back in Poland.

Among Staszów's roughly one thousand Jews at the time was a young couple, Rubin and Fayga, who welcomed a son, Zelman, sometime around the turn of the century. One of Zelman's classmates in his early religious schooling—which we can safely assume he received at least a few years of—was Munis, the son of Kuna and Minel. Perhaps on the way home from school, in the marketplace, or through their parents, they came to know Eva, Wolf and Basia's daughter, as well as Sweva, Meylich's daughter.* You have surely noticed that none of these children or their parents had surnames: Zelman was simply Rubin's son, and Eva was Wolf's daughter. As had been the tradition for millennia, Jews used patronymics rather than surnames.†

These four children—Zelman, Eva, Munis, and Sweva—were born into what would remain an eventful and tumultuous era, even after the Partitions were settled. While their parents did their best to raise them in such trying times, things only got worse. Austria hardly waited to place restrictions on Jewish commerce, reimplement the harsh and unfair taxes of the seventeenth century, and force Jews to adopt local customs—including surnames.

The Austrians had already done much of the same work before, most recently to the Jews of Galicia when Austria first received part of the territory in the First Partition. This time, however, Jews were allowed to pick their own surnames, and many protested Austrian control by choosing somewhat outlandish, nonsensical, and occasionally fantastical names. Zelman and Eva, who had married in the early 1800s and in 1806 had a son named Froim Rubin (in part after his grandfather), opted to pick the surname of Knobel (pronounced "kuh-noble"). I have no idea where this name came from, although it is suspiciously similar to *knobl*—the Yiddish word for garlic. Was it a favorite food? Was it to ward off gentiles who may be put off by the odor of garlic breath? Was it just the first thing their eyes saw when they had to come up with a name? We may never know. In any case, Froim Rubin Knobel had at least two siblings: Basia and Michael.

---

* As far as I am aware, the name of Sweva's mother is lost to time.
† Here and throughout, I will use spellings of Polish, Hebrew, and Russian names that will help the average English speaker easily understand their pronunciation. For example, Eva was "more accurately" spelled Chawa, but this mix of Polish and Hebrew phonetics is replicated closely enough by using Eva.

Meanwhile, Munis had become a butcher, most likely following in his father's footsteps. This was a serious job in the shtetl, and given that Munis had to abide by the strict rules for animal slaughter and butchering (*shehitah*), it is quite possibly an indication of his piousness. In any case, after his marriage to Sweva, he chose to adopt Goldflus as a surname, which translates to *gold river* or *gold flow*. Was the name a matter of wishful thinking? Or an intentional irony as they most likely lived in an overcrowded wooden shack with several other people on the side of an often-muddy road? Whatever the reason, Munis and Sweva Goldflus had a little girl (Gitla Brandla) in 1807, followed by a son (Kuna, named after Munis's father) and another daughter (Etla). Both the Knobel and Goldflus families probably had many other children I was unable to discover. I know of no siblings of Munis, Sweva, or Eva, but Zelman had a brother, Szlama, from whom Froim, Basia, and Michael had at least six cousins to grow up with.*

Hardly anything else is known of this "first" generation of Knobels and Goldfluses other than, despite having siblings and cousins to share in whatever childhood mischief, schooling, and religious holidays possible, Froim's and Gitla's childhoods were defined and overshadowed by the misery that followed the Austrian (and later Polish and Russian) government's reactionary reforms.

In the midst of the Napoleonic Wars and Napoleon's ill-fated invasion of Eastern Europe, Staszów and its surrounding areas were transferred to the so-called "Duchy of Warsaw" in 1809, a temporary

---

* The descendants of at least one of these cousins, Szlama's son Haiyim (Chaim) Rubin Knobel, have been traced to the present day; I have even been in touch with one of them. Haiyim's descendants in my generation are my seventh cousins; our common ancestors are Rubin and Fayga, my sixth great-grandparents, eight generations back. It's an interesting thought to imagine Froim, my fifth great-grandfather playing along the shore of the Czarna River in Staszów with Haiyim as young boys, likely completely unaware of the immense family trees they would create.

state created by Napoleon that soon fell under Russian control. Russian and Polish governments alike worked together to openly and intently "fix" the Jews, at first hoping to assimilate them into the Polish population. This meant that Rubin, Wolf, Kuna, and Meylich, as well as the younger males Zelman and Munis, had to shave their heavy beards that were part of their cultural identity, abandon their traditional dress and adopt Polish fashions, and learn to read and write the Polish language rather than Hebrew or Yiddish. It also meant that the Knobel and Goldflus families and all other Jews were now in constant fear of being driven out of town at any time, as the expulsion of Jews had been restored. Many of these "reforms" turned out to be much easier to pass into law than to implement and enforce, but they certainly did not make life any better.

One restriction that was often strictly enforced dictated where Jews could live. All across Poland, they were no longer permitted to settle in the main areas of towns or among Christians, but rather in areas specifically designated for them. In Staszów, Jews were allowed to live in the narrow corridor between the Czarna River and Dluga Street, more or less in the area of their synagogue. Moreover, Staszów, along with all the towns in its home province of Radom, was forced to pay considerably hefty taxes to support Poland's military—and thus, effectively, the Russian Army, the terrifying abductor of Jewish children and destroyer of Jewish spirits.[50]

Perhaps it's no surprise, then, that the Jewish community was pushed into bankruptcy and was consequently liquidated in 1822. Yet despite the dramatically increasing economic and social impoverishment in Staszów, Jews who had been evicted from nearby villages under similar conditions began arriving. The inflow was significant enough to lead to additional decrees limiting how many Jews could live in a single residence, as well as the kinds of work that they were permitted to do. For several decades in the early to mid-nineteenth century, the government and even some leading rabbis encouraged Jews to move further into the countryside, take up agriculture, and establish their own villages; few attempts lasted, although a small number survived into the twentieth century.⁵¹

Despite such difficult times, Jewish life persevered as it had for millennia before. On December 30, 1826, in the midst of so much chaos, Zelman Knobel and Munis Goldflus came to the courtyard of Staszów's synagogue to consent to the marriage of their children, Froim Rubin Knobel and Gitla Brandla Goldflus. As the Knobels were presumably crushing a glass at their wedding and celebrating the start of a new life together, Staszów was starting to resemble the characteristic shtetl image that many are familiar with: poor, miserable, and oppressed. But just as all the disruptions of the early nineteenth century did not stop their parents from carrying on and starting their own families, these difficulties did not stop Froim and Gitla. They had their first son, Meyer, in 1827, providing Gitla's father Munis with his first grandchild before he passed away in 1829. Unfortunately for Froim, Gitla, and the other family members, Munis was interred far away from his ancestors: the Staszów Jewish cemetery, the one that had been guaranteed to its Jews for all posterity only a century earlier, had been forcefully relocated to a new one inconveniently far outside of the town in 1825.

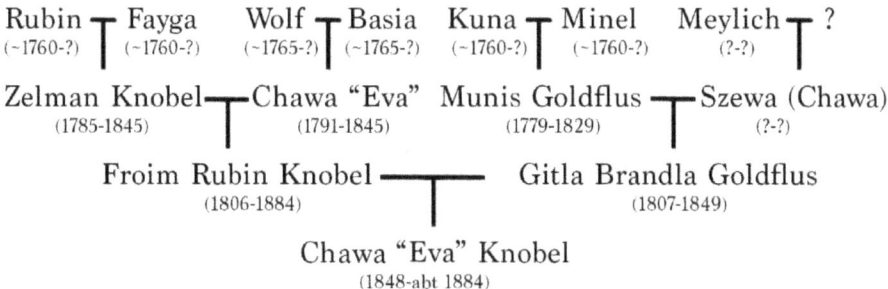

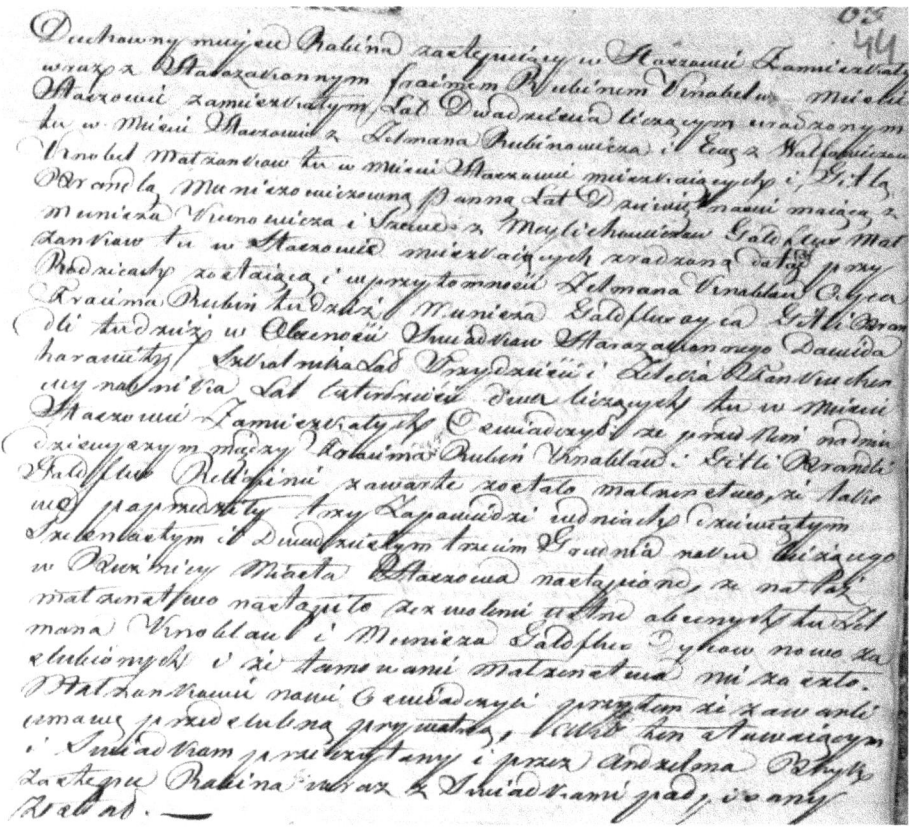

Froim and Gitla Knobel's marriage record. His name can be made out in the middle of the second line, and his parents' names on the fourth line in the center right; Gitla's is seen at the end of the fifth and the start of the sixth lines, with her parents named at the start of the seventh line.[52]

As Froim and Gitla Knobel were starting their family, Poland was rocked by the November Uprising of 1830, which, even in remote Staszów, was quickly crushed by the Russian Army. In response, Russia effectively reversed the autonomy it had previously given to Poland, after which a new level of fear must have permeated every Jewish family in the country. In the aftermath of the revolt, additional Russian troops, the agents and symbols of a gentile, anti-Judaic (and increasingly antisemitic), and cruel Russian government, were stationed in Staszów.[53]

NEXT YEAR IN AMERICA

Still, under such harsh and restrictive conditions, Froim and Gitla had seven children together, the last of whom—a daughter, Eva (Chawa)—was born on May 28, 1848.* Tragically, life for Eva's generation would turn out to be no easier than it was for their parents. Indeed, for many, it would be worse. The third major outbreak of cholera in the nineteenth century began in 1846 and reached Moscow by early 1848. It reached Staszów by 1849 and the Knobels' household by fall of that year: Gitla Knobel, Eva's mother, likely succumbed to the disease on October 9, 1849; Eva's five-year-old sister Mirla had already passed away nine days earlier.[54]

Of course, the Knobels were only one of the many families who were suddenly dealing with the horrors of unreliable water quality in Staszów. Not far away from the Knobels lived Leizer and Haia Tyszgarten, who were expecting their third child in 1848.†

But tragedy soon struck the Tyszgartens too. By the time Haia Tyszgarten gave birth to their son on January 12, 1849, Leizer had already been dead for three months. Just six months after the death of his brother, Leizer passed away on October 7, 1848, almost certainly due to cholera. His wife, who miraculously survived, opted to name their son Leizer, after her husband.

A year and a long-lost family story later, Haia Tyszgarten and Froim Knobel were married on January 11, 1850, just three months after Gitla's death and a little over a year after Leizer's. Perhaps they quickly formed

---

* She was preceded by two brothers, Meyer and Munis (named after his maternal grandfather), and four sisters, Fayga (named after Froim's grandmother), Rivka, Leyba, and Mirla. Her name, of course, was almost certainly a tribute to her paternal grandmother, who died three years before she was born.

† "Tyszgarten" may have been a Polonized form of "Tiergarten," analogous to the German for "zoo." Leizor was born in 1800 to Michael and Fayga, and he had several brothers: Zanwel, Michael, Icek, and Faywel (Fajwel). Haia (Chaia) was born in 1809 in the nearby town of Bogoria to Icek Herszenhorn and Estera, daughter of Moishe. She likely moved to Staszów to marry Leizor. Their first two children were Faywel and Michael.

a bond through the shared experiences of losing their spouses, particularly as both had young children; they also could have bonded over their abundance of grief, with the passing of Froim's parents in 1845, the deaths of at least two of Froim's children by the time of his remarriage and at least one of Leizer and Haia's children, and, of course, the sudden passing of their spouses.

Unfortunately, still more tragedy came to Froim and Haia Knobel when, after a few quiet years, cholera returned in the mid-1850s—and with a vengeance. In 1855 and 1856, it appears to have killed Eva's brother, Meyer; her sisters, Rivka and Fayga; and her half sister, Sarah, one of the two children Froim had had with Haia. In total, only three of Froim's nine children were still alive by 1856: Eva; her brother, Munis; and her half brother, Zelman (the other of the two children Froim had with Haia). In addition, both of the children of Froim's daughter Fayga, who died of cholera in 1856, died in childhood, in 1851 and 1859. So in the span of only fifteen heart-wrenching years, Froim lost eleven close family members: both of his parents, his first wife, six out of his nine children, and two grandchildren.

Yet like all the remaining Jews in Staszów, he persevered. By the second half of the nineteenth century, despite the extreme deterioration in living standards and security, the Jewish community managed to reclaim their commercial dominance, reasserting their position in industries from grain to timber and beer to gypsum.

A second uprising in 1863, however, reminded the Jewish community of their fragile standing within Polish and Russian society. Antisemitism had already been on the rise in the years leading up to the uprising, including in Staszów's own neighborhood. A demonstration two years earlier in Opatow, a shtetl ten miles to the northeast, quickly turned into a violent display of antisemitism, with demonstrators attacking Jewish homes and smashing the windows of Jewish businesses, stealing and looting while they were at it. Much of this antisemitism could be traced back to rumors that the Jews were spying on the Poles on behalf of the Russians and thus were enemies of the Poles. The Jews of Staszów, in particular, had been accused of passing information along to the Russian government about a local revolt that was part of the Polish Uprising in 1863, which ultimately ended with the Russian Army occupying and revengefully plundering the city. Miraculously, and perhaps surprisingly, the army did not even touch any Jewish homes. Of course, in reality, Jews had neither participated nor assisted in the revolt. But Staszów's Jews bought the looted goods back from the Russians while the army was on its way out, and they immediately returned everything to its rightful Polish owners after the Russians left—without asking for anything in return. In fact, the only thing they got in return was the spreading of the myth that the Jews had spied on the Polish.

I have no idea whether Froim, Haia, or anyone in their shaken-up family played a part in any of this, but they were certainly aware of what was going on. And as hard as it is to imagine the fear they must have felt as the Russian Army occupied their hometown, they continued on with their lives as best they could.

Indeed, Froim got to see at least two of his children marry and start their own families. Zelman, his youngest child, married Hannah (of the Steinberg family) sometime in the early 1870s, with whom he had nine children; at least two survived into adulthood and had kids of their own. Then, in January 1873, Froim attended yet another wedding only made possible by the chaos and tragedy of the nineteenth century.

On January 4, 1873, nearly a half century after his parents' wedding in the same place, Froim granted permission at Staszów's synagogue for his daughter Eva—the last child he had with his first wife, Gitla, before she died—to marry Leizer Tyszgarten, the son of Leizer Tyszgarten and his widow Haia, who had remarried to Froim. Yes, dear reader, you read correctly. The step-siblings (who, thankfully, were not related by blood) married. As with Eva's father's remarriage to Leizer's mother, this story, too, is lost to time. Was it their shared experience of having only ever known one biological parent while also growing up in the same household together so close in age? Or was it a matter of convenience—or maybe social necessity—for Froim, who may have been insistent on carrying on his family by any means necessary by this point? One would have to have been there to know.

In 1874, the year after a fire ravaged Staszów's Jewish quarter, Esther Gitla Tyszgarten was born to Leizer and Eva (Knobel) Tyszgarten on October 3.

Fascinatingly, perhaps revealingly, Eva gave Esther her own mother's name as her second name. The choice to permanently attach her birth mother's name to her daughter's identity—the name of a mother she never knew, a name she could only have ever known through her father—is a subtle and perhaps poetic nod to the impact of Eva's upbringing and the emotional weight of her life experiences. Through something so simple as a name, several things become clear: that Eva held her mother close to her, even in her effectively lifelong absence; that even after her father remarried, her family tried to preserve her mother's memory; and that these were both things that were significant to Eva, significant enough that she chose to forever call her child by her mother's name, literally keeping her mother's soul bound in the bundle of life.

At the time of her birth, Esther and her parents were three out of roughly 4,000 Jews in Staszów, who made up about 60 percent of the town's population. Leizer and Eva soon had a second child, Moishe, followed by at least one more, another Froim. This young Froim was likely named after Eva's father, who, after a long and emotionally difficult seventy-eight years of life, had passed away three years earlier on February 16, 1884.

Despite the great tragedies and misfortunes of the 1840s and 1850s, it is comforting to know that Froim Knobel at least was able to witness two of his children marry and to know several of his grandchildren. Esther would have almost certainly remembered him, as she would have been just shy of ten years old when he passed.

It never ceases to amaze me, even as I write this, that my own grandfather—Esther's grandson—knew somebody who knew Froim—*a man born in 1806*. I can only hope that Froim has since been without worry; may his soul be bound in the bundle of life.

Northern Poland: Gąbin

Our next stop is Gąbin, a Polish village just south of Płock and about forty miles west of Warsaw. The story of its history shares great similarities with that of Staszów's. By the 1850s, a decade of relative order compared to the onset of Polish/Russian control that characterized the preceding decades and the political upheavals that defined those after it, approximately three hundred Jewish families called Gąbin home, creating a Jewish population numbering a few thousand. Among those families are two of interest to me: the Lefcovitch and Lazarus families.

Very little is known of them; their origins—and even their names— were among the most stubborn unknowns that I encountered while researching this book. I had practically accepted defeat until, thanks to good luck, modern technology, and human generosity, I finally found a lead in an online DNA match. Incredibly, this match was already familiar with my last name, Shiroff: she had been well acquainted with one of my great-uncles, a Shiroff, who had been a good friend of one her great-uncles, a Lazarus. After a few email exchanges, she found a note stored away in an old folder explaining how our great-uncles knew each other: my great-uncle's mother (Sarah Lazarus) and her great-uncle's father (Abraham Lazarus) were siblings. Put another way, her great-grandfather Abraham and my great-great-grandmother Sarah were brother and sister. They were both born to Icek and Bena Lazarus in the shtetl of Gąbin in the middle of the nineteenth century—Sarah at some point in February 1851. Seven months later, Nysen Lefcovitch was born in September 1851. His parents are unknown at the time of this writing. Nysen and Sarah married some twenty years later, all but certainly in some outdoor space near Gąbin's famous wooden synagogue.*

Unfortunately, Gąbin's records are not as easily accessible as Staszów's are (if they are accessible at all). If they were, perhaps I would be able to follow Nysen and Sarah's ancestors back several generations, as I was fortunate enough to be able to do for the Tyszgartens and Knobels. But the Jews of Gąbin would have shared many common experiences and understandings with the Jews of Staszów.

Gąbin's wooden synagogue, built in 1710, renovated in 1893, and burned down by the Nazis in 1939. The interior of the synagogue was as renowned for its beauty as its exterior, earning it a place in Poland's national register of historic buildings.[55]

---

* Thank you, Sylvia! Thirty-five years ago, it turns out, her great-uncle's older brother Phillip (Harry and Phillip were two of nineteen children!) provided his niece with all the information he knew about his father's family. I was able to confirm Gąbin as the Lefcovitch hometown after cross-verifying with the immigration papers of Nathan and Sarah's first child, their only child born in Poland.

The Bema of Gąbin's synagogue.⁵⁶

Nysen's unknown parents and Icek and Bena Lazarus were almost certainly born in the first quarter of the nineteenth century, during the eventful and turbulent years in the aftermath of Poland's destruction in the Partitions. They were all roughly the same generation as Froim Rubin Knobel, the perpetually and cruelly unlucky grandfather to Esther Tyszgarten. Indeed, Froim likely would have implicitly understood Isaac, Bena, and Nysen's parents' life experiences as so much would have been familiar, even if the exact details were different. All grew up in the early age of the shtetl, in an era of rapid, frequent, and often undesirable political change—after all, they were among the first generation to be born into the world of the Pale. Each likely came of age in a household that, despite great personal challenges, tragedies, and religious persecution, took great pride in its Jewish faith, traditions, and values. They would have immediately understood each other's strained relations with the gentile world; they would have understood the business struggles and successes, their fears and worries, and empathized with their hopes and dreams.

Nysen and Sara would start their family in Poland and then leave for London in the early 1870s, nearly a quarter century before any of my other ancestors. I am not sure why they left when they did or why they left relatively earlier than many of their peers. It's possible that they were affected by a particularly bad crop harvest and subsequent famine in 1869, which most acutely affected the northwestern Pale, quite likely including Gąbin. It's also possible that after the Polish Uprising in 1863, they felt uneasy and sought a safer, more stable place to live to start a family. Sarah had brothers already in London; perhaps they assured her things were simply better there. Whatever the reason, they left. Eventually, they found their way to the United States, where their descendants met Esther Tyszgarten's descendants—and a century and a half later, here I am.[57]

With the Lefcovitch family out of Poland, let us return back to Staszów to bring the story of the Polish shtetl into the twentieth century.

Poland at the Turn of the Century

The next time we hear from Esther Tyszgarten in Staszów's records is when we're informed of her marriage to Hersh Isaiah Waksman, my great-great-grandfather, on February 9, 1897. At the time of their marriage, Hersh and Esther were two out of roughly five thousand Jews living in Staszów, where Jews now made up nearly two-thirds of the population. Hersh was already familiar with the Knobel family when he married Esther, a Knobel through her mother, Eva, as Hersh's sister Beyla had married a son of Fayga Knobel. Fayga's father, Hayim Knobel, was one of Froim Knobel's cousins. Through their common great-great-grandparents—Rubin and Fayga—Beyla's husband and Esther were third cousins. So it is well within the realm of possibility that Hersh first encountered, met, or was introduced to his future bride thanks to his older sister's marriage.

Unlike Esther, Hersh's ancestry is much harder to trace. Hardly anything is known of his family. Hersh's parents—Icek Waksman and Shaindla Moskowitz Shulman—are as far back as we can go. Both seem to have been born in Staszów, but their parents are entirely unknown, perhaps other than the guess that Shaindla's father's name was likely some variant of Moses. Icek and Shaindla had seven children: Moishe, Beyla, Hersh, Rochma, Mendel, Keila, and Leibel, from oldest to youngest, with Hersh, my great-great-grandfather, being born on February 19, 1875.

Perhaps making up for the lack of information about Icek and Shaindla's parents, a much clearer picture of Staszów and the lives of those who lived there exists for the period around Hersh and Esther's marriage than for any earlier period. I rely heavily upon the memoirs of former Staszówers in the hopes of relaying the warmth, personality, and depth of their recollections.

By the start of the twentieth century, most of the shops in Staszów's central marketplace were owned by Jews, except for the pharmacy and pork merchant. Jews lived near the marketplace, whereas most of the town's Poles were farmers. Stories survive of Jewish children hiding in Polish farmers' wagons, stowing themselves away so they could have the opportunity to leave the shtetl and explore the nearby forests for the day.

Jews worked in all kinds of trades: as shoemakers, tailors, carpenters, blacksmiths, bakers, butchers, painters, watchmakers, and merchants. While most were able to make an income, poverty was never completely eliminated; beggars would pass door by door for anything they could get, and dedicated tables were even set aside for beggars at weddings and funerals.

The marketplace was surrounded on all four sides by two-story buildings whose owners lived upstairs and kept stores downstairs. At its center were the market building and town hall, which survive to this day—along with the belltower used to alert the town if a fire broke out, as it did in 1873. The marketplace made for a warm and lively town center. In Staszówer Pinchas Goldhar's words:

> Two sides of the marketplace had rows of trees, one of chestnut trees and the other of lilac trees. The lilac trees were very enjoyable between Pesach and Shavuot because of the pleasant aroma that they gave off and the chestnut trees at Succoth time because of the chestnuts, a fruit we could not eat, but they had very shiny skins and served as weapons for pranksters who didn't dare to throw stones.[58]

The Czarna River was the only source of water, which both Jewish and gentile Polish water carriers provided to the town. The river froze in the winter, and the ice was chopped up and stored away until summer, when it was used for cold drinks and ice cream and to keep cool. The river's water also washed the town's clothes.

Occasionally, the river rose past its banks, which the town's Jews treated as a reenactment of when Pharaoh and his army drowned. The river was a gathering spot for all kinds of purposes, aided by its enchanting natural beauty and religious aura.

Life followed a consistent and regular pattern. Sundays had Jewish stores closed on the insistence of the town's Christian population. Mondays were noisy and busy, with merchants who came from near and far to crowd into the marketplace and sell their goods—and who often left late in the evening after having become intoxicated, much to the locals' amusement. Tuesdays were calm, empty, and slow, mostly spent cleaning up from the day before. Wednesdays were even quieter, and Thursday brought a smaller-scale version of Monday's market mayhem. Fridays were particularly joyful:

> Friday was a day that lived not with its own spirit. Friday was "erev Shabbes" [eve of the Sabbath] and was lit up

like the moon and the sun of the Sabbath. First, we studied only two or three hours in cheder, and as soon as we left the cheder, from the oppressive jail to the fresh air, we ran straight to the woods to Nachum Garber, the only Jew in Staszów who lived like a Pole, alone, one kilometer away from the town. We played ball and a game of jacks using buttons from Russian uniforms, and we brought special baked goods from home. Bubies and Zadies were handing out Shabbat goodies to all their grandchildren. The preparations for Shabbat were in full swing. The baking and cooking for Shabbat cost more than for the whole rest of the week. The strudel, the egg cookies, the soup full of "eyes" of fat on top, the chickens and the geese, the cleaning of the house, scrubbing the wooden floors, bathing and washing the hair of the children (between a half and a full dozen children in each family), the running of the older people to the ritual bath (mikveh), the cleaning of the silk and velvet jackets, coats, and shtraimels [fur hats]. In short, everything smelled of erev Shabbes.[59]

Even if observed weekly, the Sabbath was always a special, joyous occasion when Jewish homes contained a happy atmosphere and plenty of singing. Many hardly ate during the week, often only cabbage and potatoes, but on the Sabbath, one typically enjoyed a several-course meal. It was a wonderful break from the reality of life: for school children, there was no school; for merchants, businesses were closed. It was truly a day of rest.

As was typically the case in the Pale, life was culturally rich in Staszów, even as it was economically impoverished and burdened by discrimination and fear. Staszów had three fiddlers and several trumpeters. Musicians played as their parrots flew around them—the birds could allegedly even curse in Yiddish. Staszówer Yechezkel Kirszenbaum recalled:

> A blind violinist would come to Staszów each year right before Pesach; he was the herald of spring. The piercing strains of his violin would express boundless sadness, and when he would accompany his playing with a song on the [1903] pogrom in Kishinev, the whole picture of the terrifying events would be visible before my eyes.[60]

Children played ball games of all varieties, swam in the river, and created games with stones. Competitions were held among them to see whose skipping stone would make the most waves, go the fastest, or most accurately hit a target. Great efforts were undertaken via teamwork to aim stones into windows—glassless ones, the children would pray. Children attended school and were taught by strict, tough, and pitiless teachers. In school they learned of the entire Jewish story from the destruction of the Temple to their present day, of their forebears' bold sacrifices and remarkable triumphs, which, as Moshe Rotenberg recalled, instilled a sense of "respect for our ancestors and deep despair over our powerlessness in the long and dark Diaspora".[61] Tisha B'Av, which marks the destruction of the Second Temple, was always marked as a day of mourning.

The Jewish community was centered around the synagogue on Bóżnicza Street, near Złota Street today, on the west side of the town and far away from the church on the east side. It was outside of this synagogue where Hersh and Esther were married in 1897, in the same space as all of Esther's ancestors.

Staszów's synagogue was more than just a religious site; it was the center of Jewish life, where the community gathered. Moshe Rotenberg recalled:

> After prayers, everyone has a chat about business in the shops, about the prices of kerosene and candles, herring and salt, and about how much money they took in. Some talk about politics. Everything interests them: What's happening in Port Arthur? What's doing with the

[Mendel] Beilis trial? Kaiser Wilhelm? Other important world problems? They don't simply inquire; they resolve questions, and give advice to the leaders of the world. And it's no one's fault that the rulers don't listen to their advice and run the world as they think fit. And that's why the world's in such great shape...and, of course, on the nights of Chanukah, there were plenty of pranks played by the heder children and yeshiva boys, who threw snowballs at the balemer [Torah-reading platform], and the like. During the days of Chanukah we began to make dreydls, carving them out of wood or pouring lead into molds. The latter was a job requiring great care, because often we burned our hands.[62]

Looking east toward the church on Staszów's Koscielna Street, circa 1900[63]

While the church had a stone-paved road leading to its well-kept and gardened cemetery, the original Jewish cemetery was, according to Pinchas Goldhar, "like a forest of crooked, half-sunken, almost unreadable headstones, surrounded by a wall with breaks here and there, with sheep grazing and jumping over the headstones."⁶⁴

No pogrom ever occurred in Staszów, at least to the best of my knowledge, but much of the Jewish population lived in fear of their Christian neighbors anyway, particularly on holidays—and most especially around Christmas. During Christmastime, usually right after Hanukkah, Jews hid in their basements, shuttered their windows, and reinforced their doors with iron bars *just in case* a pogrom broke out.

The bema of Staszów's synagogue⁶⁵

But yet again, just as their ancestors had done for generations, Hersh and Esther carried on. They had their first son, Sroel, in 1897, followed by Froim in 1900 and a daughter, Fayga, in 1904, each one born in the little world of Staszów. Not long after Fayga's birth, however, they chose to leave the colorful, culturally rich world of Staszów behind—a world as filled with warm familiarity as it was with reminders that it was merely a stop along the Diaspora and never really home.

A goat roams free down Koscielna Street, one of Staszów's main roads, circa 1895.[66]

Staszów's mill, pictured in 1910.[67]

Chapter 3
JEWISH UKRAINE

◆────────────◆

What looked like a provincial rural settlement to the outsider was the center of the world for its Jews...the shtetl was a dynamic place and a dynamic concept, moving through stages and changes, edifying and modifying itself along the way. The shtetl] embodied action—economic and manufacturing, religious and educational, political and civic, cultural and criminal...had Russia come to grips with the shtetls' character and activity, its relations with its Jews would have taken a different path.[68]
~Yohanan Petrovsky-Shtern

By the mid-seventeenth century, Ukraine was home to tens of thousands of Jews scattered across a few hundred towns, the vast majority of which were in right-bank Ukraine. Unfortunately for both you and me, there are a few confusing terms that will be quite useful in this chapter, so let's try to get them down now: the left bank refers to *eastern* Ukraine, while the right bank refers to *western* Ukraine.

That's right: on a map of Ukraine, the *left* bank would be on the *right* side, while the *right* bank would be on the *left* side. This seemingly nonsensical nomenclature, however, actually made perfect sense in an age when hardly anyone had ever seen a map. Imagine that you are on a boat sailing from Kyiv down the Dnieper, the river that runs through the middle of Ukraine. Since the river flows from north to south, the riverbank on your right would be western Ukraine, and the one on your left would be eastern Ukraine. The distinction between the left bank and right bank is often an important one when discussing Ukraine, so remember that the left bank is the side of Ukraine geographically closer to Russia, while the right bank is the side closer to Poland (and, historically, Austria).[69]

We should also pause for a brief moment to clarify that at least in this period, when I refer to "Ukraine," I mean to refer to the area of modern-day Ukraine. In this period, and indeed until just over a century ago, there was no country called Ukraine to be found on the map. While a state called Poland has been around for a while (at least in name), the same is not true for Ukraine. Until the rise of the Ukrainian national idea in the nineteenth century, "Ukraine" was more of a geographic reference than a political one; indeed, the name "Ukraine" means something like "at the borderlands" in most Slavic languages. In the absence of a Ukrainian state in this time period, its lands were split between the two powers of Eastern Europe: the Polish-Lithuanian Commonwealth and the Russian Empire.[70]

As was mentioned briefly in Chapter 1, the general absence of Jews in the left bank (eastern Ukraine) in the seventeenth century is largely explained by the expulsion of the Jews from Lithuania (which ruled over much of the left bank) in 1495 and by the tumultuous rise to power of Russia, which was granted the bulk of the left bank by the Truce of Andrusovo in 1667. However, Chapter 1 did not explain what led to the Truce of Andrusovo in the first place. Given our focus on the Jews of Eastern Europe, I cannot give a full account of what happened. But because the truce concluded a conflict in which the Jews of Ukraine suffered so terribly that its memory remained in their cultural consciousness for centuries to come, I must tell at least part of the story.[71]

The Cossacks, descendants of whom are still around today, originated along the coast of the Black Sea in what is now southeastern Ukraine and southwestern Russia. A proud, truculent, and democratically inclined people in an area historically unfriendly to the democratically inclined, the Cossacks were almost naturally prone to launching large-scale revolts whenever they felt their rights were being violated by the ruling power of the day—be it Poland-Lithuania or Russia. In 1648, it was the Polish who ruled over them. That year, as Western and Central Europe marked the end of the brutal Thirty Years' War, a Cossack named Bohdan Khmelnytsky began a revolt after land was stolen from him with the tacit approval of the Polish court system.

The Khmelnytsky Revolt, however, went much further than the typical Cossack revolt. It quickly got out of hand, with Khmelnytsky's forces taking out the entirety of the Polish Army in only a few months, after which the Cossacks marched terrifyingly close to the Polish capital. The Polish Army, however, was far from the only victims. While Khmelnytsky took the summer off in his hometown of Chyhyryn, not too far south of Kyiv, his supporters continued north through the Ukrainian countryside, where they attacked landowners, the nobility,

Catholics (the Cossacks were Orthodox), and, most destructively of all, Jews. It is difficult to provide an estimate of the number of Jews living in the area of modern-day Ukraine at the time, but it was probably not much more than forty thousand at most. Nonetheless, the Cossacks killed somewhere between fourteen and twenty thousand of them, meaning that as many as half of Ukraine's Jews were killed. Consequently, Jewish life in Ukraine was significantly affected and would take over a century to fully recover.[72]

In Ukrainian history, Khmelnytsky is traditionally seen as something of a hero, as a national leader who took the first steps toward creating the modern Ukrainian state, or at least a man who stood up against the oppression of a foreign state. Naturally, this has long complicated Jewish-Ukrainian relations—in Jewish memory, Khmelnytsky and his revolt are responsible for the massacre of half their population at the time. But one should always be mindful of the dangers of basing relations in the present day on events that occurred several centuries ago; doing so often distorts historical events into something more like pseudohistory, which is then more easily used to justify a particular identity for a nation or to retell a nation's history with a particular underlying narrative. While there are many examples of this sort of exploitation or misuse of history, it is hard to think of a more powerful reminder of how far this can go than Russia's war against Ukraine at the time of this writing, which Russia justifies with its own pseudohistorical account of what happened next in the Khmelnytsky Revolt story.

Khmelnytsky's military successes against the Polish were, to a great extent, only possible thanks to the support of the Crimean Tatars, a Muslim-majority group from Crimea who shared many of the Cossacks' complaints against the Polish. But the Tatars also had other interests, and before long Khmelnytsky realized he would need to swap out the Tatars for a new, more reliable ally. The best option turned out to be Tsar Alexei of Russia, to whom Khmelnytsky and his officers gathered to swear allegiance as their sovereign in the Ukrainian town of Pereiaslav in 1654.

The most immediate consequence of the Pereiaslav agreement was Russia's entry into the offensive against Poland, starting the war to be settled by the Truce of Andrusovo thirteen years later. Another important consequence, which took some time to fully develop, was the concretization of the idea that the Russians were "supposed" to have sovereignty over the Ukrainians, that Ukraine would be destined to be forever ruled by Russia. Indeed, for Russian historians, politicians, and propagandists alike, Pereiaslav has represented a "reunification of Russia and Ukraine," referring to the half-truth, half-mythical separation of the so-called Slavic nation—Kievan Rus—some five centuries earlier. In fact, Vladimir Putin's propaganda uses Pereiaslav to justify the assertion that an independent and sovereign Ukraine does not, should not, and cannot exist—even though that is certainly not what either the tsar or Khmelnytsky was thinking in 1654.[73]

Before we return to the story of the Jews of Ukraine, allow me to offer two takeaways—which, for the record, are as important anywhere else in the world as they are in Eastern Europe. The first is that history matters, that it matters a lot, and that far from merely being an academic pursuit, it has the power to influence decisions of life and death. The second is that history is what we make of it. If we allow ourselves to portray the important historical figures in our national history as perfect or godlike, to freely reinterpret historical events in whichever way best justifies our current behavior or beliefs, or to overwrite our historical narrative with propaganda, we are all but certain to be weaponizing history in one way or another—and history, as we know, is important.

Jews in Early Modern Ukraine

As just described, the Khmelnytsky Revolt inflicted a major blow to Jewish life in Ukraine, and thus not too much can be said of it in the century following 1648. Those who remained in the "Polish" side of Ukraine—the right bank—continued to grow their numbers, thanks to the mutually beneficial economic arrangement Jews in Poland had with the Polish nobility. Those on the "Russian" side—the left bank—fared differently. In addition to the expulsions mentioned earlier from the Empire in 1727 and 1742, as many as thirty five thousand Jews fled Russia between 1742 and 1753 according to some reports.[74] But then, as I'm sure the reader recalls, came the Partitions of Poland; all of a sudden, the Russian Empire had far more Jews within its borders than it could reasonably expel.

As we saw in the previous chapter, the division of Poland-Lithuania was terrible news for Polish Jews from just about day one. Ukraine's story, however, was a bit different.

For one thing, the Empire saw Ukraine as a long-lost part of its natural domain.[*] Ukraine also had the advantage that it was more Orthodox-inclined than Poland, had experienced significantly less industrialization and centralization than Poland, and was much more sparsely populated than Poland. These factors combined to create something of an authority power vacuum in the first few decades of Russian rule as the tsar and the decaying Polish nobility worked out their living arrangements. The factors also slowed the Empire's efforts to transform Ukraine into something more Russian. For much of the first half of that century, particularly in western Ukraine, the contested power left Ukraine's Jews with a somewhat absent ruler—or, more

---

[*] This claim deserves far more attention than I can give it here. It is far more mythological and historical, of course, but remains a core tenet of Russia's (and Putin's) official nationalist ideology. For further reading, see Orlando Figes, *The Story of Russia*, First edition (New York: Metropolitan Books/Henry Holt and Company, 2022); Nicholas V. Riasanovsky, *Russian Identities: A Historical Survey* (Oxford ; New York: Oxford University Press, 2005); Nicholas V. Riasanovsky and Mark D. Steinberg, *A History of Russia*, Ninth edition (New York: Oxford University Press, 2019); "Russia and Ukraine: Did They Reunite in 1654?" in *The Frontline: Essays on Ukraine's Past and Present*, by Serhii Plokhy, Harvard Series in Ukrainian Studies 81 (Cambridge, Massachusetts: Harvard University Press for the Ukrainian Research Institute, 2021), 37–54.

accurately, one who paid far more attention to the observance of these rules in Poland than in Ukraine. If anything, for the first fifty years after the Partitions, the Russians were more interested in winning the allegiance of the Ukrainians from the Polish than going full throttle in Russifying them. These dynamics yielded what Yohanan Petrovsky-Shtern refers to as the "golden age" of the shtetl—for a moment, thanks to a power vacuum and no immediate rush toward hard-core Russification, Jews in Ukraine enjoyed and thrived in a brief period of stability, economic opportunity, and laissez-faire governance.[75]

Of course, this certainly does not mean that Jews had complete religious, social, and economic liberty in that time and place; they most certainly did not. On average, though, they fared better than their Polish peers. As hinted above, one reason for this is that the Jews in Poland lived and worked alongside Poles, who the Russians were world-class experts in hating by that time. Indeed, after realizing that they had played a crucial role in the Polish economy that had created so much wealth for its nobility, Russia saw Polish Jews as a threat—hence all the prohibitions on what kinds of work they could do, as we saw implemented in the previous chapter, and why Russia so forcefully put down the Polish revolts in 1830 and 1863.

The Russian Empire felt differently about Ukraine. The left bank had already been part of the Empire for over a century, and as a whole, Ukraine was culturally, linguistically, and historically more aligned with Russia than Poland had ever been. Also, despite having a lingering presence, the influence of Polish nobility was decaying and falling out of favor with much of the Jewish population. In fact, some Jews were even excited to be ruled by Russians rather than by Poles and saw the change as something of a liberation. All this meant that Russia did not feel the need to punish the Jews in Ukraine, to tightly restrict their economic activity, or to immediately begin converting them into Russians—all of which the they had done in Poland. And while neither Jews nor Ukrainians at all satisfied the Empire's criteria for

Russianness, they both (though certainly the Ukrainians more than the Jews) were at least closer than the Poles. In time, the Russians even managed to convert the Ukrainian Jews to their view of Poland. As will be seen in later chapters, even in America, non-Polish Russian Jews looked down upon their Polish peers—and some Jewish immigrants from Poland even felt the same way about themselves.[76]

For a brief moment, it looked as if the Empire might manage to successfully bring Jews into its fold. Russian acts of goodwill, essentially unheard of in the Polish part of the Pale, not only occurred in Ukraine but were warmly and gratefully received by the Jews. Some Jews even found the Russians to be—again, at least at first—protective and good-willed rulers. Many fostered patriotic feelings toward the Empire, as is evident in the fervor with which many Ukrainian Jews sided with Russia in its fight against Napoleon, not only in words but in actions. Jews donated food and money to the Russian Army during the Napoleonic Wars, supplied the government with reconnaissance accumulated while traveling during merchant work, and even chased down Polish generals, messengers, and spies. For a split second, these actions earned Ukrainian Jews the trust and respect of the Russian Empire, and the respect was mutual.[77]

In the complete reverse of Mary Antin's frightened and scornful memories of the tsars' saint days, some Jews celebrated these days with great zeal, patriotism, and pride. On at least one occasion, a massive portrait of Tsar Nicholas I was hung from Berdychiv's Great Synagogue before a crowd of eight thousand, mostly Jews, who prayed for the health of the emperor, his family, and all government authorities—before cheering him! There was hardly ever such a level of patriotism and respect among Polish Jews for the Empire (which, of course, was not without justification).[78]

Again, we shouldn't get too carried away here; not everything was perfect. Though Jews could serve on town councils, for example, the law dictated that they could do so only at the cost of shaving their beards and dressing like traditional Russians. You might recall from the previous chapter a similar law in the early days of Russian rule in Poland—but note that while this law was just about serving on town councils, in Poland it applied to everyone. Indeed, in both Poland and Ukraine, this rule seems to have been inconsistently enforced. But this inconsistent enforcement left plenty of room for abuse by authorities (where there were any, at least), as well as for bribery, which became almost a way of life for Jews and gentiles alike in Ukraine just trying to go about their business. And bribery, on top of all the taxes one already paid, was expensive. Nonetheless, at least in the first two or three decades of the nineteenth century, Jews were generally better off under Russian rule in Ukraine than they were under Russian rule in Poland.[79]

The situation did not last, of course. Perhaps the first clear sign that the Empire was changing its tone was Nicholas I's implementation of the cantonist conscription system, as discussed in Chapter 1, which marked the end of any kind of warm relations between Russia and its Jews. The Polish uprisings in 1830 and 1863 (along with the many uprisings and revolutions across Central and Western Europe in 1848) only further stressed the urgency and importance of enforcing Russian nationality and loyalty to the tsar, and no longer would the Empire tolerate non-Russian identities within its borders. When progress toward these goals failed to materialize, in the late nineteenth century, government policy shifted away from attempting Russification and instead toward enforcing and preserving the lesser status of Jews in the Empire. This brought a new wave of reactionary laws—most notoriously 1882's "May Laws"—which restricted Jewish access to higher education, prohibited Jews from moving to or buying land in most rural areas, and imposed further regulations on Jewish businesses. Jews were also barred from tavern-keeping and the liquor trade, two of the best economic opportunities available to them. The tide had turned, and life in Ukraine—and throughout the Pale—became increasingly intolerable for the approximately four million Jews residing there.[80]

Before we take a closer look at a few Ukrainian towns, I'd like to introduce a quote from Symon Petliura, the commander of Ukraine's armed forces during its war for independence immediately after the First World War. We'll come back to this quote and the story that prompted it in Chapter 6, but I feel obligated to include it here, given the story told thus far and the ongoing war in Ukraine. In a declaration admonishing his troops for instigating and taking part in violence against Ukrainian Jews during Ukraine's first true stand for independence just over a century ago, Petliura offered an interesting and important perspective:

> It is time to realize that the world Jewish population...was enslaved and deprived of its national freedom, just as we [Ukrainians] were...[Jews have] been living with us since time immemorial, sharing our fate and misfortune with us. I resolutely order that all those who incite you to carry out pogroms be expelled from our army and tried as traitors to the Fatherland.[81]

While the story of the first half of this book is of Russian oppression of the Jews in the seventeenth through twentieth centuries, an experience shared by the Ukrainians and many others, today it is the Ukrainians who are on the other side of Russia's imperial tendency toward oppression and aggression. Even over a century after the last of my ancestors left Ukraine, Russia is attempting to deprive a nationality—the Ukrainians, this time—of their right to self-determination in a vain attempt to bring them into the Russian nation, where the Russians believe they truly belong. This is not too dissimilar to the experience of the Jews in the Russian Empire (and in the Soviet Union). But while that story has all but ended for the Jews, the Ukrainians have not been so lucky.* We may not share the same fates and misfortunes with Ukrainians on the front lines today, but if we stand aside in indifference, we very well might one day. Indeed, not only Jews but the West itself will, in the long run, share the fate of the Ukrainians; whether that fate is victory or destruction is up to us.

With this in mind, let's begin our tour of Jewish Ukraine and meet my Ukrainian ancestors.

Right-Bank Ukraine: Bershad and Kyiv

We begin our journey in Ukraine's right bank, which was where the Russian Empire began its exploration of these new lands too. After all, while most of the left bank had been part of the Empire for nearly a century and a half, the right bank was mostly new. Moreover, much these new lands were a good bit farther away from Russia and its government; they were not as familiar and easy to imagine as the left bank was. Thus, it was precisely to the right bank that Russia dispatched its explorers and scouts to find out what, exactly, was actually there.

The Russians fell in love with what they found—or at least the geography of it. Traveling through the southern part of the right bank, one Russian officer noted that it "looked like a gorgeous orchard…wonderful land, fantastic climate, beautiful places. [You] get amazed and start thinking: it is here that you would like to live."[82] Thus, despite its remoteness, by the start of the nineteenth century, even a town like Bershad, a small shtetl roughly 150 miles south of Kyiv and twenty miles northeast of Moldova's modern borders, already had Russian courts and government offices established in it.

---

* To be clear, the Ukrainians are far from the only nation challenged by Russia's imperial tendencies. Belarussians, for example, remain "deprived of national freedom" under president-dictator Lukashenko's Russophilic rule. Nor is Ukraine the site of post-communist Russia's first war of imperial aggression; for further reading, see Ali Askerov, Stefan M. Brooks, and Lasha Tchantouridzé, eds., *Post-Soviet Conflicts: The Thirty Years' Crisis* (Lanham: Lexington Books, 2020).

Bershad was home to just 250 Jews in 1776, due to the various and seemingly perpetual wars and antisemitic violence in the area going back at least to the seventeenth century. Indeed, Bershad's Jewish community was attacked during Khmelnytsky's Revolt, during which (according to legend) its Jews were massacred in the Dokhna, the river that runs through that shtetl. Centuries later, local Jewish superstition still held that one must absolutely not bathe in the Dokhna unless a sacrifice had been made in the water, lest one wished to be cursed. But true to the resiliency of the Jewish people, Jewish life recovered and was even flourishing by the early 1800s, even after Bershad became part of the Pale of Settlement. The Jewish population swelled from that 250 in 1776 to 2,941 in 1853; by 1889, it reached 7,200.[83] And it is during that time of growth when our story in Ukraine begins. On (or around) January 15, 1864, my great-great-great-grandfather Israel Wexler was born in Bershad.*

I think a side note may be necessary here. Wexler is a surname by no means unique to my family—in fact, I would feel comfortable making a bet that most readers with a connection to the Jewish world know at least one person with that surname. "Wexler" itself comes from the Yiddish and/or German word for money-changer, a person who would exchange coins of any of the innumerable currencies of the pre-modern world into any other currency—a precursor to modern foreign exchange markets. Money-changing was a predecessor of banking and foreign exchange, but contrary to popular belief and stereotype, Jews were far from the only participants in money-changing; they were hardly the only participants in most financial activities, for that matter.[84]

In fact, the use of the surname may say more about the Jewish response to forced cultural assimilation than anything else, including

---

* It will become a recurring theme that birthdates in the Pale not confirmed in official records are almost comedically unreliable. The Wexlers, however, will wind up being above and beyond the most inconsistent about their own birthdays.

the adopter's occupation. When Jews throughout the Russian Empire were forced to adopt surnames, many Jews in the Ukrainian provinces Volhynia and Podolia, where the Wexlers lived, often chose artificial and even outlandish surnames mostly of German origin in mockery of the mandate, just as their counterparts in Austrian Poland had done.[85] Also, of course, "Wexler" was not how any Wexler would have spelled it, at least before they Americanized. When they first spelled it in the Latin alphabet, they typically opted for Wechsler, Veksler, or any variation along those lines—but, of course, they certainly were not writing in the Latin alphabet in the Pale!*

Regardless, as Israel grew to adulthood, Bershad became home to a central synagogue, seven additional houses of worship, and nine Jewish schools. Jews owned the vast majority of shops in the city center, and Bershad even elected a Jewish deputy mayor in 1874.

The city also became a center of Chasidic Judaism thanks to the widespread popularity and influence of the teachings of Rabbi Raphael—of Bershad—from earlier in the nineteenth century.[86] Perhaps I am a bit biased, but one of my favorite quotes from the Jewish world happens to be attributed to Raphael:

> When I go to the heavenly court, they'll ask me, "Why didn't you learn more Torah?" And I'll tell them that I'm slow-witted. Then they'll ask me, "Why didn't you do more...for others?" And I'll tell them that I'm physically weak. Then they'll ask me, "Why didn't you give more to charity?" And I'll tell them that I didn't have enough money. But then they'll ask me, "If you were so stupid, weak, and poor, why were you so arrogant?" And for that, I won't have an answer.[87]

---

* Like German, its nearest relative, Yiddish has no "w" sound. "Veksler" is likely closer to how Israel and his family would have pronounced their surname.

Raphael's insistence on the wearing of tzitzit and tallit* proved particularly influential in the region and led to Bershad's emergence as the preeminent manufacturer of tzitzit and tallit in Ukraine, a trade that became an important source of income for many Jewish families. Only after the mass emigration to be discussed in subsequent chapters did Bershad lose its status as the producer of the finest tzitzit and tallit—indeed, the entire industry faded away there.

The historical record loosely suggests that Israel's parents were David and Mimie Wexler, but I cannot know for sure. His entire childhood is unknown, but we can assume with reasonable confidence that it was a religious childhood: family tradition preserves the fact that he was a pious man with an incredible knowledge of the Torah. His immersion and education in the Jewish faith likely began at a young age and never ended; indeed, even a few decades later and several thousand miles away, Israel would one day help run a Hebrew school in Philadelphia.

In 1882, at eighteen years old, he married Hannah Berdichevsky, a girl born twenty miles away in the nearby shtetl of Teplyk in March 1864. Hannah's family name certainly implies that some part of her family had roots in Berdychiv, another important and much larger center of Chasidism about 120 miles northwest of Teplyk and Bershad. Yet I know of no record that confirms Berdychiv to be one of my ancestral hometowns—in fact, the only other thing I know about Hannah's family is her father's name, Manuel.

Israel and Hannah had two children in Bershad: Hannah (known to the family as Anna, which I'll abide by to avoid confusion with her mother) in 1885, followed by Jacob in 1888.† By that time, the quality of

---

* Tassels modeled after those worn in Ancient Israel and a prayer shawl, respectively.

† Even though the year varied when he was asked, I'm somewhat confident this is the correct year. I'm far less confident about the exact day or even the month.

life in Ukraine had deteriorated considerably, including in Bershad, resulting in the Wexlers leaving their home—and the Pale entirely—around Jacob's fifth birthday. We'll pick up their story later.

Bershad's Great Synagogue, date unknown.[88]

Sometimes it is in February, other times in May, and rarely was the same day given twice. In fact, only one was: February 8, 1888. That would be my best guess for my great-great-grandfather's birthday, but I would not put too much money on it; his younger brother (born in America) later claimed the same date (although in a different year).

Bershad's only remaining synagogue, whose interior has been unchanged for one hundred years, and its preserved Torah.[89]

NEXT YEAR IN AMERICA

Now, let us turn to a place far more likely to be a familiar name to the reader: Kyiv. While today it is an enormous city that sprawls across both sides of the Dnieper, eighteenth-century Kyiv was much smaller and primarily concentrated on the right bank. Of course, the city's value was significant enough for the Truce of Andrusovo to include Kyiv in the lands transferred from Poland-Lithuania to Russia, even though Russia was supposed to only get the left bank. Although it was certainly a larger city than Bershad, Jewish life in Kyiv was not too dissimilar from that in the shtetl. In fact, the main differences were due to its larger size and thus its greater perceived importance by the Russians.

The Jewish community of Kyiv had hardly ever known stability: they had been kicked out of the city in 1654 and only allowed to return (without welcome) after the second Partition of Poland in 1793, after which Nicholas I banned them once again in 1827. However, in recognition of the significant positive influence Jews had in the regional economy, the actual enforcement of the tsar's eviction order was postponed twice until the tsar finally got his way in 1835. Yet even banishment was still far from the end of Jewish life in Kyiv. Owing to their prevalence in the marketplace, Jews continued to attend Kyiv's fairs (where they made up about half of all merchants), and by 1850, they were permitted to return to the city so long as they lived in specifically designated inns—*and* as long as they brought their own food.[90]

Another decade later, the inns were somewhat swapped out in favor of simply levying heavy taxes upon any Jew who sought to reside in the city; in return, they were allowed residency in two suburbs, Lybid and Podil. The expense was clearly worth it: the number of Jews living in Kyiv rose from only three thousand (3 percent of that city's population) in 1863 to almost fourteen thousand (12 percent of the population) only a decade later. Kyiv's Jews ranged from wealthy merchants and industrialists to shopkeepers, laborers, artisans, and everyone else in between.[91]

In response to the assassination of Tsar Alexander II in 1881, a pogrom—supported by Kyiv's own governor—broke out, which ultimately became among the worst of the Empire-wide programs triggered by the assassination. Nearly 800 Jewish families were financially or materially ruined; many lost their lives, and several businesses were looted or destroyed. In the aftermath of the pogrom, Kyiv effectively decided that Jews once again would no longer be welcome in their city, at least certainly not as residents. Any who resided in town without the proper permissions to do so—which were many—were hunted down and removed. Even those who had their papers in order could not be sure that they would be spared.[92]

Under such conditions, Pinkus and his wife, Clara (Leafin) Satalof, were born, raised, and married in Kyiv, whether they had the legal right to be there or not. Pinkus, born in 1860 to Abraham and Hannah Satalof, seems to have been a tailor of some kind, whereas nothing is known about Clara's family, other than that she was born sometime around 1865. They likely married in the years leading up to the 1881 pogrom; shortly thereafter, they had their first child, Abraham, in 1884. The Satalofs would go on to have seven more children, although none of them would be born in Kyiv; only three were even born in the Pale. As with the Wexlers, circumstances deteriorated to the point where they, too, had to leave, and we will return to their story in a few chapters.

Left-Bank Ukraine: Chernihiv and Novhorod-Siverskyi

Somewhat more sparsely populated than the right bank, left-bank Ukraine was—and remains at the time of this writing, despite hosting the front lines of an ongoing war—a beautiful, serene, and rural region. I must note, however, that the towns described below, along with many, many more on the left bank, have been shelled, occupied, and ransacked by the Russians at one point or another since they began their full-scale invasion in February 2022; both Chernihiv and Novhorod-Siversky, the main towns of focus here, were brutally occupied in the early days of the invasion. It is a terrible fact that to this day, Russia continues a strategy of violence, oppression, and impoverishment in the same places where my ancestors (and quite possibly yours) endured similar hardships over a century ago. Once again, we should not be indifferent.

As far back as I can trace, each of my left-bank ancestors was born and raised in Chernihiv Province, in the northeast corner of Ukraine. In 1869, the province had a total population of over one and a half million, of whom 35,624—roughly 2.2 percent—were Jews. As one might guess, Chernihiv was and remains the capital of the province. Like the other Ukrainian towns, it has a complicated but long history with Jews. They were there as early as the thirteenth century but were soon expelled and did not return until the start of the seventeenth century; then, despite surviving a threat of expulsion in 1623, the community was destroyed again in 1648 during the Khmelnytsky Revolt, after which Jews did not return to Chernihiv until the creation of the Pale of Settlement over a century later. After all, since Chernihiv had been under Russian control since 1667, effectively no Jews could legally live there until it was made part of the Pale in 1794, and few lived in the region until well into the nineteenth century.

In the 1840s, Chernihiv's 2,600 Jews made up about a fifth of the town's population of approximately 14,000. By the end of the century, however, the 8,800 Jews who called the area home made up just over a third of the population, and Jewish growth outpaced gentile growth at nearly double the rate. While not as large as Kyiv, Chernihiv was a relatively big town, perhaps the second largest of any Eastern European city we'll explore in this book. Roughly 26,400 people lived in Chernihiv, according to the 1897 census, and an additional 136,000 lived in the immediate district. It is worth mentioning, however, that many Jews from Chernihiv were more accurately "from Chernihiv": only 10 percent of the Jews in the province lived in Chernihiv proper. Many lived in smaller, rural villages (most of which could be called shtetls) until doing so was banned in 1882, at which point they moved to Chernihiv proper or out of the Russian Empire entirely.

In Chernihiv, the growing Jewish community had opened their own elementary schools, a school for children of poor families, and a vocational school for girls. In addition to the common occupations of tailoring and shoemaking, Chernihiv had a strong tobacco industry, where many Jews worked in one way or another. By the mid-nineteenth century, several Jews had made their way into the merchant class, even if it still did not guarantee wealth, well-being, or even safety. The merchants made their money typically by selling agricultural goods, while the vast majority of the others were craftsmen—specifically tailors, the vocation of 30 percent of Chernihiv's Jews.[93]

Though my great-grandfather was of the impression—at least when he was well into his nineties and began discussing his family with me—that his parents were from Kyiv, they were certainly not. His parents, Pearl Rabinowitz and Mottel Shusterman, were both born in Chernihiv—his mother on May 15, 1888, and his father on June 1, 1885. Though fortune has so thankfully passed down a photograph of Pearl and her father, I have only partial confidence in her father's name—Yehuda—and only uncertain guesses at her mother's. On the other hand, I know Mottel's parents were Herschel and Hannah and that Mottel had at least five siblings: Samuel ("Ovsey" back in Chernihiv), David, Abram, Sarah, and Bessie.

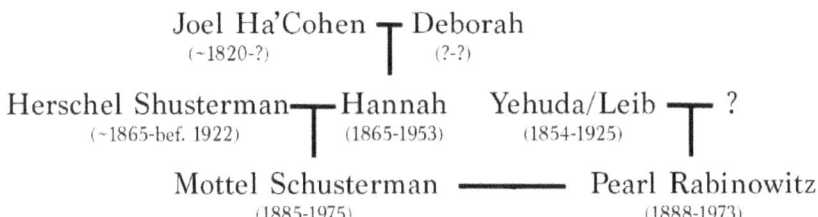

Chernihiv circa 1910, as Mottel and Pearl would have remembered it.[94]

Chernihiv's market square shortly before the Russian Revolution.[95]

Family tradition maintains that Pearl's father was a cantor or rabbi of some sort. What I discovered long after first hearing that story was that curiously enough, Hannah, Max's mother, was the daughter of a rabbi. I know nothing else about him other than his name, which is recorded (in Hebrew) on Hannah's tombstone as Rabbi Yael Ha'Cohen—Joel "the priest." Mottel and Pearl met and fell in love in Chernihiv, but they married 4,725 miles away in the New World; we will return to their story later.

Pearl and her father photographed before she left Chernihiv.

NEXT YEAR IN AMERICA

Contemporaries in time but strangers to Mottel's parents were the innovators—perhaps inventors—of my family name: the Scherovskys.* Tucked away in the northeastern-most reaches of Ukraine (though still in Chernihiv Province), Benjamin Scherovsky had at least two children, Yehuda (born in 1844) and Hannah (born around 1860). Yehuda, who was some sort of a merchant, married Masha or Menya—the record is unclear—Estrin in the late 1860s, with whom he had at least six children. By the mid-1880s, Yehuda and his family were living in Novhorod-Siverskyi, a relatively major outpost about one hundred miles northeast of Kyiv in northeastern Chernihiv. By that time, Yehuda's sister Hannah had married Hersh Yakubson, with whom she would have several children, including Abraham, their first, in 1881.

Other branches of the family, most likely related either through Masha/Menya's side or through the Yakubsons, were the Rosenbaums and Mitteroffs, who were living in Nosivka and Nizhyn on the outskirts of Chernihiv's capital. The reader's guess as to how Mendel Rosenbaum, son of Schmerl Rosenbaum and Sonia Mitteroff, was a nephew of Hersh Yakubson or Hannah Scherovsky is as good as mine.

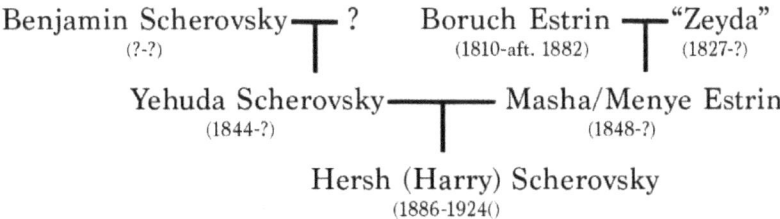

---

* In the original Cyrillic, Щеровский.

Yehuda and Masha had at least their sixth child in Novhorod-Siverskyi, most likely on June 20, 1886: Hersh Scherovsky, my great-great-grandfather.*

Jews had lived in Hersh's native Novhorod-Siverskyi ever since they had been permitted to at the start of the seventeenth century. A small community had even lived there some time earlier. By the end of the nineteenth century, the town's 2,941 Jews made up a third of its population, had established five synagogues and prayer houses, and maintained six Jewish schools. But despite its remoteness and the Jewish community's prominence, Novhorod-Siverskyi was just as prone to antisemitic violence as anywhere else. Three hundred fifty years after a terrible pogrom killed nearly all of the town's Jews in the sixteenth century, fifty-nine Jewish families were killed in a pogrom in 1905 that was part of a series of pogroms that began two years earlier in Krinshev; another and more deadly one occurred fifteen years later.[96] Whether Hersh's family survived either pogrom is unknown, but Hersh had luckily already left a year before the 1905 one. The absence of any information, mention, or record of his parents—including anything passed down to my grandparents—always led me to suspect that, whether due to the pogrom or something else, neither survived for long after their son came to America, and it's possibly they weren't alive then.

Little is known of Hersh's life in Novhorod-Siverskyi. We know that like so many other Jews living in the Pale, he was a tailor, while his cousin Mendel was some sort of a painter (likely not as an artist but for work). But if his childhood was anything like that of most boys growing up there, he came of age in a culturally rich Jewish community. Most likely, he attended school to study ethics and theology via the Torah, Talmud, and many other great Jewish texts, and he spent his summers

---

* May 5 was once given as a birth date, but all other times he always gave the same June date, even if his birth year changed from 1886 to 1883. As we will see, the change in birth year may have just been to make his wife feel better.

playing with his peers along the serene, forested shores of the Desna or perhaps even in the river.

Novhorod-Siverskyi's main street circa 1900.[97]

Novhorod-Siverskyi circa 1910.[98]

However, glimpses into his personality traits later as an adult seem to suggest that there were a few things that perhaps separated him from his peers. While he most certainly had been steeped in a traditional Jewish education, he also seemed to have a natural business acumen that went far beyond anything required for the normal day-to-day life of a tailor. Additionally, he seemed to have an easy go at learning languages well enough to speak, read, and write them fluently, even though he may never have come across them prior to becoming an adult. And the scrappy grit required of a boy growing up in rural Ukraine was seemingly easily replaced, as if he always understood what a refined life lived well would look like.

We'll get back to his story soon. First, we need to check in on the Lefcovitch family, who'd emigrated from Gąbin, Poland, back in the 1870s to London.

Novhorod-Siverskyi's riverfront, captured by a Nazi soldier in April 1943.[99]

The Desna near Novhorod-Siverskyi, which flows onward to Chernihiv and Kyiv.[100]

Chapter 4
BEYOND THE PALE

✦────────✦

[The] masses made their own decision. Millions would soon tear themselves away from the land that held the dust of their ancestors; millions would leave the [shtetls] and cities in which they had built their life, their Houses of Study and burial societies, their wooden synagogues and paintless houses, their feeble economy and thriving culture. Obsolete artisans, socialist firebrands, bewildered wives, religious fanatics, virtuosos of the violin, illiterate butchers, scribblers of poetry, cobblers, students, luftmenshen—above all, the numberless ordinary Jews, the folksmasen for whom being a Jew was not an idea or a problem but the vibrant substance of their lives—now began to ready themselves. And not merely because their life in common was weak, but because as Jews they knew themselves to be strong.[101]

~ Irving Howe

As the nineteenth century entered its final quarter, the approximately five million Jews within the Pale of Settlement were approaching a breaking point. The list of grievances and difficulties was long. The pan-European revolutionary episode in 1848, along with the Polish rebellions in 1830 and 1863, reinvigorated the Russian Empire's efforts to oppress and suppress non-Russian culture, nationality, and politics, with generally disastrous consequences for the Jews. By the end of the century, Jews were restricted from owning land (in most cases, at least), were effectively barred from tavern-keeping and the liquor trade (a couple of the best economic opportunities available to them), had strict quotas implemented on their enrollment in high schools and universities (some of the very few opportunities to leave the Pale), and were barred from most positions in the civil service (one of the only pathways into Russian life).

Then, in addition to discrimination and oppression, there was the belated arrival of industrialization to the Empire. Industrialization brought along the decline of the goods- and crafts-based local economy of the Pale, which in turn impoverished the majority of Jews who had been earning their living in the local marketplace for over a century. The Empire's rapidly growing railroad network helped speed this process up by shifting economic activity from production to marketplaces toward more urban centers. Ultimately, trains drained the shtetls of population and economic opportunity. Compounding things was the even more belated abolition of serfdom within Russia in 1861. The reorganization and relocation of non-Jewish serfs (the Jews were never serfs, owing to their separate and distinct legal status) both in the Pale and in the Empire at large created major changes in the Pale's economy, hardly any of which benefited the Jews.[102]

The Emigration Question

Unsurprisingly, emigration became an increasingly attractive idea. But its consideration also imposed the consideration of another question: to where?

The perhaps self-evident answer for the vast majority of those who chose to leave was the United States of America. Despite being much farther—a transatlantic crossing farther—than the (relatively) more liberally and democratically minded nations in Western Europe, at least four out every five Jews who fled the Russian Empire between 1870 and 1925 headed to the United States. Indeed, even many of those who did not go to America at first eventually found their way there, including, the Lefcovitch and Lazarus families from Gąbin, Poland.

Next Year in America

As those who intended to go straight to America knew, and as many who first went to Western and Central Europe soon found out, antisemitism was quite in style across much of Europe at the time. While just about anywhere might have been better than the Russian Empire, if one were to go through the immense ordeal of emigration, it would have to be worth it, understandably.[103]

America, on the other hand, was mostly free of the perception that it may be more trouble than the emigration process was worth—but this seriously understates how positively many Jews in the Pale felt about the United States. As early as the 1820s, America had taken on a nearly promised-land-type representation in the collective imagination as a land of opportunity, freedom, and security; it was the *goldeneh medina*— "the golden land"—to many Yiddish-speaking optimists.

Of course, there were plenty of positive things to say about the United States' relations with its Jews. In his famous letter to the Jewish community of Newport, Rhode Island, George Washington expressed his sincere aspiration that "the Children of the Stock of Abraham, who dwell in this land, continue to merit and enjoy the good will of the other Inhabitants; while everyone shall sit in safety under his own vine and fig tree, and there shall be none to make him afraid." Meanwhile, in the year after Washington's letter, the Russian Empire created the Pale of Settlement. The stark difference between religious freedom in America and religion-based oppression in Russia was as clear to many Jews in the Pale as it is to us today.[104]

By the second half of the nineteenth century, networks of print media—even Jewish print media—had developed enough that literate Jews, who made up a far greater share of their population than literate Russians, could learn about America, at least if they had the time and money. Mary Antin recalled her uncle owning secular, Western books— *Robinson Crusoe*, for example—that had been translated into Russian or Yiddish.[105] Jewish immigrant and memoirist Ben Reisman was lent a copy of a book about Christopher Columbus's discovery of America written in German.[106] Evidently, Eastern European Jews were interested in travel, discovery, and foreign worlds—most of all, though, as Mary Antin put it, "America was in everybody's mouth":

> Businessmen talked of it over their accounts; the market women made up their quarrels that they might discuss it from stall to stall; people who had relatives in the famous land went around reading their letters for the enlightenment of less fortunate folk...all talked of it, but scarcely anyone knew one true fact about this magic land.[107]

And what a magic land America was considered to be: in justifying why one would go through with emigrating, despite its tremendous hardships, a group of early Jewish emigrants argued that:

> [America] is the most civilized region, and offers the most guarantees of individual freedom, freedom of conscience, and security of all property...and endows every one of her inhabitants with both civil and political rights.[108]

Minnie Goldstein recalled her father's explanation to his wife, justifying the move overseas (emphasis added):

> I want to go to a country where heavy labor is no disgrace. I want to go to a country where everyone is equal, where the rich also work, and work is no disgrace. I want to go to America, where a Jew does not have to take off his hat and wait outside to see a Pole. In other words, *I want to go to a country where I can work hard and make a living for my wife and children and be equal to everyone.*[109]

This kind of sentiment instilled in the Jewish psyche to the point that it found its way even into lullabies: "In America, they say / There is never any death / It's a paradise for all / A real heaven on earth," went one.¹¹⁰ Sometimes it was the simple things: Rose Cohen remembered her grandmother, anxious about her son's soon departure for America, "consoled herself by saying, 'Oh, but socks are cheap out there, as no doubt everything else must be, and they say that it is not as cold in America as in Russia.'"¹¹¹

In addition to economic opportunities and religious freedom, some also sought the excitement and adventure in the journey and concept of emigration. One Jewish immigrant recalled many years later (emphasis added):

> I am a tailor and I was working piecework on Russian officers' uniforms. *I saved up a few dollars and figured the best thing was to go to the U.S.A.* Those days everybody's dream in the old country was to go to America. We heard people were free and we heard about better living. I was seventeen when I came in 1905. I was the first to leave from my family. My father didn't want me to go...*I figured, I have a trade, I have a chance more or less to see the world. I was young.*¹¹²

The hint of spontaneity, the "I guess I may as well," though evident here, is a clear statement that, at least to some, the long and unimaginable voyage could be worth it just for the adventure alone. (I often wonder if this quote describes Hersh Scherovsky's mindset coming here.) Some younger boys were sometimes perhaps a little too eager to get away from the *yeshiva* and get out and see the world (emphasis added):

> When mother saw me copying the addresses she asked me where I [a ten-year-old boy] was going. To my surprise, she said, "Very well, you can go." She looked over the addresses I had copied to make sure they were correct. The next day she assembled a few items...and tied it all in a large multi-colored handkerchief. She gave me 40 groshn [ten cents] and a post card with my home address on it, and she told me to mail it as soon as I

crossed the Russian-German border. *She took me to the railroad station, kissed me goodbye, and put me on the train with no railroad ticket, no ship ticket, no passport.* She probably thought this would be another escapade and that I would be back home as usual, though what was really in her thoughts I will never know. Thus my venturesome journey to America began.[113]

But not everyone was sold. Especially at first, those most excited by America—and those most likely to emigrate—tended to be the younger generations. They had hardly known life before industrialization, but with much of their life still ahead of them, they were concerned about their economic outlook in the Pale. And having been born several generations after the destruction of the Polish-Lithuanian Commonwealth, they also felt little attachment or nostalgia toward their homelands—they had only ever known it as a place of oppression and poverty. Many saw traditional ways of making a living being taken away from them, either by government restriction or by economic obsolescence. Those who tried factory work were often disappointed by the pitiful and discriminatory wages and found that they were unable to compete with the factories outside of the Pale anyway; the value of yearly output per person was five times higher in Russia as a whole than it was in Pale by 1913.[114]

Those who were not so excited about America or emigration itself tended to be among the older generations or the more religious and traditionally minded.[115] Their views on America were quite different. As "children played at emigrating," Mary Antin remembered, "old folks shook their sage heads over the evening fire, and prophesied no good for those who braved the terrors of the sea and the foreign goal beyond it."[116] In the late nineteenth century, conservative voices within the Pale opposed emigration to America on the grounds that it was "a corrupt and sinful land where the Sabbath is no Sabbath [and even] on Yom Kippur they don't fast."[117] Some were also worried about whether the economic opportunities in America were really available. Antin recalled the shock and disappointment in her father's first letter back to his family in the Pale. While Antin's father had indeed found that there was no "disgrace to work at a trade" in America, that all children went to school, and that "the cobbler and the teacher had the same title, 'Mister,'" he also found it demotivating and difficult to establish himself there. "It was plain, from my father's letters, that he was scarcely able to support himself in America, and that there was no immediate prospect of our joining him."[118]

The older, more conservative Jews' opposition to emigration meant that many younger ones—including Ben Reisman, who was told by his soon-to-be bride's uncle that "only impious people went to America"—kept their intentions secret.[119] Reisman and many other single Jewish males sought to be married as soon as possible in hopes that their bride's dowry would help finance the trip to America, but this required going through great lengths to avoid any suspicion of a desire to emigrate. Even the suggestion of emigration was unacceptable to some, including memoirist Rose Silverman's father, who scolded her for just hinting at her desire to leave; she would only "go to America over my dead body."[120]

To be clear, those who did choose to emigrate were anything but a group of progressive apostates. The vast majority were still practicing Jews, but their practice was already beginning to look different. For the younger Jews working in the industrial economy, the spaces in which they worked, the people with and for whom they worked, and the goods they made were far less Jewish than ever before. Accordingly, work no longer accommodated their religious and cultural practices and preferences as easily or comfortably as had been the case some decades earlier; gone were the days of Jewish self-employment, which had enabled complete observance of religious protocol. To avoid starvation and make rent, things had to change—something the older generations and many religious authorities were fundamentally opposed to. Their authority and influence, however, was increasingly questioned. After all, the Empire's oppressive policies had affected and impoverished just about every Jew in the Pale, resulting in what Eli Lederhendler referred to as "declassification." Aside from perhaps 1 percent of the population, everyone was in the same boat—so who were they to dictate your life?[121]

The First Steps Beyond

At some point between 1872 and 1876, the newly married Nysen Lefcovitch and Sarah Lazarus had made up their minds: there was no future for them in Gąbin and certainly not for their newborn son. It was time to leave. I am not entirely sure what brought them to this decision exactly when they made it; the exodus from the Russian Empire didn't truly begin until the next decade. But even though they may have left relatively early, their choice was undoubtedly motivated by the same reasons as the two million Jews who fled over the subsequent half century: the same grievances outlined above.

One difference, though, was that rather than heading to America, they went to the United Kingdom—more specifically, to London. Needless to say, Nysen and Sarah were hardly the first Jews to arrive in London or the United Kingdom. In fact, the earliest confirmed Jews in the British Isles came from Rouen with William the Conqueror as part of his conquest eight centuries earlier in 1066, at his invitation. Since Jews were not religiously forbidden to lend at interest and already had a proto-banking network with contacts throughout Europe, they played an integral role in England's economy by the eleventh and twelfth centuries. This came to an end in the thirteenth century, however, when, despite their economic benefits and value as human beings, Edward I forcefully expelled all of the British Isles' roughly 3,000 Jews. Not until after the English Civil War four centuries later were they permitted to return.[122]

But despite that history, London became one of the main destinations for Jewish migrants in the nineteenth century, largely due to the city's tolerance for Jews. In 1831, Jews were granted the "freedom of the city," which greatly expanded their available economic opportunities and granted them a number of social and political privileges. London effectively forced Parliament to lift the ban on Jews sitting in Parliament after they voted in Baron Lionel de Rothschild not once but twice and had the first Jewish lord mayor in 1855. And, of course, the London-born Benjamin Disraeli became the first—and so far only—Jewish-born prime minister of the United Kingdom.[123]

Between 1850 and 1881, London's Jewish population almost doubled from about 35,000 to 60,000. That rapid rise as a destination of choice for migrants like the Lefcovitches was, in large part, due to its Jewish population's notorious hospitality. Though the heart of London's Jewish quarter was in Whitechapel and Spitalfields, by the second half of the nineteenth century, some Jews had become wealthy enough to move from London's traditionally poorer East End to the wealthier West End. Yet those who found success did not forget about where they came from and set up charities and programs to assist the typically poor and uneducated or undereducated new arrivals. The Jewish Board of Guardians serves as a prime example: set up in 1859 by a group of wealthy Jews, it provided food, shelter, financial assistance, and skill training to Jewish immigrants, eventually becoming an invaluable system for newcomers.[124]

With their greater experience in London, wealthier Jews also encouraged immigrants to assimilate and blend into English culture as best they could—far less forcefully, of course, than the Russians did. To that end was the Jewish Free School. Established in 1732 and still open to this day, operating true to its name as a free school for the children of Jewish immigrants, it was also a school of English culture with the mission to take in Eastern European Jews and turn out anglicized ones. After all, the incoming migrants almost universally arrived without any knowledge of English or of life in London; they came only with whatever skills they learned at home, which became increasingly outdated, irrelevant, or unnecessary outside of the shtetl economy. Without charities like the Board of Guardians and the Jewish Free School, many immigrants would have been unable to find any means by which to support themselves in their new home; some may have had to return home.[125]

Even with the help of charities, though, life was still far from easy for an immigrant. Without being able to communicate with native Londoners or work on the Sabbath, Jews often had no one else to turn to for employment but other Jews. Though the employing Jews understood the struggle and had likely been in their employees' shoes only a few years earlier, such employment by was often unpleasant and exploitative. The majority found work in the common professions back home, as tailors, shoemakers, or cabinetmakers, but many others worked as tobacco merchants or grocers, while some worked in sweatshops, mines, and other exhausting and dangerous industrial labor. Women were provided with work opportunities, too, typically in the home, thanks to the close-knit nature of Jewish communities.[126]

Despite the encouragement of the Jewish elite, Jewish assimilation into London only went so far. In both the Pale of Settlement and London, Jews typically refrained from adopting local customs. Contemporaries could immediately recognize immigrants as Jewish because they were visually distinct from other groups by their dress and linguistically distinct by their use of Yiddish. "But for the street architecture," one commentator claimed, "one might easily imagine the place to be the busy quarter of an Eastern town."[127]

In Jewish London, an area of several miles by the final quarter of the nineteenth century, one heard nearly exclusively Yiddish. Indeed, despite the fact that many Jewish immigrants learned English, language barriers often remained a problem. Contemporary stories tell of a Polish girl who got lost and was taken to an asylum by the police (who misunderstood her and thought she was insane) and of a rabbi who was married by mistake after stopping by a register office with the intent to get a few basic questions answered. These stories may or may not have been entirely true, but the problem itself was real; London's police eventually had to be taught Yiddish.[128]

The foreignness left most Londoners with little interest in interacting with the Jewish community. So too did its lowly state: in no small part due to overcrowding, the streets of the Jewish quarter were often messy, littered with rotting food and vegetables. Nothing about the Jewish community made sense to the English:

> The state of the windows, condition of curtains, fixtures and flowers...advertised the Jewish presence. Clean curtains, tidy blinds, wax flowers, fruits displayed under a glass case in the front window—these, the signifiers of respectability, were significant absences from Jewish homes. But if not respectable, Jews were not rough. It was the singularity of Jewish culture and customs that was most striking. The newcomers, though quarrelsome and noisy, were essentially private people not much given to brawling and boozing or the lower forms of street life. Their home-centeredness found expression in the attention lavished upon children, in the rarity of wife-beating and in their generally orderly conduct. The 'Jewish type' of child, said Inspector Reid, was fairly dressed, clean, well-fed and booted. 'Jews rarely get drunk', said Inspector Barker, his colleague from the Benthal Green Division. 'Jew women as a rule lead happier lives than Gentile women, more respected by the husband and more faithful'. Jews, in short, did not fit easily into the language of class...Immigrant Jews, it seemed, lived within English society but were not part of it.[129]

Due to overcrowding and economic isolation, poverty in the Jewish quarter was widespread and of a different—and worse—nature than that seen in other immigrant communities. The slow but steady overcrowding of Jewish London meant that several families were often cramped into each small home, regardless of wealth. Inside, these homes were generally reported as "dirtier" than those lived in by Englishmen of similar class. Charles Booth, the sociologist famous for his work on poverty in London at the turn of the twentieth century, figured about 75 percent of London's Jews were poor; the poorest could be seen "sleeping on landings." Their cultural, linguistic, and religious differences left Jews unable to find work outside of the Jewish community, which could only employ so many people without leading to a fall in wages or mass unemployment. By Booth's time, despite the best efforts of Jewish charities, there were simply many more Jewish immigrants who needed help than could receive it.[130]

The Making of a Temporary Home

Perhaps on the advice of more well-established Jews in London, Nysen and his children—before long, there were six of them!—quite quickly anglicized their names. He became Nathan, while his son Mosiek (the only of his children to be born in Poland) became Moses, and Mordecai became Mark (sometimes Max). His three other boys were given English names at birth: Abraham, Jacob, and Samuel. This leaves us with his only daughter: Fannie, whose name was likely an anglicization of the Yiddish Feigel or Fayga or perhaps the Polish Fejga. In any case, Fannie is one of my great-great-grandparents.

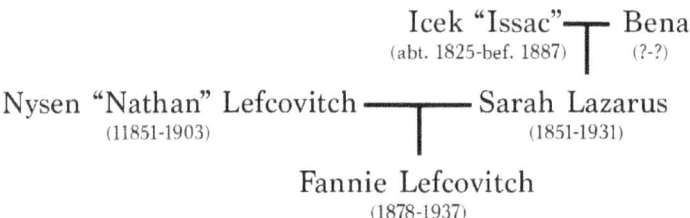

In addition to having anglicized names, Nathan and Sarah's children also attended secular state-run schools. While there were state-run schools in the Pale, they were certainly not secular, and hardly any Jews bothered or wanted to attend them, even when they were allowed to. These schools taught children the English language; they, in turn, evidently taught it to their parents over the course of their stay in London. Sarah, my Gąbin-born great-great-great-grandmother, whose native language was almost certainly Yiddish, supposedly developed an English accent, which she was allegedly quite fond of, much to the envy of the rest of the family!*

It is likely the tough economic situation of the area that explains why Fannie's birth on July 16, 1878, was not in London's traditional Jewish quarter but rather in Mile End New Town, a neighborhood further east where Jews had then only started moving into. Their home at 5 Regal Place, not far from where the Mile End Underground station is today, and was well beyond where the Jewish quarter "ended" only a few decades earlier. However, the inflow of so many Jewish immigrants meant that there was no choice but for their quarter to expand; Whitechapel had become too expensive and too overpopulated for most to live in. Territorial disputes over which immigrant community "owned" which streets became common, particularly between Irish and Jewish immigrants. The Jews generally won.[131]

Evidently, though, things were not much better on the new periphery of the Jewish quarter. The Lefcovitch family—which included six at the time—shared their residence with the Cesleys, a family of four. While their home was not as small as it could have been, it is certainly still difficult, perhaps even unpleasant, to imagine ten people living in it. So, too, is the thought of their children making the hourlong walk to and from the Jewish Free School, which their oldest sons Moses and Abraham attended.

But having spent the first twenty-five years of his life in the Pale, such difficult economic conditions were nothing new to Nathan. In London, he and many others found work as tailors; unlike most of his peers, though, Nathan became a master tailor with three of his own

---

* I cannot thank Richard, a fellow descendant of Nysen and Sarah, enough for sharing this information and more with me.

(presumably Jewish) employees by the time of the 1881 Census. Being the employer and not the employee is suggestive of some relative success, given the circumstances. Moreover, his three employees could not possibly have been his own children: Moses was in school, while Abraham was five, Fannie three, and baby Mordecai only a year old. In fact, Moses remained in school for three more years, until he left at twelve years old. Of course, it was the Jewish *Free* School, but keeping your child in school still came with a large opportunity cost because doing so meant they could not work at home, with you, or do anything else that might bring in extra income.

Nathan, it seems, never employed any of his children—instead, the children all went to school. Abraham followed in his older brother's footsteps and began attending the Jewish Free School when he turned six. Fannie, Mordecai, and even the just-under-four-year-old Jacob all had their first day of school on May 18, 1885, at the Berner Street School. Quite unlike the Jewish Free School, the Berner Street School was not run by a Jewish charity but was one of the first schools opened by the publicly funded School Board of London (by the location of the school, however, many of its students were Jewish). Samuel joined them there after his fifth birthday in 1888, though Mordecai seemingly "graduated" to the Jewish Free School in 1887. The only part of the school still standing today is its doors, quite possibly the ones through which the Lefcovitch children walked on their first day in 1885.[132]

The Lefcovitch children were extraordinarily lucky to attend such good schools—this opportunity was unavailable for both their parents as well as many other children in immigrant quarters. A description from a visitor to the Berner Street School from 1885—the year Abraham, Fannie, and Jacob all enrolled—is worth quoting at length:

> [We] visited the cookery class of Jewish girls; the teacher was giving a demonstration lesson on a fruit pie; only a gas stove was in use. After this part of the lesson, which took one hour, the class was divided, one-half attending

the demonstration lesson and the other half writing it for an hour...the laundry room we next visited was large, with closets, boiler, tubs, ironing tables and stove with flat irons. A similar class to the cooking class was receiving a lesson from the black-board in washing cretonnes and colored cloths. After this I saw the girls washing at the tubs, one tub being fitted for washing colored articles, and the other for white silk scarfs or handkerchiefs which the girls had brought from home. I saw some of their laundered work also, cuffs and collars—very good; the girls evidently enjoyed the work very much. [The new schoolhouse] was a fine large building, with well-lit rooms, sliding partitions largely of glass, big halls and play-grounds for boys on the top of the building...the pupils of the school are nearly all Jews, Russian or Polish, some German...all have to be taught the English language...some of the teachers were Jewish; the teacher of the upper class was selected in order to conduct their religious exercises suitably. The cookery classes also have special provision for meeting the Jewish code with regard to food.[133]

Thanks in no small part to these schools, Nathan and Sarah's children knew London very well. By the time Fannie was fifteen, the streets around her were not a mystery to unravel as they were for her parents but the only place she knew, and most likely knew well. Having the schooling and ability to read and write enabled her to not only experience but to understand the world around her in a way that must have been difficult for her parents. She was surely also aware of things like class structure, which was not only an important reality of British society but also apparently visible in her own family. Aaron, her mother's brother who had immigrated to London a decade before the Lefcovitches, apparently managed to do quite well for himself in that city—well enough to have an entire home occupied exclusively by his own family and a live-in servant! Seeing her cousins—her mother's brother's children—in the synagogue or perhaps on holidays and recognizing the difference a better income made seemingly left a lasting impression on her, as it did for many struggling Jews who saw those around them living more comfortably. That impression, perhaps, was what led her to develop a style and bearing that assured others she was a woman of refined taste—though she also developed a reputation for being rather theatrical, as did her brothers.

Even if there were no intrafamilial comparisons, surely Fannie and her family were among the Jews in Whitechapel strolling along the promenade, hoping to see and be seen. That was the reputed place where matchmakers were on the alert, ready to do their magic, so of course, everyone dressed in their best. Then there were the theaters and halls for entertainment. Perhaps because of the horrible and harsh conditions Jews were often forced to suffer, they have long turned to the theater, to music, and even to comedy for entertainment and relief. Everywhere they settled, theaters and places like Wonderland, an amusement venue that sported boxers and entertainers in Whitechapel, sprung up. Surely Nathan and Sarah took their young family members to enjoy the shows at least once, which possibly even inspired a few of them: many years later, when they were in the United States, two of Fannie's brothers boxed in a Vaudeville troupe.

Even with its few comforts and new amenities, life in London reminded many a little too much of life back in the Pale. London, especially its Jewish community, was taking in many more immigrants than it could absorb, at least without living standards plummeting. By 1905, 150,000 Jews lived in the city—a tripling of the population in only twenty-five years! Of course, Jews were not the only ones arriving in large numbers. England received about 100,000 immigrants between 1861 and 1871 (net of emigrants, deaths, and naturalizations) and another 120,000 between 1871 and 1881. Between 1881 and 1891, England netted 198,000 immigrants, followed by a whopping 247,000 between 1891 and 1901. Many of London's Jews, including the Lefcovitches, who had already seen how difficult it was to live in the Jewish quarter, probably knew it would not be getting any better.[134]

The leaders of London's Jewish community, the longtime residents whose careers in banking, finance, or insurance had allowed them to move to the West End and fund London's Jewish philanthropy, soon began to discourage permanent settlement in the city, and not entirely without reason. Charles Booth, the famed sociologist, described the state of Jewish London in 1902:

> The [Jewish] newcomers have gradually replaced the English population in whole districts. Formerly in Whitechapel, Commercial Street roughly divided the Jewish haunts of Petticoat Lane and Goulston Street from the rougher English quarter lying in the East.* Now the Jews have flowed across the line; Hanbury Street, Fashion Street, Pelham Street, Booth Street, Old Montague Street, and many streets and lanes and alleys have fallen before them; they fill whole blocks of model dwellings; they have introduced new trades as well as new habits and they live and crowd together and work and meet their fate independent of the great stream of London life surging around them. [They] usually live on specked potatoes, stale bread, wurst (a kind of sausage), bagels (a light kind of bread), which they soak in soup made up of the coarsest parts of animals, stale or decayed fish.[135]

Then came antisemitism. Margaret Harkness, writing under the pen name John Law, expressed the feelings of many Londoners through a character in her book *Out of Work*:

---

* The area of Wentworth Street and Brick Lane today.

> Why should they come here I'd like to know? London ain't what it used to be; it's just like a foreign city. The food ain't English; the talk ain't English. Why should all them foreigners come here to take our food out of our mouths, and live on victuals we wouldn't give to pigs?[136]

Among the most aggrieved were London's native-born working and merchant classes, who felt that Jewish workers and merchants had become too successful and prominent:

> These Jew foreigners work in our trade [shoemaking] at this common work 16 or 18 hours a day, and the consequence is that they make a lot of cheap and nasty stuff that destroys the market and injures us.[137]

> Mrs Lee, a tailoress...spoke bitterly of the Jews..."When you go to the warehouse they are there, a whole row of them, ready to take everything." Mrs Goodey, a trouser machinist, [said]. "The Jews had caused the fall in prices...every time the work comes in they take a 1/2d. or 1d. off the price." Others called for action and not words: "If we broke the heads of fifty Jews down here in Whitechapel", said one irate workman, "something would be done to prevent this immigration".[138]

Nathan Lefcovitch and his two oldest sons were, of course, tailors.

London's growing antisemitism was further encouraged by the public outcry after the Jack the Ripper murders, which took place in heavily Jewish Whitechapel in 1888. Locals were convinced that the murderer was Jewish. The crimes were simply too violent to have been committed by an Englishman, many felt; therefore, a Jew must have done it. Even more damaging to the reputation of the Jewish community was the on-record attestation by an assistant police commissioner that the murderer was a Polish Jew living in the East End.[139]

Next Year in America

Suddenly, London must have felt like the Pale—something the Lefcovitches could have told you themselves. By 1891, Nathan was unemployed, and the family moved again (though this time only down the street to 25 Morgan Street). Fannie was thirteen at the time, an age when she'd be acutely aware of any social sting associated with the move. With the dream of upward economic and social mobility still mostly unfulfilled, their oldest son, Moses, was now no longer living with them, nor was he even in London—instead, he was in search of better opportunities on the other side of the Atlantic, in Philadelphia. Before long he was joined there by the rest of his family; the Lefcovitches only sojourned in London.

Chapter 5
HOW THEY LEFT—AND WHY

Either we get civil rights or we emigrate. Our human dignity is being tramped upon, our wives and daughters are being dishonored, we are looted and pillaged; either we get decent human rights or else let us go wherever our eyes may lead us.[140]
~Max Mandelstam

The picture painted thus far of Jewish life in Eastern Europe may, on its own, be enough to give the reader at least *some* idea of what eventually drove millions to flee in one of the largest and fastest migrations in human history. But before we finish answering the question of *what* made them leave, let us first turn to the process of emigration and coming to America. By running the narrative a bit out of order, we can come a little closer to truly understanding how terrible life had to have been in the Pale—as we will see, the journey to America was typically an incredibly unpleasant one as well.

In this chapter, I borrow heavily from the memoirs of those who left Eastern Europe in much the same way and at the same time as my ancestors and many millions of other Jews. Unanimously, these are stories of fear, anxiety, discomfort, and terror, with occasional moments of excitement and optimism sprinkled throughout. But the fact that so many millions of Jews fled Russia this miserable way anyway only further darkens the imagination of Jewish life in Russia. As we recall the awful emigration experience, keep in mind that the Jews of Eastern Europe *still* overwhelmingly voted with their feet against remaining in the Russian Empire. Regardless of the costs, pains, or discomforts, leaving the Pale was clearly worth it.

Escaping the Pale

Though a small number of mostly Polish Jews fled Russia in the 1870s, the enormous wave of emigration out of the Pale began in earnest after the pogroms of 1881-1882. Thus, these were not merely migrants seeking a new home; they were refugees fleeing terror, poverty, and violence.

A perhaps surprising fact about this era is that even though emigrating from Russia was technically illegal, it was largely tolerated by the government—in fact, the government may have even occasionally encouraged it.[141] The tsar and his ministers ultimately came to see the Pale of Settlement as a solution that was better than nothing—i.e., better than allowing Jews to live anywhere in the Empire—but not as good as if there were simply no Jews around in the first place. To be clear, the evidence suggests the government was *not* thinking of genocide; they were hoping that the Jews would leave on their own. Though he later attempted to walk back this comment (which he himself had approved for publication), Kyiv's own public prosecutor said in an 1882 interview that while "the Eastern frontier [Russia proper] is closed to the Jews, the Western frontier is open to them; why don't they take advantage of it?"[142]

In the late 1880s, the governors of the Kyiv and Podolia regions—where the Satalofs and Wexlers lived, respectively—went so far as to ask Tsar Alexander III to encourage poorer Jews to emigrate, something the tsar thought would be "very useful."[143] Of course, the governors certainly did not want all the Jews to go: the government was aware of the inconvenient fact that Jews were indeed a critical component of the local economy. But as time went on, the government did increasingly little to prevent mass emigration.[144]

This era of migration began with refugees pouring into Brody, a town near L'viv in Western Ukraine. There they anxiously waited—often while starving, homeless, and sleeping on the streets—for an opportunity to travel to the ports of Northern Germany, where they could then flee to America by boat. Brody was quickly overwhelmed. A town of only about fifteen thousand at the time, it became the temporary home of as many as twenty thousand refugees. As conditions worsened with limited and already-scarce food and shelter available for so many, various charitable organizations were set up to alleviate the pressure on local communities and help make the journey of the Eastern European Jews to Germany easier. These organizations created discrete information centers along the travel route, secured low rail and steamship ticket prices for those leaving Russia, and even negotiated with several governments on behalf of the refugees to ease the entire process. Over the next many years, their efforts led to a somewhat consistent process by which millions left the Pale.[145]

By the 1890s, several agencies—part charitable organizations, part corporations—had just about perfected a process that facilitated the emigration of millions of Jews. The passenger steamship companies that would ultimately bring the emigrants to America, such as Norddeutscher Lloyd, worked with what became known as "forwarding firms," which sold tickets and helped transport passengers from their home shtetls to the ports of Northern Germany.

The largest forwarding firm was Johann Friedrich Missler's: between 1885 and 1923, 1.8 million passengers booked trips through Missler, earning him an annual salary equivalent to a million dollars today. Firms like Missler's operated ticketing agencies throughout Europe, with Missler supposedly having several thousand ticket agents in Galicia alone. Ticket agents often doubled as innkeepers, teachers, or religious leaders—ordinary people in the Pale who were not hard to come by. And to secure future customers, those who used Missler's service were asked to send home letters written on Missler-branded stationary.[146]

To the great benefit of millions, most ticketing firms tried to make the process as easy as possible. They worked in one of two ways: either a migrant connected directly with an agent, or an earlier arrival to the New World paid for a ticket and sent a notice to the recipient with a receipt and instructions. Once a ticket was purchased, the soon-to-be emigrant would simply select a departure time. These were usually announced through leaflets disseminated throughout Eastern Europe, often discreetly to avoid catching the tsar's attention—while the tsar was not opposed to Jewish emigration, his government held that actively encouraging it was tantamount to treason, and it remained officially illegal.[147]

If tickets had been purchased for you by a relative already in America, they were sent to you by mail. Sometimes when these mysterious things arrived in the mail, it wasn't immediately clear what they were:

> The letter was heavier than usual. And when we opened it, two yellow tickets fell out from among the two closely-written sheets. "What is this?" we all asked at once. "Not money. And this writing must be English." We handed the tickets to grandmother who held out her hand for them. Suddenly her hand began to tremble and she said, "Perhaps these are steamer tickets. Quickly read the letter."[148]

Travel arrangements were then made to get from the emigrant's hometown to the port of departure, which was almost always either Bremen or Hamburg. By 1905, Russia had a relatively advanced rail network of over 30,000 miles of train track, a network that connected those in remote areas—even the small towns of Bershad or Novhorod-Siverskyi—to the major cities of Central Europe, where they could then get to the German ports.[149]

As "easy," if one could call it that, as ticketing firms like Missler's had made the logistics, there was just about nothing that they or anyone else could do to make the personal ordeal of emigration any easier. The decision to leave was a difficult familial, communal, and sometimes even religious one to make. It was also a very emotional decision; choosing to leave meant choosing to leave behind family, friends, neighbors, and an entire community there was no guarantee that the emigrant would ever see again.[150]

The anticipation that built up in the days and weeks prior to departure filled the emigrant's family with worry. "You will write us, dear?" Marcus Ravage recalled his mother insistently begging him. "And if I [his mother] should die when you are gone, you will remember me in your prayers."[151] When the fateful day came to board the train to take them away from their home, it was marked with deep solemnity. In his memoirs, Ravage compared the sense of loss to that of a person dying: the "whole community turned out and marched in slow time to the station, and wept loudly and copiously, and remembered the unfortunates in its prayer on the next Saturday." He recalled:

> At the moment of departure, when the train drew into the station, she [his mother] lost control of her feelings. As she embraced me for the last time her sobs became violent and father had to separate us. There was a despair in her way of clinging to me which I could not then understand. I understand it now. I never saw her again.[152]

It was emotional for the emigrant too. Many years later, Rose Cohen recalled the thoughts running through her mind as she began her journey to America:

> Could there be anything more painful than parting from those dear to you? Will this ache in my heart always be there? And yet, how strange! It is but a few hours since I have left grandmother and the children and their faces have already become indistinct, as though I had left them a long time ago…oh, I can't bear to think of it! Suppose something happens now and I could not go to America but had to go home. Would I be glad? Glad to go back to those four smoke-covered walls? No! I would

be disappointed, more than that—life would hardly be worth living.

Once one had departed from the shtetl on their way out of the Pale, the next step was to get to a major city outside of Russia but relatively close to the border, which meant they often found their way to Vienna or Berlin first, or sometimes Minsk. This was the riskiest and perhaps even the most difficult part of the entire process; indeed, Rose Cohen's father's first attempt to leave Russia ended when he was arrested at the border.[153] Getting from the shtetl to the border was manageable, even if it often required many transfers between several trains, something few Jews of the Pale had any experience in. Actually *crossing* the border, however, was just about a nightmare. Because they were expensive and inaccessible to most Jews, essentially none of them had passports—legitimate ones, at least—and therefore they had to get off the train at the last stop before the border and wander through the countryside, typically at night, praying they would make it to the other side undetected.[154] But while most emigrants knew to fear border guards, many were unaware of the risks of being misled or even robbed of what few possessions they had during the trip. Abraham Cahan's experience captured both difficulties quite well:

> We made a strange group going across fields and meadows in the night, halted suddenly every few times by the tall peasant [who was guiding them] holding up his finger and pausing to listen for God-knows-what disaster...we stumbled on endlessly. It seemed as if the border were miles away. Then the peasant straightened up and announced we were already well inside Austria.[155]

Once they made it to a major city in Austria or Germany, the next stop was a port city. By this point, even if an emigrant had left their hometown alone, they often merged into a larger group of Jews making the same journey and were frequently joined by assistants and guides who were employed by the ticketing firm. Language was often a barrier, so migrants attached cards to their caps or shirts identifying them and their destination.[156]

Making it across the border was still far from the end of possible trouble, and certainly far from the end of fear and discomfort. An 1892 cholera outbreak in Hamburg closed the ports and borders entirely; they reopened in 1894 after a rigorous health check and quarantine period was added to the emigration procedure. Now, even for those who managed to bribe the border guards or get across the border by train undetected, a deeply uncomfortable procedure of disinfection and examination awaited them at the station where they exited. Unhealthy immigrants were usually turned away upon arrival in the United States, and since the emigration agencies would need to cover the cost of the return ticket, migrants were screened at border stations to detect unhealthy passengers before departure. It was not a pleasant experience, made no better by the fact that the doctors only spoke German. Mary Antin eerily recalled being treated "like cattle":

> This was another scene of bewildering confusion, parents losing their children, and little ones crying; baggage being thrown together in one corner of the yard, heedless of contents...a man came to inspect us, as if to ascertain our full value; strange looking people driving us about like dumb animals, helpless and unresisting...our clothes taken off, our bodies rubbed with a slippery substance that might be any bad thing; a shower of warm water let down on us without warning...they are only making us ready for the continuation of our journey, cleaning us of all suspicions of dangerous sickness. Thank God![157]

If one was lucky enough to pass the medical examination, which not all were, the next step was to get to the port of departure. As a final check before being allowed to proceed to the port, they needed to provide paperwork and proof of disinfection and healthiness before being transferred to another train to a port town. The trip from the border station to the port likely took at least another twenty-four hours, not including any time required to transfer trains; by this point, most migrants would have been in transit for at least a week, and often for much longer.

Bremen and Hamburg were the two major ports of emigration from the mid-nineteenth century onward, with a staggering 4,863,199 Eastern European migrants escaping Europe through Bremen alone between 1831 and 1910 (for reference, Bremen averaged about 100,000 residents in this period). Yet another million would leave by the start of World War II. At the end of the nineteenth century, nearly all these migrants were Jews escaping the terror and poverty of Eastern Europe.

Still, arrival in the port cities did not grant the emigrants any comfort or security. Yet another round of quarantine and disinfection awaited them: "two weeks within high brick walls, several hundred of us herded in half a dozen compartments...with never a sign of the free world beyond our barren windows," as one such emigrant remembered it.[158] While finally having an actual bed—more accurately a cot—to sleep in again came as a relief, it was only a temporary one:

> Before we were on our cot for very long we saw that sleep was out of the question. The air in the room was so foul and thick that it felt as if it could be touched. From every corner came sounds of groaning and snoring. But worst of all were the insects in the cot...after sitting up a while she [her aunt] remembered seeing a wagon with some hay in it under the shed in the yard, and we decided to go there.[159]

Migrants most commonly stayed in provided lodging for at least a week in order to quarantine, either in overpacked homes or hostels. Surprisingly, there were supposedly decent living spaces in the later years; Missler's forwarding ticket agency even offered lodging that included kosher food and rabbinical services. However, the lodgings were often overwhelmed by the sheer volume of migrants, and many migrants spent several nights on the floor in a densely packed warehouse or dance hall, sharing food, a living space, and a toilet with several dozens of other families. It was a miserable ordeal, with still more starvation, theft, and discomfort to come after—and even during—the quarantine period. Locals in Bremen and Hamburg, even including some Jews, took advantage of the desperate and often clueless emigrants, urging them to buy all kinds of nonsense—one story recalls a young man being encouraged to drink a whole bottle of whisky to avoid seasickness. Thankfully, such cruel behavior was slowly eliminated as the migrants became more familiar with the process over time when many had guidance from the family already overseas. On the plus side, at least the similarities between Yiddish and German allowed the migrants to communicate with the Germans with some mutual comprehension.[160]

It was also in the port cities (and sometimes in the cities on the train journey to them) where many emigrants from the Pale got their first real glimpse of modernity, city life, and advanced industrialization. Until the late nineteenth century, industrialization had hardly progressed beyond its early stages throughout most of the Pale. Many amenities already common in the cities of Western and Central Europe and in America were entirely new to the immigrants, including Mary Antin, who recalled her simultaneous amazement and anxiety in her first experience of modern public transportation:

> We were marched up to a strange vehicle, long and narrow and high, drawn by two horses and commanded by a mute driver. We were piled up on this wagon, our baggage was thrown after us, and we started on a sight-seeing tour across the city of Hamburg. The sights I faithfully enumerate for the benefit of my uncle include carts drawn by dogs, and big cars that run of themselves, later identified as electric cars [streetcars]...something

made me think of a description I had read of criminals being carried on long journeys in uncomfortable things—like this? Well, it was strange—this long, long drive, the conveyance, no word of explanation; and all, though going different ways, being packed off together. We were strangers; the driver knew it. He might take us anywhere—how could we tell?[161]

The defining experience of the port city, however, was of course all the waiting around that took place there. Rose Cohen and her family "stayed in Hamburg a week. Every day from ten in the morning until four in the afternoon we stayed in a large, bare hall waiting for our names to be called."[162] There you would wait until an official announced the arrival of whichever ship and read off the names of those who would board it—after all, most of these emigrants likely had no idea the name of the ship they were taking. When that time finally came, each emigrant (or sometimes just the head of the group) met with an emigration officer to record some final details and get final clearance to board the ship. This could be a scary moment: "the scoundrel," as Cohen's aunt referred to the officer, "threated to send us home. He said he had the power to send us home!"[163]

As eagerly anticipated as the day to board the boat that would bring them to America was, the time spent on board the ship was often among the worst parts of the entire emigration process. It was a terrible ordeal—and not just because of how confusing, disorienting, and unfamiliar the experience of crossing the Atlantic Ocean must have been for most former shtetl dwellers. Of course, the transatlantic journey would have been difficult to imagine within the mental geography available to the average Jewish resident of the Pale; after all, few traveled much farther than a few towns over from their own, and if they were not a merchant of some kind, often not even that far. But the distance and imaginative discomfort aside, the ocean voyage was one of tremendous real and material discomfort.

Those on board had little to no idea what to expect. This couldn't be clearer than in Rose Cohen's recollection of the first few days on board. The journey began with fear, but this was soon replaced with serenity:

> [On the first day] I dreaded crossing the ocean for I had heard that the water was rough. The boat rocked fearfully, and there was sickness and even death. But when some time passed and I saw how smoothly and steadily the boat went along over the quiet water, I felt relieved. I sat quietly...watching the full moon appearing and disappearing behind the coulds, and listening to our fellow travellers. Their faces, so worried and excited for weeks, looked peaceful and contented as they sat grazing at the moon and talking quietly and hopefully of the future in the new world. "How beautiful," I thought. "This is the way the rest of our journey will be."[164]

But, of course, this soon turned out to not be the case, and this serenity quickly vanished into a nightmare:

> [Over the next three days] we were deathly seasick...During that period I was conscious, it seems to me, only part of the time. I remember that once when I opened my eyes I seemed to see the steamer turn to one side and then disappear under water. Then I heard voices screaming, entreating, praying. I thought we were drowning, but I did not care. Nothing mattered now.[165]

To make matters worse, by the time a migrant finally stepped onboard the ship to bring them to the United States, they had already been traveling, quarantining, and sleeping in unfamiliar and uncomfortable places for weeks—yet they were roughly only in the middle of their entire emigration process. Even before the ship left the dock, the soon-to-be immigrants were physically and mentally exhausted.

Once onboard, emigrants were cramped into the steerage of the steamship, where they ate, slept, and spent much of the trip praying it would soon be over. In Morris Raphael Cohen's recollections:

> We were huddled together in the steerage literally like cattle—my mother, my sister and I sleeping in the middle tier, people being above us and below us...we could not eat the food of the ship, since it was not kosher. We only asked for hot water into which my mother used to put a little brandy and sugar to give it a taste. Towards the end of the [fourteen-day] trip when our bread was beginning to give out we applied to the ship's steward for bread, but the kind he gave us was unbearably soggy.[166]

Similar descriptions of the voyage's cramped and miserable conditions can be found in the memoirs of just about anyone who went through it. One recalls becoming "utterly dejected" being "herded together in a dark, filthy compartment," where extreme seasickness led many to become so ill they feared they were close to death; a contemporary account described "crowds everywhere, ill smelling bunks, uninviting washrooms...the odors of scattered orange peelings, tobacco, garlic and disinfectants meeting but not blending."[167] The food was "miserable," and, as Morris Cohen experienced, rarely kosher (though this changed over time). A government report found that "everything [onboard] was dirty, sickly and disagreeable to the touch. Every impression was offensive."[168]

Making matters even worse, there was essentially nothing to do onboard, except for the rare few who reportedly brought Russian-English dictionaries with them or those who brought cards for card games. There was nothing to distract the passengers when they were not overcome by the disgusting and close-quarters conditions of steerage, no excitement or intrigue to counter the ever-present fear and worry. "More than the physical hardships," Morris Cohen recalled, "my imagination was occupied with the terrors of ships colliding...one morning we saw a ship passing at what seemed to me a considerable distance, but our neighbor said that we were lucky, that at night we escaped a crash only by a hair's breadth."

Others worried about what was to come: "The sky was blue—stars shining. But in my heart it was so dark when I went up on the ship...in Grodno I was at least someone in the store. But in America, without language, with only a bit of education...young people laughed and joked even though in my heart it was like the storm at sea."[169]

The trip did, however, offer an opportunity for the emigrants to get a head start in adjusting to life outside the Pale, as Oscar Handlin argued:

> The crossing involved a startling reversal of roles, a radical shift in attitudes. The qualities that were desirable in the good peasant [and non-peasant] were not those conducive to success in the transition. Neighborliness, obedience, respect, and status were valueless among the masses that struggled for space on the way. They succeeded who put aside the old preconceptions, pushed in, and took care of themselves.[170]

In a very literal sense, the Jews arriving in America perfectly matched the description found in the poem adorning the base of the Statue of Liberty, passed by the vast majority of immigrants: they were tired and poor huddled masses, yearning to breathe free.

Why They Left: Persecution and Poverty

By now, we have seen how terrible life had become in the Russian Empire by the end of the nineteenth century, both through the impoverished and terrifying state of life at home as well as through the fact that so many left even though the emigration process was so miserable. Indeed, the despair, poverty, and terror that characterized life in the shtetls of the Pale was only getting worse as the nineteenth century went on, and the mood throughout the Pale grew even more frightened and miserable. Mary Antin's recollection of Passover shortly after the violent expulsion of Jews from Moscow in 1891 is telling:

> Passover was celebrated in tears that year. In the story of the Exodus we would have read a chapter of current history, only for us there was no deliverer and no promised land. But what said some of us at the end of the long service? Not 'May we be next year in Jerusalem,' but 'Next year—in America!' So there was our promised land, and many faces were turned towards the West. And if the waters of the Atlantic did not part for them, the wanderers rode its bitter flood by a miracle as great as any the rod of Moses ever wrought...the open cities becoming thus suddenly crowded, every man's chance of making a living was diminished in proportion to the number of additional competitors. Hardship, acute distress, ruin for many: thus spread the disaster, ring beyond ring, from the stone thrown by a despotic official into the ever-full river of Jewish persecution.[171]

Life for the Pale's roughly five million Jews was reaching a breaking point, and the time to leave was rapidly approaching—even for many of the most reluctant. But what was it that finally pushed people over the edge and motivated so many to leave? Asked why she left the Pale, Rose Silverman put it succinctly: "Things were bad for me and hardship drove me to leave my old home. It's just that simple."[172] Most, if not all, Jews had a poor quality of life, from which either poverty, starvation, religious discrimination, dehumanization, or misery could be accurately singled out as motivations for leaving. We can get a closer and more personal glimpse into what motivated so many to leave by returning to the stories of the families we met in the preceding chapters.

Next Year in America

The Satalofs, from Kyiv, were the first in my family to come to the United States.* In fact, religious persecution within the Pale had already forced them to leave home once before by the time they left for the United States in 1892. The nineteenth-century renewal and revival of Jewish life in Kyiv stalled and turned violent after the 1881 assassination of Alexander II. Police began hunting down Jews living within the city without the proper rights to do so. Over the next five years, nearly six thousand Jews were evicted from Kyiv, about a quarter of its Jewish population.[173]

Pinkus and Clara Satalof and their son Abraham, all born in Kyiv, were seemingly among these six thousand Jewish evictees. While Abraham was born in Kyiv in 1884, by 1886 they had relocated to Kaharlyk, a small shtetl roughly fifty miles south. There they had three more children in the following few years, including my great-great-grandmother—another Esther—in 1890. But Kaharlyk would not be the Satalofs' forever home.

By the time their daughter Lena was born in January 1893, Pinkus and Abraham were already in the United States, having departed via Bremen six months earlier. As was often the case, the wife and younger children were left behind, sometimes for a few years, in order for the husband and perhaps his oldest children to earn enough money to bring the rest of the family over. This was an incredibly difficult experience for many women in the Pale: the family, which had been the core of shtetl life, was temporarily broken up and scattered across the world. As her husband worked hard to establish himself in America, sometimes the most a wife left in the Pale could do was to make sure her younger children would not forget about their father:

Sleep, my baby, sleep. Your father is in America.

---

* At least among my direct ancestors. Technically Nathan Lefcovitch's oldest son was here first, but I am a descendant of Nathan's daughter, Fannie, who came in 1893.

In that wonderful country he eats white bread every day.
When there is a sound at the door, he does not flinch;
It is not the officers of the Czar but only the wind.
Sleep, baby, soon you will join him.[174]

The husband's absence, of course, was usually quite hard for the children too. "My childhood days were not happy ones, because my father was not with us," recalled an immigrant whose experience must have been much like Esther Satalof's, my great-great-grandmother, who was only two and a half years old when her father left for America.[175] However, even a mother's best attempts to make up for the father's absence were complicated by the need to keep the family going financially. Left without the income of their husband and often of their oldest children, many women had to take up brutal work in factories, take on the risk of housing boarders, or, if they were lucky, take over their husband's business. Even when they arrived in America, many mothers found it difficult to reconnect with their older children who went earlier—and some found that their spouses hadn't quite been so faithful.[176]

These were unimaginably difficult times for many Jewish women. Needless to say, however, the ability and determination to suddenly step into their husband's role is a testament to the endurance, dedication, and toughness of the women of the Pale. In fact, for the children whose formative years were spent watching their mother take care of the family on her own, it implanted the idea that women could be as strong and independent as men—if not more.[177]

The Wexlers were lucky: as best as I can tell, Israel; his wife, Hannah; and their two children, Anna and Jacob, left Bershad together as a family in 1893. Almost surely, the same increasingly dreary state of Jewish life that had driven the Satalofs to America a year earlier inspired the Wexlers to emigrate too. Their hometown of Bershad had fallen into a truly dilapidated state by the late nineteenth century. Many years later, another—presumably unrelated—resident of Bershad recalled the scene:

> Even on the main streets of the town there were no pavements, in spring and autumn there was impassable dirt...there were no trees or flowers. On the Lag Ba Omer holiday, Jews went on a picnic outside the city. They walked past the Valley and Yerushalimka—areas of the poor, past shacks with earthen floors, but with geraniums on window sills and embroidered curtains, along the stone fence behind which you could see the estate of the bankrupt Counts of Potocki. On the outskirts there was a new building of a rural school and a post office. The director of the school, the head of the post office, excise, bailiff, and policeman lived in this area. They spoke Russian, and the Russian language seemed very beautiful to me since childhood, because these elegant and enlightened gentlemen spoke it. Then the fields, forest, Ukrainian villages began, from where men came on the bazaar days on the sump of the town.[178]

What happened to the beautiful, serene environment described only fifty years earlier by the visiting Russian officer quoted in Chapter 3 as so nice that he could imagine living there? A journalist visiting Bershad in the late nineteenth century described how "industry has been reduced to a minimum, trade is bad, and there are too many traders for each to...have the means to live; the grain market in the town on market days is crowded with exhausted Jewish figures, hoarsely trading."[179] The poorest—those doing manual labor, perhaps making bricks or tiles, refining sugar, or working as tanners or furriers, as Israel Wexler did—were almost better off than the merchants, since "at least bread is provided" for them. But work was hard to come by for anybody, and the town economy was in a state of collapse thanks to Russian restrictions against cross-border trade, unfair tax burdens, and a shrinking population. Rail first came to the region in the 1870s, with Bershad being connected to the Kyiv-Odesa line in 1897. But while the railway temporarily boosted economic activity in Bershad, the poor dreariness of small-town shtetl life led many to seek bigger towns with more opportunities—namely, Kyiv and Odesa.[180]

The big towns did not prove to be consistently or permanently welcoming toward Jews either, as we have seen, so many sought to flee the Pale altogether. The journalist concluded that "all these conditions gave rise to the 'over the ocean'-desire again. Emigration fever boils with renewed vigor, and dozens of families are leaving their native place for the sake of an unknown stranger."[181] Indeed, the Wexlers, too, were far from immune from "emigration fever": when Jacob Wexler was all but five years old, his family left Bershad for good to come to the United States. They arrived in New York on July 25, 1893, after spending thirteen days aboard the SS *Stuttgart* sailing from Bremen. Jacob would have likely had similar memories of this journey as the Satalofs' oldest daughter, Esther, who was about the same age when she left Ukraine. Though they were only two of millions of Jews entering New York at the time, they had plenty of time to ask each other about it—after all, they later wound up married for over half a century.

Around the same time that the Satalofs and Wexlers left Ukraine for America, the Lefcovitches were preparing to emigrate for the second time in two decades, roughly fifteen years after they first immigrated to London. As seen in the previous chapter, by the late nineteenth century, London was no longer the London that Nathan and Sarah immigrated to in the 1870s—if anything, it was closer to what they had left behind in Gąbin.

London had reached a breaking point by the end of the nineteenth century, where extraordinary population growth made conditions ever worse for Jews living there. The ever-increasing presence of these foreigners speaking a very foreign language, wearing very foreign clothes, and practicing a mostly foreign religion began to unsettle locals. And with so many immigrants clamoring for housing in a relatively small quarter of London, rents and home prices shot up, and overcrowding became a necessity.[182]

Next Year in America

In the late nineteenth century, London became an increasingly antisemitic city. Native-born Londoners resented Jewish competition in the labor market and business, even if their position was hardly enviable; many Jews slept where they also worked up to twenty hours each day. Over time, many English were all but compelled to become tailors as English employers tried to avoid hiring Jewish ones, who they felt had gained too much market power and influence. And, as mentioned in Chapter 4, the Jack the Ripper murders oddly enough fanned the flames of antisemitism, with many among the public assigning responsibility to the Jews.[183]

Thus it is no surprise that we find Moses Lefcovitch in a passenger list record arriving in New York on October 29, 1890. By 1893, he, his father, and his next-oldest sibling, Abraham, were already working as tailors in Philadelphia's Jewish quarter, where on May 8 they purchased five tickets for Sarah, Fannie, Max, Jack, and Samuel to join them there for a total of $87.50—about four months of work at Pennsylvania's average monthly wage at the time.* Sarah and her four youngest children presumably arrived in America by the end of that year. One interesting point is that Nathan and Sarah's family were the only ones to leave London for America for some time. The vast majority of their nieces and nephews—the many children of Sarah's brothers—remained in the United Kingdom. It is hard to imagine what unique pressures to emigrate they could have faced that the rest of Sarah's family didn't.

Why They Left: Violence and War

> *The pogroms taught me their lesson...I became convinced that it was not lack of high culture that was the cause of our tragedy, but that we are*

---

*It is very possible that Nathan came at the same time or shortly after Moses. He was certainly in the United States by May 1893, when tickets were purchased for his wife and remaining children to join him.

> *aliens. We will still remain aliens when we are as fully stuffed with education as a pomegranate is full of seeds...we are aliens everywhere. We have to return home.*
> ~ Moses Leib Lilienblum[184]

In addition to the same deep poverty and increasing oppression experienced by the Sataiofs, Wexlers, and Lefcovitches, my remaining ancestors were almost certainly driven to America by violence, whether by the fear of it or after an experience with it. While many Jews had long felt anxious and endangered on major Christian holidays (especially Easter), antisemitic violence became increasingly frequent, intense, and destructive in the last quarter of the nineteenth century. The assassination of Tsar Alexander II in 1881 proved to be a turning point: rumors accusing the Jews of conspiring in the assassination plot led to the worst outbreak of antisemitic violence since the Khmelnytsky Revolt over two centuries earlier. The Russian word "pogrom" was introduced into the English language by journalists describing this wave of violence, in which Jewish stores, homes, and religious centers were assaulted, damaged, and often destroyed, while Jews themselves were beaten, raped, or even murdered. In some cases, the Empire even endorsed, supported, and defended these riotous and violent uprisings.[185]

While this initial wave of violence thankfully died out after a few months, the coast was not clear. This was made painfully clear to Jews living in the Pale—and to the entire world—when one of the most infamously horrific pogroms tore through Kishinev (now Chisinau) in modern-day Moldova on April 19, 1903—Easter Sunday, per the Julian calendar. The Jewish community there, numbering about 50,000 at the time, was savagely rampaged by a mob of around 2,000 locals. It was a relatively normal pogrom at first, just on a larger scale: homes were looted; businesses were destroyed. But after it became clear that neither the Russian nor the Moldovan police, military, or clergy would step in to try to stop the assault, things quickly escalated. Indeed, rather than stopping the onslaught, one police officer stepped in to arrest a group of

Jews for defending themselves; the Orthodox bishop rode through the streets blessing the attackers. As night came, the attack intensified and grew increasingly barbarian. With "neither regret nor remorse" according to one journalist, Jews were tortured, some with nails driven through their skulls or by having their eyes gouged out (to ensure they would "never again look at a Christian child"); many were raped, and some, about four dozen, were murdered. As many as two thousand Jews were left homeless, while the riot left hardly even a scratch on any Christian home. The violence did not completely stop until the morning of April 21, after about forty-eight hours of anarchy.[186]

News of the Kishinev Pogrom spread far and fast, with then-president Theodore Roosevelt stating about two months afterward that he had never known of "a more immediate or a deeper expression of sympathy for the victims of horror over the appalling calamity that has occurred."[187] Before long, though, similar pogroms occurred throughout the Pale, particularly in Ukraine. Word had even spread to the Japanese, who subsequently decided that Russia was too barbaric to be diplomatic and negotiate with, helping lead to the outbreak of the Russo-Japanese War in February 1904.[188] Particularly after the return of violence at home, war added a new terror to daily life: the prospect of conscription. Although the cantonist system described in previous chapters had been eliminated after Russia's defeat in the Crimean War in 1856, its memory and associated traumas remained in the collective Jewish consciousness, and forms of the draft were still alive and well throughout the nineteenth century. Fears of the return of conscription turned out not to be misplaced: thirty-five thousand Jews were conscripted for the Russo-Japanese War, with about one in ten not returning.[189]

Perhaps unsurprisingly with all this in mind, in the first decade of the twentieth century, Jewish emigration hit its highest levels. While on average about 25,000 left Russia for the United States each year in the 1880s, the average annual rate between 1900 and 1910 was about 82,000, and then 75,000 between 1911 and 1914. No longer were Jews only fleeing from material poverty and social or religious oppression; now they were also fleeing from violence and death. All of my remaining ancestors left the Pale in the first decade of the twentieth century, and their timing is particularly telling.

Hersh Scherovsky left his hometown of Novhorod-Siverskyi in July 1904, a year after the Kishinev pogrom and four months after the Russo-Japanese War began. He had seen the fears of conscription turn into reality: at least two Jews from Novhorod-Siverskyi, most likely at least known to Hersh, were wounded, killed, or missing in action while fighting in yet another war for a country that tolerated violence and subhuman treatment toward them at home.[190] Having seen and experienced enough, about a month after his eighteenth birthday, Hersh set out on a nearly five-thousand-mile voyage in search of a better and safer life. He was joined by his cousin, Mendel Rosenbaum, who had moved from Nosivka to Novhorod-Siverskyi at some point before they left—I'm not exactly sure why.[*]

Their plan was to meet up with their aunt and uncle, Hannah Scherovsky and Hersh Yakubson, at their apartment (which doubled as a tailoring shop) at 636 Wharton Street in South Philadelphia. By the time Hersh and Mendel left Novhorod-Siverskyi, their uncle had already been in the United States for almost fifteen years, long enough to have anglicized his name to Harris Jacobson. For Hersh and Mendel to know where they were going, Harris likely wrote a letter to either of them with his address and a few pieces of advice for the journey ahead.

---

[*] It is unlikely that Mendel's family was banished, as his sister remained in Nosivka until Mendel paid for her to come to the United States five years after him. His father died before 1910, but it is not known exactly when. If his father died before he left, perhaps Mendel and his mother went to live with or near the Scherovskys in Novhorod-Siverskyi. It is also possible that he went on his own, perhaps to live in a more remote area to avoid the rise of antisemitic violence, or simply for work—he was a painter at the time, possibly of anything from houses to churches to pottery, which required frequent movement either in search of work or as part of the job.

Next Year in America

I can't help but imagine them carefully bringing this piece of paper with them on their journey, clutching it as if their lives depended on it—after all, they would have had no idea where they were going without it.

What their Uncle Harris did not seem to have sent along, though, was money: according to the ship's records, Hersh and Mendel paid for their own tickets. With family so relatively well established in America, this is somewhat odd. However, if they had sold many, if not all, of their own possessions before arriving—as many did, often after hearing the false rumor that immigrants could not bring items of value into America—perhaps they had no need for their uncle's charity. It is also possible that their uncle simply could not afford to pay for the tickets, as he had several children of his own to take care of. One thing is almost certain, though: their parents had nothing to do with the process. Aside from each other, they left entirely alone. As best as I can tell, none of Hersh's siblings ever came to America, nor did his parents. Mendel's sisters did come to the United States over the next decade, but his mother only left after being widowed at a much older age.

After their final, undoubtedly emotional goodbyes to family, friends, and all they had ever known, the desolate scenes of remote shtetl life in northeastern Ukraine passed through Hersh and Mendel's eyes for the very last time as the train carrying them pulled away from Novhorod-Siverskyi's first and recently built train station in the early summer of 1904. Their first stop was likely the better-connected nearby town of Novozybkov so they could transfer to another train that could get them to a much larger city—perhaps Warsaw, maybe Vienna, possibly Minsk. No matter the next stop, it was not the last: they needed to get to Bremen, which often required at least one more intermediate stop, most often in Berlin. Only after what likely amounted to over a week's worth of travel by train-hopping did they eventually arrive in Bremen. Finally, after several unfamiliar days and uncomfortable nights in Bremen, Hersh and Mendel boarded the SS *Cassel* and departed Bremen and the Old World on July 7, 1904.[191]

Rosenbaum, Mendel 28 m painter
Polirowski, Hersch 21 tailor

Harry and Mendel in the passenger list for the Cassel.[192]

After a two-week journey across the Atlantic Ocean, they arrived in Baltimore on July 21, from where one last train finally brought them to their Uncle Harris in Philadelphia. They seem to have settled in quickly. No more than eighteen months after they arrived, they had "officially" anglicized their own names, perhaps on their uncle's experienced advice. Mendel became Max, and Hersh Scherovsky became Harry Shirofsky.

Though the Waksmans left from a town—Staszów—relatively far from Novhorod-Siverskyi, they left at almost exactly the same time as Harry and Mendel, and likely for very similar reasons. Sometime between late 1903 and late 1906, Hersh Waksman left his wife and now three children behind in Staszów and left for America, promising to bring the rest of the family to join him once he had established himself in the New World.

Curiously, though all of Hersh's six siblings also left Staszów around this time, none of them joined him in the United States. His sister Rachel left for Canada, but the other five siblings remained in Europe. While Hersh and Rachel left for the New World, the remaining siblings instead opted for Hull, a coastal city in the United Kingdom. First to go was Hersh's oldest brother, Moses, sometime around 1900. Over the next decade, he was joined there by his siblings Mendel, Leibel, Celia, and Beyla—in fact, according to one of Beyla's grandchildren, Hersh's father (who by then must have been about sixty years old) went to Hull, too, where he became the president of a synagogue. Many of Hersh's siblings were likely fleeing violence too—this relative's grandfather on the other side of his family supposedly showed up in Hull in 1905 in a Russian military uniform, having deserted some time earlier—but I have no clue why Hersh (or his sister Rachel) did not stick with their families. Was there a falling out or a dispute, or was it simply the only option at the time? Whatever the reason, unlike the Lefcovitches, the Waksmans in Hull remained in the United Kingdom, where many of their descendants still live. Remarkably, not until well into the twenty-first century was either half the family aware that they had close family on the other side of Atlantic.[*]

While he all but certainly never saw his Waksman family again, Hersh was thankfully able to earn enough money to bring his wife and three children to him in Philadelphia, where he had anglicized his name to Harry Waxman. Perhaps with some help from his wife Esther's brother Froim, who became Frank after he joined Harry in Philadelphia in June 1906, Harry paid $87 in November 1906 for his wife and three children to travel aboard the SS *Pennsylvania* from Hamburg to New York, where they arrived on May 20, 1907, after sixteen days at sea. Much like their father's, their children's names were immediately anglicized: Sroel became Jacob; Froim became Frank; Feigel became Fanny. They were joined in December by Esther's other brother, Mosiek (later Morris), who opted to abridge his surname from Tyszgarten to Tishgart. Once again, their timing suggests a response to the pogroms and the war—there was no more time to wait.

---

[*] Many thanks to Laurence, the relative cited in this paragraph, for this information, as well as to Ron, who helped get Laurence and me in touch.

The record of Harry Waxman's purchase of tickets for his wife and children.[193]

Back in Chernihiv, Pearl Rabinowitz and Mottel Schusterman both faced the same pressures to leave as the Shiroffs and Waxmans; after all, Chernihiv was the capital of Novhorod-Siverskyi's province and was much less remote. In fact, a terrible pogrom broke out there in October 1905, the echoes of which reached both Nosivka, where some of Max Rosenbaum's family still lived, and Harry Shirofsky's native Novhorod-Siverskyi. However, their poverty meant that only one of them could afford to leave for safety.

Perhaps part of the reason they chose for Pearl to leave first was a matter of her sex: it was just safer for women in the States. But that raises the question: why wait to get married? The sad answer: they opted to wait to get married until they would reunite in America *just so that Pearl would not be stuck waiting if Mottel was never heard from again*. There was no guarantee that they would ever see each other again. Pearl would never really know if she were a widow. Though that may seem like an extreme proposition to think about, they were behaving quite rationally relative to their surroundings.

The family story my great-grandfather shared with us didn't speak of the poverty or fear, though. It suggests another dynamic was at play. Pearl was, by all accounts, very much a typical woman of the Pale. She was bossy, perhaps formidable, and had no problem speaking for herself. Mottel, on the other hand, was handsome and social—and something of a ladies' man. My great-grandfather's story was that Pearl managed to secure Mottel all for herself by promising that she would go to America first and work to pay for him to join her there. If that is the truth, well, it certainly worked out all right.

In any case, Mottel thankfully arrived safe aboard the *Noordland* in Philadelphia on September 2, 1907, after Pearl purchased his ticket for $34 a month earlier. The *Noordland's* passenger list indicated that he was received upon arrival by Pearl Rabinowitz, his "bride"—the only time I have seen that on a passenger list. Also according to my great-grandfather, Pearl's willingness to come to America first and pay his way was conditional on Mottel's willingness to take her last name once they married—and he did. As Great Pop Pop's version of events went, Pearl was too young to be married without parental consent in Philadelphia, so they went across the Delaware River to New Jersey to be married.

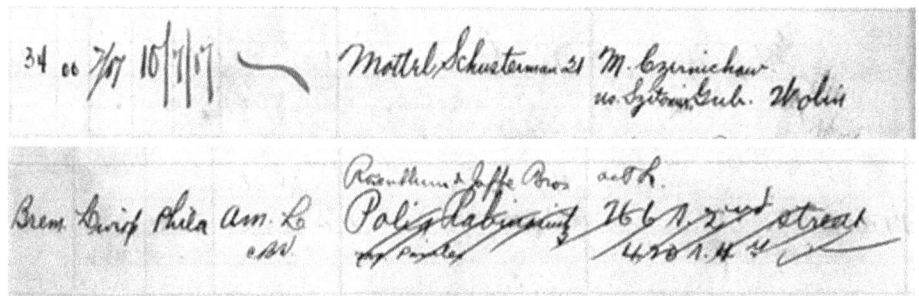

The record the purchase of Max's ticket by Pearl.[194]

I don't know how much I buy that story, given that Pearl must have been about eighteen at the time, but the trend of taking Pearl's last name bizarrely became something of a rite of passage for those coming to America with tickets paid for by the new Rabinowitz couple. It happened at least twice more, when Mottel's brothers David and Samuel both changed their surname from "Schusterman" to "Rabinowitz" on their citizenship forms. Clearly, they were not thinking of all the confusion this would cause their brother's great-great-grandson when he tried to reconnect the dots over a century later.

Those Who Came and Those Who Did Not

Of course, I have only been able to tell the stories of those who came and those who I have been able to find records on. Surely my ancestors had brothers, sisters, aunts, uncles, cousins, and other relatives who stayed behind for one reason or another. The elderly often were either not up to the great trouble of the voyage or, as we saw at the start of this chapter, were uninterested in coming to America or even opposed to it.

Consider, for example, my great-great-grandparents' generation, all of whom were born between 1874 and 1890. All eight of them were born in the Old World and ultimately came to the United States, but only seven of their sixteen parents ever joined them there. Of the seven who did, all but one was younger than fifty when they emigrated. It is no surprise that my older third-great-grandparents did not feel up to the journey. For example, Hannah Knobel and Leizer Tyszgarten, Esther Tyszgarten's parents, were both born in 1848, and would have been about sixty when Esther came to America. As far as I'm aware, Pearl Rabinowitz's parents never came, which is unsurprising given the family tradition that her father had been a cantor (or a rabbi) and a conservative man. Likely for similar reasons, Max Schusterman's father remained in Chernihiv until his death sometime between 1907 and 1910. However, Max's mother, Hannah, is a noteworthy exception to this rule. Even as the daughter of Rabbi Yael Ha'Cohen, even as a sixty-year-old woman, she eventually left Chernihiv for the United States. This was likely a practical decision: her husband had died some years earlier, and four of her children had already resettled in Philadelphia. And thus the decision was made to come to America with her daughter Bessie in 1922. Hannah, who my great-grandfather called "Baba," miraculously lived for another thirty years, dying in 1952. According to her grave, she was ninety-seven years old. I don't quite buy that—she must have been closer to ninety—but nonetheless, may her soul be bound in the bundle of life.

The stories of my ancestors are reflective of the demographics and situations of millions of other Jews who came to America at this time. In his classic history of this wave of Jewish immigration, Irving Howe offers three characterizing facts about those who emigrated: they came with their whole families more frequently than other immigrants did; they were overwhelmingly young, like most other immigrants; and they were more likely to be skilled laborers than other immigrants were.[195] Roughly a quarter of Jewish immigrants between 1899 and 1910 were younger than fourteen years old, and about four out of ten immigrants were women. The respective statistics for all immigrants in the same period are about one in ten and three in ten. About three-quarters of Jewish immigrants were between fourteen and forty-four years old upon arrival, which was about average, though also doubtlessly pushed up by grandparents who often came along when the whole family moved. Overall, the Jewish migration was largely a migration of young families.[196]

Moreover, it was also largely a migration of relatively skilled laborers. Whereas only about a fifth of all immigrants in the decades leading up to World War I were skilled laborers, roughly two-thirds of Jews were. Forty percent of Jewish immigrants worked in clothing, not too far from the estimated share who worked as tailors in the Pale. Of course, one must be a little careful here: as will be discussed in the next chapter, it is very possible—or even likely—that many lied about their profession to the immigration officers upon arrival. Also, as Howe notes, "the category of 'skilled laborer' employed by U.S. immigration authorities had only the haziest relevance to the Jewish workers who came over, since many of them were small craftsmen and artisans without industrial experience."[197] This was surely true of all of my ancestors; though just about all of the men were tailors or artisans of some sort, one can be almost certain they had never used much electric machinery or equipment until they came to the United States (with the likely exception of Nathan Lefcovitch). Nevertheless, they made do.

Still, as indicated earlier in this chapter, not everyone was interested in coming to America. "The Jewish immigrants...constituted in great part the 'dissenters,' the poor and underprivileged, the unlearned and less learned, and those who were influenced by secularism."[198] This was particularly true in the first half of the migration, at least until the turn of the century. After that, anyone who could get out of the increasingly violent Russian Empire did their best to. As Howe argued (emphasis added):

> In the years when conditions in Russia reached a measure of stability, people were able to make choices. Clearly, age was a decisive factor: the young were always a large portion of the immigrants, grown restive precisely through the stimulus created by the Yiddish cultural-political upsurge, or stirred to personal hope by reports from relatives already in America. In part, the Jewish migration was a function of the intellectual and spiritual turmoil within the Jewish community of eastern Europe; and some, if not the majority, of those who left would have wanted to get away even if there had been no hunger or persecution. At least before 1905 Jews who held strong religious or political convictions were less likely to emigrate than those who did not.[199]

This likely explains why few of my ancestors came with their parents, while others came alone, even if they were barely young adults. Whether it was old age, sentimentalism, a familial obligation, fear, or orthodoxy that kept them there, older Jews were clearly reluctant to make the journey.

And now, to offer a succinct and final answer to the question in this chapter's title—what made them come here?—let us return a final time to Howe:

> It is best to turn back to the folk voices themselves. An unpublished Yiddish memoirist writes, "They pushed

me into America"—"they" being all those forces of oppression he encountered in his youth. Another unpublished Yiddish memoirist recalls still more vividly, "A powerful storm-wind ripped us out of our place and carried us to America." No one in the path of that "storm-wind" was left untouched.[200]

Chapter 6
A LOST WORLD

◆──────◆

Ah, God in Heaven, should I ever forget them, forget me as well on that last day![201]

~ Adam Mickiewicz

By this point in this book, all of my ancestors have arrived in the United States, and the story told thus far is representative of the two and a half million Jews, something along the lines of an entire third of Eastern Europe's Jewish population, who immigrated to America. This chapter succinctly covers the remaining two-thirds.

Even before the First World War came to an end in 1918, it was clear that the "war to end all wars" had not, in fact, brought an end to warfare. The Russian Revolution, which began in 1917, guaranteed that war was not going anywhere. After Russia withdrew from the war when the revolutionaries took control of the country, the war on the Eastern Front transformed into a handful of smaller but no less serious conflicts between various Eastern European powers. Together with the mess left behind by the First World War, the rapid spread of the revolution meant the creation—and sometimes re-creation—of new (or revived) nations, including an independent Poland (which hadn't truly been seen since the Partitions of Poland over a century earlier) as well as independent

Ukrainian and Belarusian states—something which hadn't truly ever been seen before.*

It was only a matter of time before traditional territorial disputes and national rivalries would be revived, too—and, indeed, not too much time. Large-scale violence ravaged through Poland and Ukraine, in which hundreds of thousands of Jews were killed. Before the end of 1918, the Western Ukrainian People's Republic—which had split off from the Austro-Hungarian Empire—was at war with Poland over historically and culturally Polish-leaning L'viv and its surrounding territory. (This long and complicated story is impossible to sufficiently retell here.) Soon the Polish-Ukrainian War became entangled with the already-ongoing War of Ukrainian Independence, closely related to the Ukrainian-Soviet War. These wars were messy, often with more—sometimes far more—than only two sides fighting against each other. The modern Polish, Ukrainian, Belarussian, Lithuanian, and Russian states would not come into existence peacefully.[202]

Unsurprisingly, Eastern Europe's remaining Jews suffered greatly during this period, and even more so in the next under the Nazis. Unfortunately, however, it was no longer possible for those who remained in the Pale of Settlement to flee to safety in America.

The Closing of the Gates

With the pace of immigration—not just of Eastern European Jews—showing few signs slowing down as the nineteenth century turned to the twentieth, free-flowing immigration had increasingly numerous and vocal detractors advocating for shutting off the faucet. Restrictive immigration reform had been gaining popularity among the public and politicians ever since the beginning of the era of mass migrations in the

---

* Technically, there were a few independent Ukrainian states—the Ukrainian People's Republic, the Western Ukrainian People's Republic, the short-lived Ukrainian State, as well as the anarcho-communist Makhnovshchina movement.

latter half of the nineteenth century. Many well-respected and influential public figures offered fervent denouncements of open immigration policy, including Henry George and Theodore Roosevelt (the latter of whom even denounced the Chisinau pogrom against his own cabinet's advice). Their (perhaps familiar) argument was that the immigrants would never—and perhaps could never—assimilate, that they would take jobs from native-born Americans or become strikebreakers, and that they posed a threat to American life, values, and even safety.[203]

The anti-immigration influence was soon too strong for many policymakers to ignore. At first, immigration reform passed by Congress in this era sought something of a compromise, seeking to regulate immigration more than prohibit it. For example, an act passed in 1882 mandating that those who were denied entry to the United States be sent back at the shipowners' expense did far more to bring about the pre-emigration portside medical examinations and quarantine periods than it did to slow the pace of immigration. But as the anti-immigration movement grew more powerful, attempts at reform became increasingly restrictive. Entry into the country was complicated for the many immigrants who made the transatlantic voyage with tickets paid for by someone else after a law passed in 1891; that law also allowed immigration officers to deny entry to anyone who seemed "otherwise objectionable," a very broad criterion made even broader in 1903. Another law enacted in 1891 prohibited the encouragement of immigration by advertisement, something some Jewish philanthropists had experimented with in the 1880s.[204]

As the pace of immigration intensified in the first decade of the twentieth century, so did the anti-immigration movement's efforts to curtail it. In 1909, the New York commissioner of immigration, William Williams, implemented a requirement that arriving immigrants at Ellis Island would need at least $25 to be allowed entry into the United States—a very high sum relative to the typical immigrant's wealth. The change may have surprised arriving immigrants as much as it surprised those who had followed Williams's earlier reforms, which were principally designed to ensure immigrants at Ellis Island were treated courteously. But his earlier reforms did nothing to assuage the outrage of many immigrant populations—especially the Jews, who vehemently denounced Williams and his rule change in the well-read Jewish newspapers. "Most of the immigrants working in factories today came to these shores without a penny," one paper argued, yet they were "the ones who have built up the palaces, machines, food, and clothing which America enjoys."[205] It also caused great confusion in Europe:

> You can't imagine the chaos that Williams's twenty-five dollar edict has created in the towns and villages of Russia. Thousands of emigrants on the eve of departure don't know what to do. Those who had a few extra rubles, though not the entire fifty, decided to take a chance and embark...while cabling to their friends in America.[206]

While the outrage did lead Williams to partially walk back the new requirement, it was only a temporary victory. In 1917, on the eve of America's entry into the First World War, Congress finally succeeded in implementing one of the reforms most dreaded by those in favor of immigration: literacy tests. Three presidents had vetoed literacy tests three times before—in 1897, 1913, and 1915—but by 1917, the prospect of war in the context of the growing anti-immigration movement meant that there would be no veto this time around. In addition to requiring immigrants over sixteen to pass a literacy test to be allowed entry—which, of course, the majority could not possibly pass—the act also gave immigration officers even greater discretion over individual cases and all but banned immigration from most Asian countries except Japan and the Philippines (which was an American colony at the time).[207]

A few years after the First World War came to an end—a period in which hundreds of thousands of Jews suffered terribly in Eastern Europe, unable to come to America—came the official end to the period of open immigration: the Immigration Act of 1924. The act implemented a highly restrictive immigration quota system that capped the total number of immigrants of a given nationality each year to 2 percent of that nationality's foreign-born population in the United States as of 1880—the last year in which the Census was taken before the inpour of millions upon millions of immigrants, Jewish and non-Jewish alike. A quota was also placed on the total number of immigrants who could be allowed into the United States each year: 142,483, less than a tenth of the number of immigrants who entered the United States in 1906 alone. The number of Polish immigrants was capped to 5,982 per year, while Russia (still including Ukraine at the time) was capped to merely 2,248. Jewish immigration to the United States all but came to a complete halt.*

And so, on September 29, 1924, the White Star Line's *Canopic* became the last immigrant ship to arrive in Philadelphia with Jewish immigrants and refugees on board.[208]

The Russian Revolution and the Interwar Years

While all of my immediate ancestors had already left these places by 1910, many of their neighbors, families, and friends remained. There the state of life in the shtetls of the Pale of Settlement continued its steep decline, with poverty and starvation becoming increasingly common. In search of whatever economic opportunity they could find, many of those who opted to stay in Eastern Europe rather than emigrate moved to urban centers such as Warsaw, Lodz, L'viv, and Odesa, further depriving the shtetls of population and economic activity. In less than a century, Kyiv's population grew from 25,000 around 1830 to 250,000 in 1900 and then to 630,000 in 1914, while Odesa grew from 25,000 in 1814 to 450,000 in 1900; in only forty years, L'viv grew from 50,000 in 1870

---

* It is important to also note that while immigration from Europe was greatly restricted by the 1924 act, it was all but entirely banned from Asia—this time including Japan—and remained so until nearly a half century later.

to 200,000 in 1910.[209] As we saw occur in London, the rapid inflow of new residents—many but not nearly all of them Jews—made urban life tense.

The situation took a turn for the worse in 1905, when a revolutionary fervor broke out among the peasant and working classes after Tsar Nicholas II forcefully denied a petition calling for a constitutional monarchy with an elected assembly. The situation was made no better when the army opened fire on a crowd of protestors, killing over a hundred and wounding hundreds more. News of these events spread fast; only days later, workers throughout Ukraine began going on strike. The news spread far, too, as even those in the remote, overcrowded villages—shtetls and non-shtetls—joined in, with some even cutting down trees in forests owned by the nobility and attacking their homes. By the end of the year, the Russian Empire's economy had almost come to a complete stop; the people had hit a breaking point, and things were getting out of control. Times like these had always been particularly dangerous ones for Jews; only a few decades earlier, the pogroms in 1881 and the early 1860s had followed episodes of political and social unrest.[210]

This time would be no different. Accusations of everything from being sympathetic toward the tsar to being responsible for the economic decay of rural Ukraine and Poland ultimately led to a terrible outbreak of pogroms throughout the Empire. Economic angst over competition for jobs and a need to find someone to blame led to the deaths of hundreds of Jews in Kyiv and Odesa, with thousands injured, and tens of thousands of homes and businesses were destroyed. The onset of the Kyiv pogrom killed twenty-seven and destroyed 1,800 Jewish homes and businesses, with only one out of twenty-eight Jewish stores on Kyiv's main street left intact.[211] Chernihiv Province was hit particularly hard— more than half of the 630 pogroms occurred within its borders, including one in Chernihiv and one in Novhorod-Siverskyi.[212]

The tsar ultimately gave in, or so he wanted his subjects to believe, and the situation calmed for some time until the outbreak of the First

World War in 1914. This time, the tsar did not survive—literally or figuratively. The Russian Revolution put an end to the Russian monarchy, also taking out the Pale of Settlement while it was at it.

At first, the Russian Revolution might have brought Eastern Europe's approximately four million remaining Jews some relief, perhaps even optimism. After all, it was the end of the Russian Empire that brought about the end of the Pale of Settlement, and many—thought not all—Jews had developed vaguely socialist-leaning sentiments in their early years of factory work. Moreover, with Ukraine and Poland no longer under the tsar's yoke, perhaps now they would finally be free to live peacefully and without interference among themselves. Indeed, some even joined nationalist causes, particularly in Ukraine.

Whatever hopes Eastern European Jews had for life after the Russian Empire were crushed, and quickly so. Jews, of course, rarely emerge unharmed in episodes of nationalism-driven conflict or civil war. As various Russian armies battled for control of Ukraine in 1918, a wave of pogroms more violent than any since those during Khmelnytsky's revolt broke out across Eastern Europe. Many were perpetrated by the communist Bolshevik Army, including one in Harry Shirofsky's hometown of Novhorod-Siverskyi, but the vast majority were not. In fact, rather than the anti-communist White Army—who at one point even used the slogan "Beat the Jews, save Russia"—or the revolutionary Red Army, it was the army of the Ukrainian People's Republic who was responsible for about 40 percent of the pogroms. Some estimates suggest that over 100,000 Jews were murdered during the revolutionary years, with another half million left homeless.[213]

The army of the Ukrainian People's Republic at the time was under the command of Symon Petliura, a controversial figure in Jewish Ukrainian memory today. A few years later, Petliura himself was murdered in 1926 by an aggrieved Ukrainian Jew who had lost relatives in the pogroms instigated by Petliura's troops. Petliura, however, seems to have been appalled by his troops' behavior; his legacy as a violent antisemite is, at least in part, unfairly assigned. In an order written in 1919, which I briefly introduced in Chapter 3, Petliura denounced his army's behavior:

> It is time to realize that the world Jewish population...was enslaved and deprived of its national freedom, just as we [Ukrainians] were...[Jews have] been living with us since time immemorial, sharing our fate and misfortune with us. I resolutely order that all those who incite you to carry out pogroms be expelled from our army and tried as traitors to the Fatherland.[214]

Unfortunately, though at least one of his officers was tried and shot on Petliura's orders for his involvement in pogroms, Petliura was ultimately unable (or potentially unwilling) to put an end to the violence. Indeed, his army's intent to destroy, plunder, and murder Jewish communities and their residents despite Petliura's orders is indicative of widespread antisemitism in the early days of partially realized nationalism and of the communist revolution. The additional danger imposed by the nationalist dimension of these conflicts was also clear in Poland, where attempts of Jewish communities to remain neutral in the revolutionary conflicts were seen as Ukrainian sympathy. A wave of antisemitic violence broke out there as well, killing dozens in L'viv in 1918–19.[215]

Thankfully, after revolutionary fervor calmed down after the creation of the Soviet Union in 1922, so did the violence against the Jews of Eastern Europe. But the calm would only last for a decade. The global spread of the Great Depression reenergized the revolutionary spirit, with an impoverished peasant class once again looking for someone to blame. The Ukrainian peasant class in particular proved unruly. Despite the Ukrainian People's Republic's transition into a Soviet state in 1922, Ukrainian peasants did not take much interest in Stalin's collectivization campaign, with some villages along the Polish border moving as a whole to Poland. Stalin's solution was to teach them a lesson via state-organized starvation: the Holodomor, Stalin's manmade famine in which somewhere between three and a half and seven million Ukrainians were left to starve to death, including a small number of Jews.[216] Kyiv was particularly hard hit, with hundreds of thousands starving to death there. By 1934, approximately one in eight Ukrainians were killed in that tragic way.[217]

Then, of course, came the Second World War.

The scale of the destruction caused by the Nazis—destruction of life, property, and often entire communities—was unprecedented in the modern era and remains hard to conceptualize. Of the 3.3 million Jews in Poland in 1939, three million were murdered by the Nazis between 1939 and 1945; of the roughly 1.5 million in Ukraine, as many as 900,000 Jews were murdered.[218] Rather than attempting to cram a complete history of the Holocaust into these pages, I will instead return to the hometowns of my ancestors to tell the story of German occupation.*

The Nazis and the Second World War

Only a few weeks after the Second World War began with the Nazi invasion of Poland, the Nazis marched into Gąbin on September 17, 1939. Four days later, the Nazis torched Gąbin's historic wooden synagogue and then ordered the town's Jews to enter the blaze to recover doors, windows, and chairs. It was the beginning of the end of the five hundred-year history of Jews in Gąbin. In August 1941, the town's 2,300 Jews were moved into a ghetto, and soon they were sent off to concentration camps; many wound up in Auschwitz. The ghetto was closed on May 12, 1942, and any remaining resistant Jews were shot on the spot. Only 212 of Gąbin's Jews remained at the end of the war, less

---

* I encourage the reader to consult another work for a more complete treatment of the Holocaust. See, for example, Timothy Snyder, *Bloodlands: Europe between Hitler and Stalin* (New York: Basic Books, 2010).

than 10 percent of those who had called Gąbin home only a few years earlier.[219]

A little over one hundred years after the forced closing and relocation of the first Jewish cemetery in Staszów, the one that had been promised to the Jewish residents in perpetuity in the eighteenth century, the Nazis occupied the city on November 8, 1942. At least 4,500 out of Staszów's prewar Jewish population of 5,000 were murdered by the end of the war, destroying Staszów's Jewish community forever. Among the 4,500 victims of Nazi terror was ninety-five-year-old Zelman Knobel—Froim Rubin Knobel's ninth and youngest child—along with his son Boruch Knobel and all of Boruch's children. Boruch, a doctor, was remembered in Staszów's Yizkor Book as "one of the town's maskilim [a member of a progressive, enlightened reform movement] and a great lover of conversation. He was good hearted, and his smile and his joy of life—even in his poverty—never left his face."[220]

While I have been able to confirm that Zelman, one of Esther Tyszgarten's uncles, was among those murdered in Staszów (as was Zelman's son's family), the Nazis surely killed more Knobels, Tyszgartens, and Waxmans. My grandfather recalls his grandmother Esther Tyszgarten confessing toward the end of her life that either she, her husband, or their relatives had cousins who perished in the Holocaust; some even had children who made it to Israel, who she claimed she had been sending money to. I have never been able to find these relatives, as hard as I have tried. Many Tyszgartens appear in Yad Vashem's database; though none were from Staszów, they did come from towns quite nearby. Yet so far, I have not been able to link these Tyszgartens to the Tyszgartens of Staszów.

The legacy of Nazi occupation and mass murder remains visible in Staszów today. After the Nazis occupied the city, in an act designed to simultaneously dehumanize Jews and erase them from memory, they removed most of the gravestones from the "new" Jewish cemetery to reuse them as pavers for roads through nearby mud and wetlands. When no Jews came to claim the surviving gravestones after the war, as nearly all were murdered, the city government simply decided to sell them; many wound up auctioned off to local construction and landscaping companies. But some sixty years later, about 150 gravestones were discovered in a Staszów home, followed by roughly 400 fragments of gravestones in a nearby courtyard. The German government paid to restore them along with the cemetery, which included the construction of a beautiful memorial to all the murdered Jewish Staszówers. However, only a small fraction of the Jews who were ever buried in Staszów have a gravestone that survived.

As far as I am aware, not a single one of my Staszówer ancestors or any of their relatives have stones that survive to any extent. Yet nearly all were born and raised in Staszów and spent their entire lives working and living there, holding their community so near and dear to their heart until the day they died (and maybe still thereafter). In fact, my ancestors who never left, along with the ancestors of those with Staszówer roots who also never emigrated, have *still* never left—they still reside in that small town in the Polish countryside along the Czarna River. Their final resting places are unknown, unmarked, and undetectable beneath the overgrown grasses and thick weeds above. As key as they were to Staszów's culture, history, and development, and despite how central Staszów was to their lives, nearly all of Staszów's former Jewish residents lie beneath unmarked earth, the legacy of a disrespectful act of compelled forgetting. But they would only be forgotten if not for their descendants and relatives. In the words of a wonderfully written plaque placed alongside the restored cemetery's fence:

> A vibrant and spiritual Jewish community existed in Staszów for 250 years. In November 1942, the Germans and their allies deported most of the 5000 Staszów Jews to the death camps of Belzec and Treblinka. This hallowed cemetery was destroyed and its many hundreds

of gravestones uprooted. 60 years later, in 2002, nearly 150 of the original stones, found in a house on Koscielna Street, were returned here, ending their "exile" in a belated triumph over those who sought to obliterate Staszów's Jewish history. "Should I forget them, may God in heaven forget me." - Adam Mickiewicz.[221]

May they be bound in the bundle of life—and should we forget them, may God in heaven forget us.

In Ukraine, where somewhere around two million Jews lived at the start of the Second World War, roughly a million Jews—and perhaps another half million more—were murdered by the Nazis during their occupation between 1941 and 1945. Unlike in western or central Poland, however, many of Ukraine's Jews were murdered not in concentration camps but in their own hometowns. The *Einsatzgruppen*, the Nazis' dedicated military group for committing genocide, arrived in Ukraine with orders to kill anyone who stood in the way of—or against—Nazi Germany. While some Ukrainian hypernationalists and police forces were willing (some even eager) to join the Nazis in this task, many non-Jewish Ukrainians suffered greatly under the Nazis too.[222]

The scale of the Nazis' terrifying efficiency toward evil was made clear shortly after their flawed invasion of Eastern Europe, Operation Barbarossa, began. Either because they knew what was coming or because they had been called into military service, about two-thirds of Kyiv's pre-invasion population of 160,000 left the city, leaving behind about 60,000—many of whom were women, children, elderly, or unwell. On September 29, 1941, under penalty of death, Kyiv's Jews were ordered to appear at a local cemetery with all their valuables, documents, and warm clothing. Between September 29 and 30, 33,771 Jews were taken to the Babi Yar ravine and murdered in what became among the most infamous Nazi atrocities in Ukraine.[223]

A few weeks earlier, the Nazis occupied Chernihiv on September 9, 1941. As in Kyiv, many of Chernihiv's roughly 12,500 Jews had already left or joined the army, leaving behind a few thousand. After killing a few hundred in October, on November 18, 1941, many of Chernihiv's remaining Jews were called to the city's Red Square, where they were subsequently murdered. By the time Chernihiv was liberated by the Soviet Union in September 1943, at least two thousand were Jews were dead.[224]

Further east in Novhorod-Siverskyi, many of the town's Jews had already left long before the Nazis arrived in August 1941. Indeed, the town's synagogue closed at some point in the 1930s, and while about 3,500 Jews lived there when my great-great-grandfather left in 1904, just under a thousand remained in 1939. Even fewer remained by November 1941, when the Nazis brought the remaining 174 Jews to an anti-tank ditch in Ostroushky, a village just across the Desna River, where they were all murdered on November 7 and 8 by the S.S., with assistance from local Ukrainian police.[225] As in Staszów and many other towns, the Nazis also recycled many of the headstones in the Jewish cemetery for use in paving a 150-foot stretch of a local road. Some Jews returned after the war, but even before the Russian invasion of Ukraine, fewer than two dozen remained.[226]

Bershad, the origin of my family's Wexler branch, has a story quite unlike the rest. In a place where most people still heat their homes by burning wood and where streetlights are nowhere to be found, the same clay synagogue Israel Wexler—my great-great-great-grandfather—would have attended in the second half of the nineteenth century still stands, slowly decaying, but still in use. While technically occupied by the Nazis during the Second World War, the region was most under the control of Romanian fascists, who turned out to be less-effective killers than the Nazis, allowing 70 percent of Bershad's prewar population of 5,000 to survive the war. Shtetl life more or less continued in Bershad, where despite considerable emigration to Israel and the United States about a hundred Jews still live. Many of the homes in the Jewish quarter, even those abandoned by emigrants, still have mezuzahs fixed to their doorframes. Passover and Yom Kippur are still observed in the synagogue, even if achieving a *minyan*—a quorum of ten men required for certain prayers in Orthodox Judaism—is all but impossible on most other days.[227]

What keeps the spirit of Jewish life alive in a place like Bershad? Of course, there is something to be said for the endurance of Jewish life in general—after all, it has just been easy to be a Jew just about anywhere in the world in just about any point in history, yet here we are regardless. But one of Bershad's elderly Jews—a witness to the Holocaust—ascribed it to something else: "centuries of coexistence." Let us hope we may continue to live in peaceful coexistence.[228]

One final thought before we finally turn to the United States. A very rough tally of Eastern European Jews who were murdered in the first half of the twentieth century counts something like six or seven million, more than three times the number who came to the United States between 1881 and 1924. The vast majority were murdered after the end of the First World War, at which point immigration to the United States was no longer an option. Many had no way out, no alternative but to defend themselves and their community, often to their death.

There is no good—by that I mean, legitimate—reason the United States cut off immigration in 1924. If its major coastal cities were truly becoming overcrowded—a point that many were approaching, in all fairness—this was certainly untrue of much of the interior of the country. Couldn't Congress have attempted to get immigrants to settle in the often sparsely populated Midwest? Couldn't state and local governments have built up new cities from scratch, to be settled by millions of determined, hard-working immigrants? And, indeed, was early twentieth-century capitalism not dependent on a hard-working but determined working class, a class most immigrants were eager to join? In hindsight, the closing off of immigration in 1924 seems to only make sense if one believes the xenophobic and isolationist talking points of the early twentieth century.

But as seen above, cutting off immigration had disastrous consequences, not least of all for Eastern European Jews. Not only were their towns and communities destroyed by the Nazis, and not only did their vibrant culture and nationality all but disappear forever, but around six to seven million Jews were murdered, many of whom were unable to escape from Nazi (and revolutionary) terror even before it arrived. One of the reasons Jewish law considers murder to be a crime worse than any other is because its consequences do not only affect the victim: by taking someone's life, you also take all future life they might have created. Had millions of Jews (indeed, all victims of the Holocaust) not been murdered by the Nazis or by the various revolutionaries of the era, many would have likely had children, grandchildren, great-grandchildren, and so on, some of whom would still be alive today. But they did not.

Part II
AMERICA AS A NEW JERUSALEM

◆──────◆

Their [Jews who left theirs] place of origin was now a thing of the despised past: a small town, a townlet, a hamlet, a shtetl. The smaller the better—thus they could explain their escape from their particular past and their desire to become part of something universalistic, imperial, mainstream, big and important. The shtetl for them was a yardstick measuring the gap separating their acculturated present from their Jewish past.[229]

~Yohanan Petrovsky-Shtern

No matter what one had or had not done for a living [back home], being an immigrant meant starting out again from scratch, with relatively few social and material resources, and with only one hope: to master enough information about one's new life situation, quickly enough, to enable one to find a place to live, a line of work, and a companionship- or kin-based support network. It was the task and the privilege of making a new beginning, after all, that motivated the emigrants to come to America in the first place.[230]

~Eli Lederhendler

"The Jew peddler!" you say, and dismiss him from your premises and from your thoughts, never dreaming that the sordid drama of his days may have a moral that concerns you. What if the creature with the untidy beard carries in his bosom his citizenship papers? What if the cross-legged tailor is supporting a boy in college who is one day going to mend your state constitution for you? What if the ragpicker's daughters are hastening over the ocean to teach your children in the public schools? Think, every time you pass the greasy alien on the street, that he was born thousands of years before the oldest native American; and he may have something to communicate to you, when you two shall have learned a common language.[231]

~Mary Antin

TAYLOR SHIROFF

My grandmother's tree. Mildred and Harry were her parents.

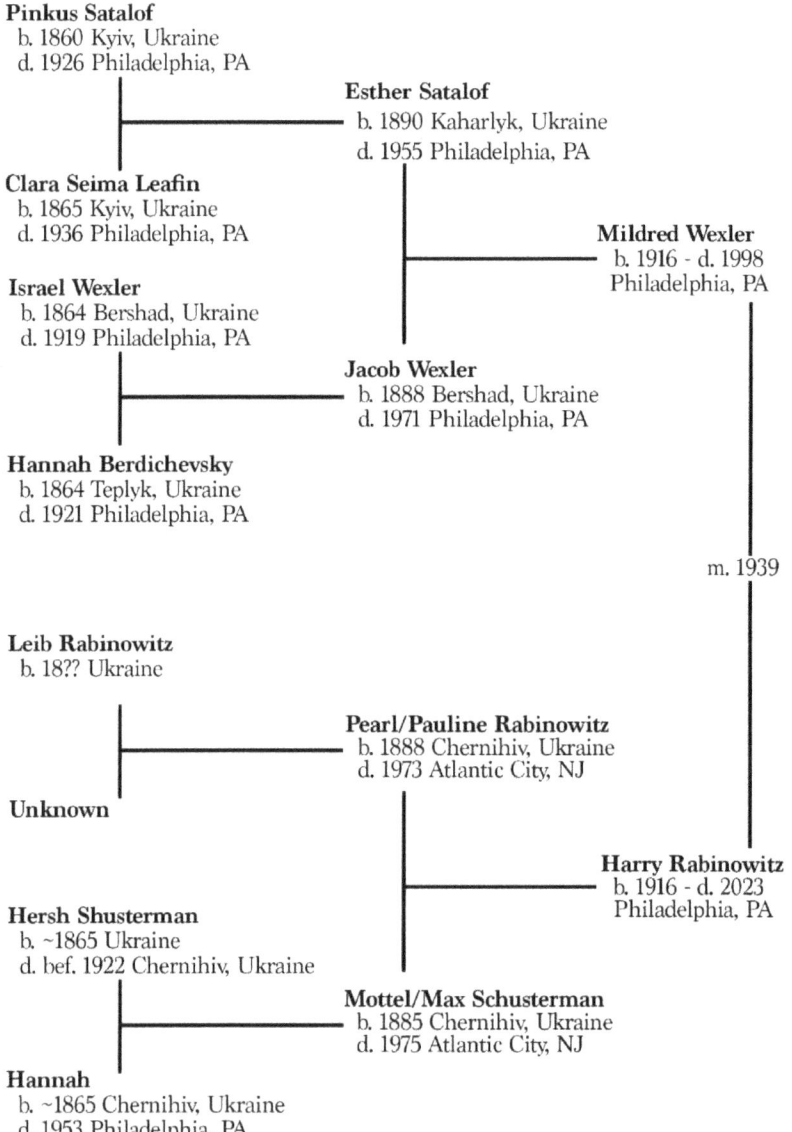

NEXT YEAR IN AMERICA

My grandfather's family tree. Pauline and Victor were his parents.

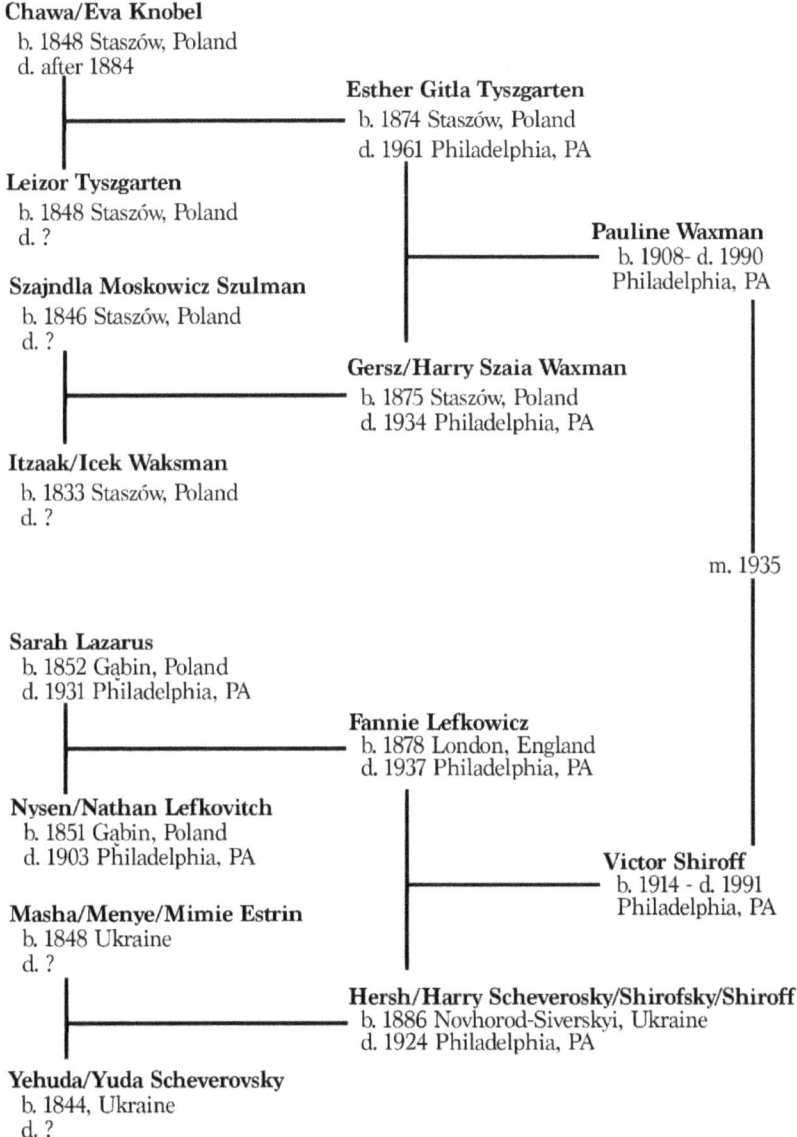

Chapter 7
ARRIVAL IN AMERICA

◆━━━━━━◆

The Jews who came to America were a people infatuated with ideas of the future, not so much for themselves as for their children. The future was their dream, the 'fix'.[232]

~ Irving Howe & Kenneth Libo

A full decade before the invention of air conditioning, a five-day heat wave brought daily highs of nearly 100 degrees to New York City between July 25 and 29, 1892. On August 2, four days after the heat wave broke, Pinkus Satalof and his son Abe stepped off the SS *Elbe* and onto Ellis Island on a comparatively comfortable seventy-three-degree Tuesday. With their first steps off the boat, they became the first of my father's ancestors to step foot in America.[*] All of my father's other ancestors soon made similar journeys over the next fifteen years. The

---

[*] Perhaps more accurately, their arrival is the earliest that I have been able to confirm. It is possible that Nathan Lefcovitch was in the United States before the Satalofs arrived in the summer of 1892, as we know that his oldest son, Morris, came to America in October 1890 and that Nathan had presumably joined him there by 1893. Yet Nathan does not appear along with Morris in the passenger list. It is possible that they were recorded separately but indeed were on the same ship or that Nathan came after Morris but before his wife and children, though it is also possible that he came after they arrived in late 1893.

table below details how, when, and from where each of my immigrant ancestors came, along with their families.

Ancestor	Last Residence	Departure Date	Arrival Date	Family Dep. Port, Arr. Date
Nathan Lefcovitch	Gąbin, Poland / London, England	? ca. 1890-1893	? ca. 1890-1893	Wife Sarah, with children Fannie, Jacob, and Samuel London; arr. late 1893
Pinkus Satalof	Kaharlyk, Ukraine	Bremen 7/22/1892	New York 8/2/1892	Wife Clara, with children Morris, Esther, and Lena Bremen; arr. 7/8/1896
Israel Wexler	Bershad, Ukraine	Bremen 7/12/1893	New York 7/25/1893	Almost certainly came together
Harry Shirofsky	Novhorod-Siverskyi, Ukraine	Bremen 7/7/1904	Baltimore 7/21/1904	Unknown
Harry Waxman	Staszów, Poland	? ca. 1904-1906	? ca. 1904-1906	Wife Esther, with children Jacob, Frank, and Fanny Hamburg; arr. 5/20/1907
Pearl Rabinowitz	Chernihiv, Ukraine	? ca. 1904-1906	? ca. 1904-1906	"Groom" Mottel Schusterman, Bremen; arr. 9/2/1907

Arrival in America

What an overwhelming occasion it must have been to step foot on American soil: a new language, a new climate, a new culture, coming to the senses all at once as they wandered ashore into a new country—and what a very, very different country it was from whence they came. But there would be no time for new arrivals to explore and get acclimated to their new homes at first. There were many officers, doctors, and tests to be dealt with before they were free to wander about the country.

An interview with an immigration officer typically came first. Amazingly, this was not always as terrible of an experience as one might have imagined—that is, unless you were the first of your family to arrive. With little idea of what questions would be asked—or the "right" answers to them—and with few, if any, contacts to provide as a reference, the interview was often incredibly anxiety-provoking for the pioneer immigrants. The immigration officers, particularly at Ellis Island, tended to have far more autonomy than perhaps they should have and could deny immigrants entry for just about any reason. Immigrants who were sick, had a physical deformity, were symptomatic of mental illness, were completely unable to answer the officer's questions, or had no contacts in the United States faced a very real threat: being sent back.[233]

But for those who came after a family member had already arrived, the process was much easier: the family member in America would write home with their address, often along with tips and recommended responses to the customs officers' questions. Miraculously, even those who had never seen or heard the English language before or who hardly knew anything of the immigration process were able to make it through; in fact, it was an incredible and amazing process to some. Jewish autobiographer Aaron Domnitz described the "privilege" of how he was treated at Ellis Island:

> My first contact with my new country was the brief conversation between me and the immigration officials. We were put into short lines as we entered the large buildings at Ellis Island. Each line had to go by a small table next to which officials sat who questioned each immigrant in his language. The new immigrant felt right at home. My line spoke Yiddish. Hence, a big, strange country recognized my language that I had brought here with me from abroad as an official

language. In Russia and Germany, I did not receive any such privilege.[234]

The questioning was simple—basic questions about character and political and religious inclinations. Who paid for your trip? Was someone meeting you? And the like. But they still posed a dilemma to many immigrants, particularly those who were the first in their family to arrive: should you tell the truth? Those who came penniless or destitute often, and understandably, did not want to appear as such. But there were also wrong answers that could cause the immigrant trouble. For example, the correct response to "Do you have a job waiting for you?" was no: by a law passed in 1885, the importation of contract labor was illegal. Luckily, organizations like the Hebrew Immigrant Aid Society were created to advise understandably clueless immigrants on such matters, among other things. HIAS continues to exist to this day; it now helps resettle Ukrainian refugees, doing work quite similar to what it was doing over a hundred years ago.[235]

Then came the doctors. Since most Jews arrived via the Bremen or Hamburg processes, they had already been screened for many, but not all, of the illnesses and other potential problems that could result in being denied entry. Nonetheless, this pre-screening did not excuse them from the deeply uncomfortable (and often medically questionable) tests upon arrival. At Ellis Island, immigrants were examined by three doctors. The first checked for basic issues, such as troubled breathing, deformities, or mental issues, followed by a second doctor who checked for various diseases. After these two was the third, and thankfully final, doctor. He was the most feared one:

> [He] stands directly in the path of the immigrant, holding a little stick in his hand. By a quick movement and the force of his own compelling gaze, he catches the eyes of his subject and holds them. You will see the immigrant stop short, lift his head with a quick jerk, and open his eyes very wide. The inspector reaches with a

swift movement, catches the eyelash with his thumb and finger, turns it back, and peers under it. If all is well, the immigrant is passed on...most of those detained by the physician are Jews.[236]

There were legitimate reasons for doctors to worry about the spread of disease. Had Israel Wexler come to America only a few months later than he did, he would have been sent back, likely before he even left Europe, as immigration to the United States was temporarily paused after outbreaks of typhus in the United States and cholera in Germany in the fall of 1892. And with the image of the steamships from Chapter 5 in mind, it is unsurprising that the ships themselves often hosted outbreaks of all kinds of sicknesses.

As daunting as the questioning and medical examinations must have been, the next step probably felt even more overwhelming: getting to your final destination. The unimaginable confusion and difficulty of navigating a new and decidedly foreign country is likely what led many to simply stay where the boat arrived (which, for most, was New York City). The fortunate new arrivals—derogatively referred to as "greenhorns" at the time—who had family to join elsewhere often arrived with train tickets to their final destinations already in hand, as that was part of the packages sold by the ticketing agencies, and usually even had the exact address of their families.[237]

When Sarah Lefcovitch, Esther Satalof, Esther Waxman, their children, and Mottel Schusterman were finally brought over by their families in America, they likely arrived with train tickets to Philadelphia and addresses in hand, significantly easing the physically and surely also emotionally tiring process of reuniting with their loved ones.

But for all the first arrivals without family to join, and for Harry Shirofsky and his cousin Mendel (who paid their own way), there probably were no pre-purchased train tickets, nor would there be anybody to meet them at the port to guide them to their new home. Yet once again, the most basic kindness of immigration officers and ordinary Americans, along with that of those who had recently immigrated themselves, helped ensure new arrivals safely got to where they needed to go. The memory of Benjamin Reisman's experience with this kindness may be preserved in somewhat dry prose, but his recollection is still among my favorites:

> When my turn arrived [to go through the immigration officers' questioning], the officials asked me how much money I had...they asked if anyone was coming to pick me up. I said that I expected my brother-in-law to come. An official turned to an officer and told him to ask me the street and the address. I said, "179 Eldridge Street." He told them to show me where the ferry was and they took me and showed me...I saw many people going to the ferry. I followed them. On the ferry I recognized a Jew and asked him how to get to Eldridge Street. He told me that he would put me on the right streetcar himself and wrote on a piece of paper for me to show the conductor. The conductor let me off at Grand Street and showed me which way to go.[238]

How could Benjamin—or any other new arrival to America—possibly have gotten to where he would need to go without the help of the immigration officer, the fellow Jew, and a compassionate streetcar conductor?

Whether arriving in New York, Baltimore, or conveniently in Philadelphia, the city of arrival could only have been unimaginably larger, more complex, and modern than could possibly have been conceivable to those who had hardly known anything other than the shtetls of the Pale. The city could be as unsettling as it was amazing. "Having come from a little bit of a village with a few houses, it [the East Side] was to say the least disturbing," one immigrant recalled; another recalled their shock that American children had shoes and stockings to wear every day and not only for special occasions.[239] But some were also surprised by the urban poverty they found in American cities, as recalled in one immigrant's memories of their first impressions of New York's East Side, the city's main Jewish quarter (emphasis added):

> It was a long walk, especially on a hot summer's day...Orchard Street. The crush and the stench were enough to suffocate one: dirty children were playing in the street, and perspiring Jews were pushing carts and uttering wild shrieks. A far from pleasant first impression...*was this the America we had sought? Or was it only, after all, a circle that we had traveled, with a Jewish ghetto at its beginning and its end...with their dark tenements, filthy sidewalks; saloons on nearly every corner; sinister red lights in the vestibules of many small frame houses—all these shattered my illusions of America and made me feel terribly homesick for the beautiful green hills of my native Vilna [Vilnius].*[240]

Many immigrants had indeed come to America with perhaps overly high hopes for what life would be like here, as we have seen. Even though it was truly a far freer land than from whence they came, their arrival would suddenly drop them into new, challenging, and difficult economic and social circumstances. In their first few years in America, most immigrants were poor, lonely, and exhausted. This started on day one: "Loneliness, weariness, and, at last, night under the roof of a stranger who shared his home with me...closed my first day in the United States," one immigrant wistfully recalled.[241] Between the economic adversity and the difficulties of adjusting to the modern, secular, and largely non-Jewish society around them, some immigrants, including the one from Vilnius quoted above, even became somewhat nostalgic for the Old World. As one wistfully put it, "I am overcome with longing—not only for my Jewish world, which I have lost, but also for Russia."[242]

Abraham Cahan, a Jewish novelist and immigrant of this era, expressed the sense of many demoralized immigrants in a letter to a Russian newspaper: "Curse you, emigration...accursed are the conditions that have brought you forth! How many lives have you broken, how many brave and mighty have you rubbed out like dust!"[243]

The early years were most difficult. Immigrants had to adjust not only to American culture (Mary Antin's earliest memories in America are of her father introducing her to bananas, rocking chairs, and iron stoves) but also to the American economy—one that was far more modernized and industrialized than they had ever known back home. For years, poverty, cramped apartments, and harsh working conditions were the norm. The transition into the idealized kind of American life imagined by many immigrants was a quick one. The trip to the final destination—in the case of all my ancestors, Philadelphia—was only the beginning.

What Is Philadelphia?

> *On the train to the border, when we hear the word America we rejoice. [Another emigrant:] "So you're going to New York! We're going to Philadelphia." [Aleichem:] "What is Philadelphia?" "A town like New York." "Wait a minute. Philadelphia is no more like New York than Atsheshcok is like Vilna or Otvozk like Warsaw."*[244]
> ~Sholom Aleichem

It is hard, if not entirely impossible, to say exactly what brought something like a quarter of a million Jews to Philadelphia in this period. Though nowhere close to rivaling the size of New York's Jewish community, Pennsylvania—and Philadelphia, its largest city—did have the *second* largest Jewish population in the United States in the first few decades of the twentieth century, regardless of how Aleichem may have felt about it. Indeed, the number of Jews in Philadelphia grew significantly faster than it did in New York between 1907 and 1918, when it more than doubled to 322,000. But all of Philadelphia was growing too: whereas Jews made up roughly 15 percent of the city's population shortly after 1900, this figure declined to about 11.5 percent in 1918. Even at the end of the era of Jewish mass immigration, Jews made up just under 4 percent of Pennsylvania's population and about 10 percent of the entire United States'.[245]

When the first Jewish refugees from Eastern Europe arrived in Philadelphia, they settled in the southeast part of the city known as Society Hill—a neighborhood that had fallen a long way from the place where the elites of George Washington's day—including Washington himself—gathered and danced. A century after our country's founders lived there, many of the once-magnificent homes and mansions in the area covering a quarter of a square mile contained by South Seventh Street, Walnut Street, Washington Avenue, and the Delaware River had fallen into disrepair and deterioration.

Before the Eastern European Jews claimed these streets as their own, the residents of this neighborhood were anything but Jewish or Eastern European. They were largely Irish, with some Germans, Danes, and Scots—though the typical resident was more likely to have moved from Delaware or New Jersey than Europe. In 1880, the apartment that would be home to the Waxmans by 1909 was occupied by a New Jersey-born husband and his Pennsylvanian wife and daughter; the Lefcovitches' future apartment was rented by five Pennsylvanians and a Delawarean, with the rear unit leased to an Irish immigrant and his Missouri-born children; Harry Shirofsky's future workplace and home was the residence of a single man, born in North Carolina to a German immigrant.* It was a working-class neighborhood, home to water boys, box makers, salesman, sail makers, druggists, firemen, and cigar makers, in addition to a number of saloons. South Street, near Society Hill's

---

* Technically, these are all just immediately south of Society Hill. The Jewish quarter quickly expanded to include this territory.

southern border, was already well on its way toward becoming the business hub of South Philadelphia. The stalls of South Second Street's New Market sold produce and basic goods, driven in—by horse, that is—from throughout the tristate area.[246]

From the beginning, southeast Philadelphia, particularly Society Hill, attracted nearly all of Philadelphia's Jewish immigrants. This was a result of its proximity to the Washington Avenue docks, where the immigrants—and later their families—arrived, in addition to the availability of cheap rent as well as employment and commercial opportunities, most commonly in the tailoring sweatshops that defined the early decades of the Jewish quarter or at the uncountable businesses of Dock Street or South Street. Apartments within the homes on the surrounding South Street could be rented for the relatively low cost of only a few dollars, a deal made even better by the proximity to Strawberry Street and Bank Street, where the clothing and garment industry was headquartered. The immigrant Jews "found South Street to be the most prominent business street in South Philadelphia" when they arrived, an editor of a Yiddish paper wrote at the time. "Several German Jews had businesses on South Street. The Russian Jews could talk to them and the new arrivals began to settle around South Street."[247]

The German Jews were among the roughly 15,000 Jews who called Philadelphia home before the first Eastern European Jews arrived in 1881, most of whom had immigrated in the decades leading up to the Civil War (indeed, often with the help of much earlier versions of the same Bremen-Hamburg system used by their Eastern European peers many decades later). Also among the earlier Jewish residents in Philadelphia were Sephardic Jews who had either immigrated to America themselves or were the descendants of the few who had called America home since before the American Revolution. But those communities were of no interest the Eastern European immigrants, it seems: Society Hill, preferred by the Eastern Europeans, was about as far south of Market Street as the German American Jewish community in Northern Liberties was north of it. There were significant cultural, religious, and political differences between the arriving Eastern Europeans and the German Jewish establishment, who also had a particular dislike for the Yiddish language.[248]

While these factors collectively explain why Eastern European Jews settled in Society Hill, they do not get us very far in understanding why they came to Philadelphia in the first place. It is important to remember that many—particularly those who were the first in their family to leave—were willing to go to wherever they could get to; the exact final destination didn't really mater, as long as it was not within the Russian Empire. As we saw earlier, many immigrants opted to remain in the city of their port of arrival, which naturally made New York City home to far more Jews than anywhere else in the United States. But for those desiring to avoid the increasingly overcrowded Jewish neighborhoods in Manhattan, Philadelphia was within reach from just about any of the ports on the eastern seaboard. Hence, in addition to those who sailed directly to Philadelphia, many others got to the city by train, typically arriving at the only half-functional rail station at Ninth and Brown Street in what was then in the territory of Philadelphia's German Jewish population. Of course, not all who came to Philadelphia stayed there. The trains of the Pennsylvania Railroad also backed down to where the steamships docked at the Washington Avenue wharf for the ease of all who were heading westward to cities like Chicago, Cleveland, or St. Louis.[249]

In fact, if Philadelphia was consciously chosen for any particular reason, it may have had something to do with the Pennsylvania Railroad. As early as 1873, a prominent Hebrew journal read by learned Jews throughout the Pale regarded that railroad as "the best and most reliable for emigrants who are going to the American West." Others may have looked to the Pennsylvanian city because they heard the somewhat prominent rumor that the doctors, examiners, and immigration officials at Ellis Island were stricter than those elsewhere and thus sought to avoid entering through New York.

While we don't know for sure what brought all of them, we can say when the very first group of Eastern European Jews arrived in Philadelphia. On February 23, 1882, the steamship *Illinois* arrived after a roughly two-week voyage from Liverpool. Aboard were 329 Jewish refugees from Odesa, Kyiv, and Warsaw, each fleeing the tragic pogroms sparked by the assassination of the tsar just short of a year earlier. This was only the beginning: over the next two decades, about 60,000 more followed.[250]

Philadelphia's German Jewish community had heard the news that the refugees were coming some weeks in advance and had arranged to use an old railyard—coincidentally, one owned by the same Pennsylvania Railroad that was lavishly praised by the journal quoted above—as a temporary shelter. Yet their hospitality had limits. While they were willing—some even happy—to provide basic necessities (and sometimes more) to the Eastern European Jewish refugees, German Jewish charity was definitively curtailed to exclusively support existing refugees already in America. Not only did they refrain from directly supporting Jews still in the Russian Empire, but they campaigned with a number of Jewish organizations and charities to avoid encouraging more Jewish immigration. It was the beginning of what would remain a complicated relationship.[251]

It should be said, however, that the German Jewish associations and charities of Philadelphia made a genuine and meaningful effort to help the refugees, particularly in the early years, and perhaps even more so than their equivalents did in New York City. Russian refugees had a particularly strong ally in Alfred Jones, the son of Jewish immigrants from the Netherlands. Five months before the *Illinois* landed in Philadelphia, Jones used his position as editor of the *Philadelphia Jewish Record* to publish accounts of the violence in Russia and to promote efforts to support the arriving refugees.[252]

Isidore Binswanger, a German-born Jewish immigrant to Philadelphia, also stands out as particularly generous ally to the Russian Jews. In addition to earning himself a fortune in the granite industry, from 1870 to 1879, Binswanger also served as president of the Hebrew Education Society, a school founded a few decades earlier to provide Jewish children in Philadelphia with a half-secular, half-religious education. In 1879, the Society established a school for the children of the earliest Polish and Lithuanian refugees; in 1885, Binswanger's daughter established a kindergarten where the "uptown" (i.e., German) and "downtown" (i.e., Russian) Jews could attend school together, with the expressed intent to "make the children good American citizens [and] imbue them with the best American ideals."[253] When Binswanger died in 1890, he dedicated a portion of his estate to go toward aiding Russian Jews.[254]

Still, few among the German Jews thought that sustained Jewish immigration to Philadelphia either could or would be possible. At first, this may have seemed reasonable; after all, only a thousand Jewish immigrants arrived in Philadelphia in 1884—of whom all but 145 left for other cities.[255] Yet by 1890, the Hebrew Education Society estimated that "about 10,000" of the roughly 27,000 Jews living in the city at the time "were born in Slavic and in Hungarian countries." The Society's further commentary on the consequences of such rapid growth in only a decade is telling:

> This large population has settled in our midst within the last twelve years, their necessities have made great and increased demands on the Jewish charitable and educational institutions, and though many of that population have succeeded in becoming self-supporting, yet but very few of them are able to contribute or do contribute in relieving the necessities and caring for the well-being of their countrymen. It is a matter of gratulation that our Jewish community, faithful to the principles of Judaism are practically applying them in

> the relief of the wants, the amelioration of the condition, and the mental and physical education of these immigrants.[256]

To be fair, it was true that the charities were increasingly stretched thinner and thinner as refugees continued to arrive. Offering everything from cash aid to housecleaning lessons to English classes to countryside picnics for children, they simply could not keep up. The United Hebrew Charities, created in 1869 by the merger of a number of earlier Jewish charitable institutions, was no exception. In 1870, they provided $13,350 of aid to 682 individuals—about $20 per person—whereas in 1894, the demand for aid had become so strong that $46,536 went to 7,986 people—less than $6 per person.[257]

As early as 1896, the United Hebrew Charities, along with most charitable organizations, began opposing further Jewish immigration, with the Philadelphia Association of Jewish Immigrants—an unsurprising anti-immigration holdout—begging their colleagues to "remember their own antecedents—their own ancestry":

> They should bear in bind...that no matter how deficient these Russians and Poles, who comprise the great mass of those who now emigrate, may appear in education and refinement when judged by the standard of our Western civilization and culture, that they are far better than their surrounding in the old world. Remember it is not their faults, crimes, or practices that have caused them to be driven hither, but the wretched issues of national prejudice.[258]

But there was no stopping the flow of refugees, at least not yet. Before long, so many had arrived that Philadelphia already had its own thriving Yiddish theater, and a well-read Yiddish press was soon up and running.[259] Then the resurgence of pogroms between 1902 and 1905 led Jews—including most of my ancestors—to flee Russia at an unprecedented scale. Philadelphians were well aware of the pogrom in Chisinau and the hundreds inspired by it. The city's Jews—together with many generous Christians—raised over $50,000 to be sent to Jewish organizations in the Pale of Settlement as aid, and on November 29, 1905, a march of mourning was organized, "perhaps the saddest sight which has ever been seen in the streets of this city":

> Ten thousand men and women, each with a black flag in hand, marched under great banners of dull black. In a line that formed on S. 3rd Street near Bainbridge, the march began. A band accompanied the marchers and played "unspeakably sad, minor harmonies." Although it rained all day, some of the older women had no head covering and only scant protection for their feet...Small black flags hung from almost every house in the Jewish streets...in the center of the parade was a chorus of forty men who at intervals sang folk songs of Russia. "At times the effect was like a great organ, and the quiet which prevailed on the streets was like that of a vast cathedral."[260]

Just about all of my ancestors were living in Philadelphia at that time, most within a block from the origins of the parade. Did they partake? If not, then surely they were standing along the route watching. Pogroms occurred in many of their hometowns, places some of them had only just left. One of the hundreds of pogroms occurred in Harry Shirofsky's native Novhorod-Siverskyi, his home until sixteen months before the parade; another broke out in Chernihiv, from where Pearl Rabinowitz left roughly a year earlier—and where her soon-to-be husband, Mottel Schusterman, still was.* The city's several Yiddish or

---

* Mendel Rosenbaum, Harry Shirofsky's cousin who immigrated with him, still had three sisters and his mother living in the outskirts of Chernihiv. He bought his sister

Jewish newspapers were all covering the tragic events unfolding back in Eastern Europe. One can only imagine the anguish, worry, and guilt felt by those who enjoyed safety in America as their friends, families, and communities were damaged or destroyed back home.

Finding Work

Although the German Jews wished to live separately from the newcomers (and vice versa), they would come to find that they had little problem hiring them as employees or leasing to them. As the Lefcovitches certainly had discovered in London, there was far less generosity, humanity, and respect than one might have suspected that members of the same faith would have for one another. The sweatshop system spread rapidly through Philadelphia, as it did in many other large cities, whereby the relatively wealthier and more established German Jews employed more recent immigrants to work under terrible conditions for terrible hours and terrible pay, most egregiously in the clothing and textile industries, but also in manufacturing and industrial workplaces. Many even worked in their own homes. The criticism of one of the many commissions set up to investigate the sweatshop system offers a view into how bad the situation had become:

> A sweatshop is a place where both residence and workshop are identical, often consisting of only one or two rooms where the occupants live and labor, year by year, the most unvarying, unprofitable and unenviable kind of life. Hope well nigh extinguished, ambition all but dead, and life a real burden. In such a place as this (where cleanliness is unknown, all the laws of health violated with impunity, and disease and death are prevalent) wearing apparel is made and sent to the stores,

---

a ticket to come over in 1906, shortly after the Chernihiv pogrom; his mother and other two sisters arrived in 1909. One can only imagine how he felt after hearing the news of the pogrom.

and I have no doubt that it often happens that such clothing is the means of spreading diseases, which undoubtedly are originated and cultivated there. There are in Philadelphia 648 sweatshops, where, in normal times, not less than 6,000 men, women and children toil.[261]

Unfortunately for most new immigrants, there was hardly a choice but to enter the sweatshops. As one scholar of Jewish immigrant labor, Eli Lederhendler, put it, "In America, one single imperative existed—to get out from under."[262] You needed to find a place to stay as quickly as you could, and you could only ever afford to stay there—and still be able to afford to eat—if you could find employment too. The general absence of modernity from the Pale made finding employment—particularly good employment—outside of it difficult, and many realizes that their own occupations were either entirely absent or fundamentally different from what they had done back in the Pale. For example, those who had been tailors back home—as the plurality of Jewish immigrants seemingly were—arrived in America to find that tailoring was much different here. The use of electricity in tailoring would have been all but unheard of to the Pale's many tailors but was the default in America by the time they arrived. Similarly, though there were factories in the Pale, there were few factories of the sort that had become commonplace in America and the industrialized world, and though artisans and craftsmen are an essential part of any society, even the nature of their work was much different in the United States than back home.[263]

It is no wonder, therefore, that many Jews settled into entirely new occupations upon arriving in America. Harry Waxman may have remained a tailor, but Harry Shirofsky certainly did not, as we will see; his cousin Mendel had been a painter back home but wound up opening a grocery store, as did Fannie Lefcovitch's brother and many thousands of other Jewish immigrants. Others bounced between trades, something much more easily done in America than in the Pale, where the Russian

Empire had immense power and control over the economy. Just about anywhere, however, the work was terrible. Yet since the majority had arrived with hardly any money at all and no longer had a place to sleep as soon as they disembarked from their arriving ship, they did what they had to do to make ends meet.

The women were subject to hard work too. Pearl Rabinowitz, who traveled by herself when she was barely an adult, took a job working as a dressmaker in a sweatshop to earn enough money to bring her soon-to-be-husband to America. Given the generally poor wages available for a young female Jewish immigrant, Pearl had to make every cent of income count. Women in her position often scoured the entire neighborhood for the best prices for food and clothing. One immigrant recalled how her mother "walked blocks to where we could get milk for a penny a quart cheaper than we could get it in the immediate vicinity."[264] Pearl's hard work paid off, though, even if her soon-to-be husband arrived with a mere $8.50 in his pocket. Nonetheless, she retired and never worked again.

Pinkus and Abe Satalof, the first of my ancestors to come to America, would have understood Pearl's dedication to earning an income to bring her loved ones over. Pinkus had left his wife, Clara, and three of their children behind in the Pale and was surely eager to get them to the Philadelphia as quickly as possible. Pinkus found work as a laundryman, while his son, Abe, worked as a tailor—likely in a sweatshop, but it would have to do. Thankfully, they soon saved up enough money to purchase tickets for the rest of their family to travel from Kaharlyk to their new home at 526 Mercy Street in South Philadelphia. Even a decade later, his four oldest children all worked in the clothing industry, in factories as tailors (for the boys) or dressmakers (for the girls). Employed as they all were, though, economic stability could never be taken for granted: the 1910 Census indicated that Pinkus had been out of work for half of the previous year. Perhaps this necessitated his fifth child, Herbert, the first to be born in the United States, to have already entered the labor force as an "errands boy" at only fourteen years old.

Nathan and Abraham both returned to tailoring in Philadelphia, almost certainly in the same sweatshop conditions as the rest. Nathan's fifteen to twenty years of experience tailoring in London's East End surely helped make the transition to tailoring in America much easier than it had been for his peers, as he had already become accustomed to the tools and methods of modern Western tailoring. Still, Abraham did not remain a tailor for life. He later opened a grocery store, as many Jews did once in the United States, including Mary Antin's father. Nathan, on the other hand, remained a tailor until his premature death on April 26, 1903. He was fifty-two, and only one year shy of being eligible to fill out his petition for naturalization. Though he was doubtlessly among the best prepared and adjusted of my ancestors for life in America after living an English-speaking country for three decades, he unfortunately died before the legal right of citizenship could be bestowed upon him.

Living Arrangements

The best-case scenario for many immigrants, given their incredibly tight finances, was finding whatever friends, family, old neighbors, or distant relatives they had in America and moving in with them. Mottel, of course, knew living with family would be the permanent arrangement before he even left for the United States. He and Pearl were engaged before she left Chernihiv and were married as soon as he arrived in Philadelphia—where he was met by "his bride," according to the passenger list. As mentioned earlier, Mottel took Pearl's last name, and before long, Mottel and Pearl Rabinowitz became Max and Pauline Rabinowitz to the outside world—even if Pauline still liked to go by Pearl within the family. For others, like Harry Shirofsky and his cousin Mendel, it was a temporary arrangement; the two lived with their uncle Harris Jacobson's family at 636 Wharton Street for no more than a year or two after arriving here before moving elsewhere.

Over time, however, many found themselves with a desire to get away from living with their families. This wasn't always personal—indeed, more often than not, it was really a desire to leave the overcrowded, dirty, unhealthy, unsanitary, dark, and deeply uncomfortable nature of most immigrant housing. The apartments—tenements, more commonly—of the Jewish quarter were, like those of most immigrant quarters, absolutely anything but luxurious.

The tenements may not have had dirt floors, nor were they easily inflamed wooden structures, the way nearly every home in the Pale was built, but they were still miserable places to live. "A weariness emanates from the Jews, from the wagons and tables and shops around which they mill," the Russian-born Yiddish playwright and immigrant of this generation Leon Kobrin wrote:

> And weariness is carried from the gray walls of the tenement houses where these same Jews with their wives and children, with their..."boarders" and "boarderesses" choke themselves in dark rooms with no light or air...where bedbugs and roaches scurry around.[265]

Rich as America was, it took many, many years for its Jewish immigrants—indeed, just about all of its immigrants—to escape the deep poverty that characterized their early years here. Naturally, the first few weeks were particularly difficult. The *Forward*, a Yiddish newspaper based out of New York (but which also ran separate editions for other cities, including Philadelphia), ran many vivid descriptions of life in these early days in its reporting, including this unimaginable—but far from atypical—story of a recently arrived family in 1905:

> The family arrived in America six weeks ago; the mother just gave birth to her first child. The father is an unemployed painter. The two-room apartment is occupied by the father, mother, newborn child, and eight boarders. Can you imagine the horror and debasement

of giving birth in the presence of eight strangers? The mother lies on an old sofa; there are piles of dirt in all the corners. The boarders sleep on old mattresses.[266]

In addition to being overcrowded, dirty, and in dire need of proper ventilation, the tenements also often doubled as the workplace. In the same edition quoted above, the *Forward* tells of a family of nine who all lived in one room, headed by a shoemaker, whose business took the tenement's other room—the one in the front, the only one with a window.

The overcrowding was not just a consequence of the family-oriented nature of this wave of Jewish immigration, though having a large family certainly did not make things any easier. Instead, many had boarders living with them, who paid rent in exchange for the ability to sleep inside rather than on the streets. While the extra income was certainly needed by the hosting families, taking in boarders not only meant more overcrowding but also more responsibility for the women. This was something of a double-edged sword. On the one hand, it let the women be their own bosses and earn incomes without needing to leave the home; on the other, it meant more cooking, cleaning, and overcrowding.[267]

Since just about all recent immigrants were poor—and it was not as if there were no impoverished city-dwellers before the immigrants arrived—there were always many more people who were able to pay to sleep in a cramped corner of a tenement home than were able to rent the tenement itself. In extreme cases, the tenements could become so overcrowded that their residents took turns sleeping in a bed, alternating nightly or hourly. To no surprise to the modern reader, these living conditions all but guaranteed terrible hygiene and even more terrible overall health. Living in poverty as they were, there was often little that could be done—or rather, afforded—if somebody became ill; living as tightly packed as they were, there was also hardly anything that could be done to prevent the illness from spreading.

As shocking as these living standards are to us, most Jewish immigrants were already used to such overcrowding before they arrived here. By the time they left the Pale, overcrowding was common—almost a way of life. Beds were shared; any open space could be—and was—made into a place to sleep:

> [My family was] six; two uncles was eight; my grandmother was nine; and my aunt was ten. And we had four rooms. And I don't ever remember going to sleep with only the four children and parents. There was always somebody else...was it a cousin? Was it an uncle? One of them. We had them, very many.[268]

Quite similar living arrangements turned out to be common in America:

> When I came to this country I went to live with my aunt who lived in a very small, little house...there were five girls in one room—three in one bed and two in the other bed...the room, I can say, was about twelve by twelve...in the front room was my cousin, with her three children; she had three little boys. She slept with three boys in one room. And then there was another cousin and her husband and three children in another room, but they stayed there only about three months. Sometimes we were fourteen, fifteen people in that little house.[269]

To whatever extent one could be used to this way of living, as unhealthy and undesirable it may have been, many Jewish immigrants really were used to it. They did not see the same problem that the early twentieth-century reformers saw in urban tenement life—in fact, they hardly saw a problem at all. It was simply the only way of living that many Jews had ever known. Moreover, wasn't squeezing in all the family—and sometimes friends or old neighbors from the Pale—that one could into your home the exact kind of hospitality that they had always been taught to show? Living space, privacy, and personal space were simply not the priorities of most of the immigrant generation, at least not at first. Though running hot water, indoor toilets, and gas ranges all became highly desired and sought-after must-haves for their homes, "virtually none of the first generation of children to grow up on these shores knew what it meant to have his or her own bed, let alone his or her own room."[270] The children of the immigrant generation would, however, seek these amenities for their own children.

Though it was not as overcrowded as New York had become and indeed largely spared of the worst of tenement living, the living situation of my great-great-grandparents, Harry and Esther Waxman, the former Staszówers who found themselves living in the core of Jewish Philadelphia by no later than 1908, is a claustrophobia-inducing example of what the home of a recent Jewish immigrant looked like. Their daughter, my great-grandmother, Pauline Waxman, was the first of my Jewish ancestors to be born in the United States—even if the actual year and date has been lost.

The 1910 Census—which records the Waxmans as "Foxmans," revealing the original pronunciation of the family name in the W-less Yiddish language—put Pauline at two years old; she was twelve in the 1920 Census, again consistent with a 1908 birthday. Miraculously, though, by 1930, her birth year began moving forward—to 1910 that year, 1913 by 1940, and, by the end of her life in 1990, all the way up to 1917. As my grandfather—her son—put it, "it was a miracle: time would pass, but she was getting younger while we'd be getting older."* But though we cannot be certain of the exact date, we can be almost certain that she

---

* This was a common trend among the women in my family, at least. While Pearl eased into becoming ten years younger, Fannie Lefcovitch consistently understated her age by ten years for almost her entire adult life. Everyone either bought it or just went along with it to keep them happy.

was born sometime in 1908 at home, which, for the time being, was 226 Monroe Street.

The picture we get of the modest 226 Monroe Street from the 1910 Census has much in common with the depiction of tenement life given above. Seven families totaling forty-five people were crammed into the 1,200 square feet of 226 Monroe's four floors—every single one of them of Eastern European Jewish descent. Emblematic of the family patterns of the Jewish immigrants, twenty-eight of the forty-five residents were younger than eighteen. Pauline and her younger sister, Molly, were two of only nine residents in the entire building who were born in the United States (all of them were children); they were also the only members of their family born here. It may not have been New York, but the quality and comfort available in Philadelphia was not much better or different than in New York.

So many of Philadelphia's Jewish immigrants settled in the Jewish quarter that it was dense enough that if the Waxmans ever took young Pauline on a stroll, leaving their front door and heading 250 feet east to South Second Street before making a left and going another 250 feet north, they would have passed a crockery store at 710 South Second, where her future father-in-law would have been working downstairs, her future mother-in-law caring for her future siblings-in-law upstairs. Or if instead of turning up South Second, the Waxmans had continued another 250 feet east along Pemberton Street instead, they would have passed by 117 Pemberton, where Max and Pearl Rabinowitz were living by 1910 (Max and Pearl would become the grandparents of a woman who'd one day marry Pauline's son).

Max and Pearl were not the only occupants of their building either, which was even smaller than 226 Monroe. They were joined by another Eastern European Jewish family of seven and also had a child of their own: Morris Rabinowitz, born November 4, 1908, the day after William Howard Taft won the presidency over William Jennings Bryan. Max had settled down as a carpenter by then, a career he stuck to for the rest of his life, helping construct rowhomes throughout Philadelphia.

More than anyone else in my family, the Rabinowitzes serve as an exhausting display of the dedication to bringing the rest of the family over. The ritual was anything but over after Pearl earned enough working on her own to bring her fiancé over from Chernihiv—that was just the beginning. After Max and Pearl were married, the family's income was primarily dedicated toward this purpose. Over the years, the household—everyone, not just Max but the children and other relatives living there too—worked to save enough money to bring Max's mother, two of his sisters, two brothers, and supposedly many more over. Some, including Max's brother David, stayed with the Rabinowitzes, who moved further south to 2213 South Front Street as Philadelphia's Jewish quarter expanded in the 1910s and '20s, just as it did in London.[*] It certainly made it easy for their arriving relatives that the Washington Avenue Immigration Station, which just about every immigrant to Philadelphia went through at the time, was almost across the street. In fact, the Washington Avenue station was not much more than a fifteen-minute walk to just about any of the apartments and tenements my ancestors and many tens of thousands of other Jews settled into upon first arriving here.

At 2213 South Front Street, Max and Pearl had their second two sons: Benjamin, on July 11, 1911, followed by Harry on September 10, 1916, two weeks before Rosh Hashanah that year. Though I (indeed, all of us) have eight great-grandparents, four of whom appear in this book, only one of them is "my great-grandfather": Harry Rabinowitz, named

---

[*] Those who are well acquainted with southeast Philadelphia food geography and may realize that Tony and Nick's (formerly known as Tony Luke's), my family's preferred cheesesteak destination, is a short ten-minute walk south on Front Street from where the Rabinowitzes lived. Later in life, from time to time, my great-grandfather (Max and Pearl's youngest son) would return to where he grew up for a cheesesteak (with no cheese, of course, to keep it kosher).

after Max's father Hershel. This is due, in large part, to the fact that I never knew any of my great-grandparents (or even grandparents) on my mother's side and that Harry was the only one still alive on my father's side by the time I was born. But Harry had not only survived into my lifetime—he was a part of my life.

For so many years until his death when I was just short of thirteen, my weekends were defined by the weekly ritual of making the forty-five-minute drive to visit him and take him out for brunch, errands, or a haircut. Though my parents and grandparents were lucky enough to hear bits and pieces of the stories contained within this book firsthand from those who actually lived through them, my great-grandfather was the only person I was lucky enough to personally know who saw this world up close and personal. May his soul be bound in the bundle of life.

Though they tended to move about frequently, nearly everybody settled down in relatively close proximity, packed tightly into the Jewish quarter. While Harry Waxman was briefly living at 226 Monroe Street, Max Rosenbaum was only a block away. A decade before Max lived at 124 Bainbridge, the Lefcovitches (whose daughter later married Max's cousin) lived two hundred feet south, on Kenilworth. The Lefcovitches also briefly lived at 202 Monroe, 250 feet down the street from where Harry Waxman would live six years later, before moving to 752 South Second, only 150 feet from Harry Shirofsky's residence at 735 South Second. And if—or when—either Harry ever walked one minute around the corner, down Pemberton Street, he would have passed by Max and Pearl Rabinowitz's home, number 117. A few blocks south were the Satalofs by 1904. Only the Wexlers were relatively far away, at Fourth and Wharton in 1910. Perhaps what is most amazing about all this is that when the descendants of those original immigrants met and married years later, there is no evidence to suggest any of those families actually knew each other.

For better or for worse—and overall, things really were better—this was their new home. Though it is false that nobody returned to Russia, very few did. Once you were here, there was truly little choice but to keep on keeping on. Thankfully, the struggles of the early years—the overpacked apartments, the factories and sweatshops, the poverty—were not in vain. Before they may have recognized it, if they ever recognized it at all, many were living the American Dream. With time, America would try its best to fulfill the hopes and expectations that its new Jewish residents had arrived with.[271]

The interior of 702 South Second Street, just a few buildings down from where Harry Scherovsky lived and worked, pictured in 1914.[272]

Photos above and to the right are courtesy of PhillyHistory.org, a project of the Philadelphia Department of Records.

Top: The interior of an immigrant tenement at 530 Lombard Street in 1914.[273]
Bottom: the southwest corner of Second and Monroe, near where the Lefcovitches and Waxmans once lived, pictured in 1962.[274]

Chapter 8
THE AMERICAN DREAM

◆───────◆

To my worthy wife...and to my loving son...I come to tell you that I am well and in good health...I am telling you that my sun is beginning to shine in America. I am becoming a person—a businessman...white bread and meat I eat every day just like the millionaires...I am no more Gedalyeh Mindel—Mister Mindel they call me in America...in America there are no mud huts where cows and chickens and people live all together. I have for myself a separate room with a closed door, and before anyone can come to me, I can give a say: "Come in," or "Stay out," like a king in a palace. Lastly, my darling family and people of the village of Sukovoly, there is no czar in America.[275]

~Anzia Yezierska

Life in America felt so extraordinarily different to its two million newly arrived Jews not only on account of its economic advancements and societal differences. Perhaps most striking to new arrivals was the freedom: in religion, in business, and in society. Though one must be careful to not describe the America of this era too strongly as a truly free land of equality—as a reality check, the Civil Rights Act of 1964 was still forty years away when the gates into America were closed—there is no question that America was a country of much greater freedom and equality than the Russian Empire.

The Jews who arrived on America's shores between 1880 and 1920 were unimaginably better off here than back home, even if things did not always work out too well here. After all, even the most economically impoverished new American Jews found themselves without the need to hide in cellars on Christian holidays for fear of a pogrom. Much freer in religious matters and without the yoke of a controlling, paternalistic, and Christian state, American Jews finally had a fair chance of success in life—with the added benefit of no longer needing to constantly fear for their well-being.

This was the American Dream in its truest form. Rather than the one typically described, where anyone can achieve great success regardless of background so long as they work hard, the American Dream was about something much more general when James Truslow Adams first introduced the term in 1931:

> [The] American dream that has lured tens of millions of all nations to our shores in the past century has not been a dream of merely material plenty, though that has doubtlessly counted heavily. It has been much more than that. It has been a dream of being able to grow to fullest development as man and woman, unhampered by the barriers which had slowly been erected in older civilizations, unrepressed by social orders which had developed for the benefit of classes rather than for the simple human being of any and every class. And that dream has been realized more fully in actual life here than anywhere else, though very imperfectly even among ourselves.[276]

As Mary Antin put it, Russia was "another Egypt" for the Jews: life was very often difficult, impoverished, laborious, restrictive, discriminatory, and even dangerous, mostly because of the ruling government's self-determined policies. These realities of the Pale were among the "barriers" that Adams accurately accused the "older civilizations" of building. Jews in the Pale could not live up to their potential because of all the barriers the Russian Empire had put in the way, as well as the construction of the Russian social order in a way that dehumanized Jews. In America, though things were imperfect, it was a different story. "What did I find in America?" Bertha Fox, a Jewish immigrant born in a town one hundred miles north of Bershad, asked. "A great deal: material contentment, free schooling, free lectures in all languages, and, above all, calm. Calm."[277]

Back in Chernihiv, Max and Pearl once had to sit down after antisemitic violence had ravaged through their hometown and figure out how they could still have a future together. But in America, things were different. Pearl, a woman on her own both during the journey here and in her first year in America, was able to find a place to stay as well as a job—something uncommon in Russia, unless she had been widowed. Once reunited, Max and Pearl were able to start a family of their own, free from the fears they would have had if they had remained at home. They were able to start that family knowing their kids would not face the same stiff, rigid, and institutionalized boundaries that they faced; they would be able to "grow to fullest development," in Adams's language, or at least much more so than they could have at home.

Despite not learning much, if any, of the English language, Max worked through nearly his entire life as a carpenter, building rowhomes throughout Philadelphia. Pearl, who gladly resumed her duties as a housewife once Max arrived, never let her feminine strength and dominance over the household subside. When her children and husband came home from work, they were to empty their pockets of change in front of her—though she would double check that nothing remained hidden anyway. Her granddaughters heard plenty of tales of her shaking the laundry upside down to ensure not a hidden cent was left unaccounted for. As mentioned earlier, most of the money that did not go toward food and rent went toward bringing the remaining family abroad to the America. She managed and controlled the household to such an extent that both of Max's brothers also changed their surnames to "Rabinowitz" once they arrived (Max's mother, unsurprisingly, did not).

When Harry Waxman ventured far overseas to America in order to look for a better life, he and his wife, Esther, knew it would be a long time before he could send for her and their three children. They also knew there was no guarantee he would ever see them again. But clearly things were so bad—frankly insufferable—that the downside of leaving Staszów for America was not as intolerable as continuing to stay there. However, in America, Harry was able to afford to bring his family over on a tailor's wages—the same job he had back in Staszów, even though he was far poorer there. In America, he earned better wages and lived in a much nicer—even if smaller and more compact—home, and, just like the Rabinowitzes, he could grow his family in comfort with the peace of mind from knowing his children would be safer and able to achieve far greater things in America. Back home, the son of a tailor would simply become a tailor just as his father; in America, Harry's son Frank went on to do much bigger and more profitable things.

The Wexlers left what was likely the second-most remote hometown of any of my ancestors to live within one of the largest cities in the entire United States. The range of opportunities in their hometown of Bershad were nothing in comparison to those offered in Philadelphia. Partly that was because of Philadelphia's much larger population and greater wealth in general, but there was more.

In Philadelphia—and in all of America—Jews were able to, simply put, "do their own thing." Back in the Pale, Jews settled into occupations not necessarily as they wished but as was needed and available; if no work was available or needed, that was it. In America, however, one could settle into a particular industry or craft, and if their employment was endangered, they could simply find another place to work. We see this in the ever-changing job path of Israel Wexler's son Jacob, who went from a hosier knitter to shipbuilder to car mechanic, likely all in response to the changing needs of his family. Some may have worked in a variety of different occupations back in the Pale, but few did so on their own free will; rather it was the result of restrictions and regulations.

The Working-Class Jewish Immigrant

One reason behind startlingly high Jewish poverty rates in the Pale was the discriminatory prohibitions on their entry into more profitable professions. At best, Jewish merchants and shopkeepers paid absurd taxes, tariffs, and fees and were harassed, obstructed, and heavily regulated and taxed in the course of their work; many could not even legally leave the Pale, even though the best markets were outside of it. At worst, Jews were explicitly precluded from taking up certain vocations or sometimes even forced into particular occupations. There was no choice; there were no options. Consequently, it was all but impossible to break free from the inescapable state of desolate poverty, no matter how hard one worked.

In America, on the other hand, that wasn't the case—and the Jews of Eastern Europe had every intention to make the most of the new opportunities here. Indeed, they brought with them the same entrepreneurial spirit and strong work ethic that had long been observed in Jewish communities—even by the Russians, who were often impressed by the seemingly always-working Jews they came across during their first expeditions into Ukraine's shtetls. Those traits had developed largely as a consequence of the deep material poverty experienced by most Jews in Eastern Europe, where it was hard to survive without sharp business skills and a willingness to work long, hard, and difficult days in often less-than-desirable industries under even less desirable working conditions. Once in America, however, it meant that Jewish immigrants arrived armed with a little extra willpower and know-how as they began establishing themselves. Their willingness to work just about anywhere and under just about any working conditions led many to into jobs that, while certainly undesirable to you and me, would later open up numerous opportunities for the immigrants and (especially) their children.

For most, it was decades before they could reap the luxurious fruits of the American Dream—higher education, suburban living, stable and well-paying jobs, and so on. In the early years and the first few decades, the priority had to be on earning an income, and until the 1920s, work was often in challenging and uncomfortable environments and for poor wages. As we saw in the previous chapter, for many this meant conforming to the sweatshop system, whereby one worked under terrible conditions for too many hours, often in their own home but sometimes in an overcrowded and poorly ventilated factory-like warehouse. This was most common in the clothing and textile industries, where many Jewish immigrant men and women spent their first many years tirelessly working behind looms and sewing machines, "enslaved in the sweatshop by the boss tailor, sweating and toiling for sixteen hours a day," as one immigrant recalled. Even after the transition into working in more familiar factories, warehouses, and industrial spaces later in the early twentieth century, working in the clothing and garment industry typically meant you were in a sweatshop, where one "toiled and bled in dark, stuffy and polluted tailor shops for slave wages."[278] It is no surprise that many Jews joined unions; some started their own, while others were tempted by anarchism or socialism. One can hardly blame them.

While Nathan Lefcovitch, who worked as a tailor almost certainly (both in London and in Philadelphia) in sweatshops under conditions similar to those described above until his death in 1905, Harry Waxman worked his way up as a tailor in a department store. But that wasn't necessarily an upgrade—the working environment wasn't always that much better, and you lost the autonomy of working in your own shop, or at least in your own home. While these sorts of jobs did typically provide some extra income, it was still often not enough for the household. Evidently, even Harry's department store gig still left the family short on income: according to the 1920 Census, the family had a

Norwegian immigrant boarding with them for extra income and had already put their son Frank, then sixteen, in the workforce. Their daughter Pauline soon followed, getting her first job soon after completing middle school.

It was unfortunately quite common for immigrant children to leave school many years too early, and not only for the girls. My great-grandfather, Harry Rabinowitz, had to quit school after the eighth grade and settle into a job making leather bags at a luggage shop where his brother Benjamin was already working, while their oldest brother Morris was a retail salesman. Benjamin's education ended after his second year of high school, whereas Morris left after eighth grade like his youngest brother; none ever attended college.

Even a family of all boys needed to work instead of attend school. Jacob Wexler, Harry's future father-in-law, had a similar childhood. After leaving school no later than the age of twelve, he and his fourteen-year-old sister Anna were already working as "hosiery knitters," almost certainly under sweatshop-like conditions. Perhaps it is for that reason that their father, Israel, lied about their ages to the Census taker: he said Jacob and Anna were sixteen and seventeen, respectively. As a young man, Jacob (albeit temporarily) left the clothing and textiles industry behind in favor of working in the ports of South Philadelphia, bolting metal sheets together to build ships—certainly not the most fulfilling or, especially in those days, healthy or safe job.

But again, occupations were not set in stone, and many immigrants moved around just as Jacob did. Indeed, his own father, Israel, spent his first fifteen years in America working as a tailor before becoming a furrier. Before long, he was also helping to run a Hebrew school in Philadelphia, a side project likely motivated by having spent the first three decades of his life in deeply religious Bershad (family tradition maintains he was a very pious man). The Wexler family's hard work eventually paid off: while Jacob never went to college, his two younger brothers did, with one becoming a dentist and the other an attorney.

Unfortunately, neither Israel nor his wife, Anna, lived to see their children succeed in America—Israel died at fifty-five years old on August 4, 1919, followed by Anna almost exactly two years later on August 1, 1921.[*]

Eager to take advantage of new opportunities and to escape horrid working conditions, many immigrants sought out job training, English language classes, and other opportunities for education. The charities mentioned in the previous chapter that were at the ready to help the new arrivals were soon quickly supplemented by a number of public and private schools established to help ease the transition into the American economy. After the working day, public schools taught basic life skills and the English language or helped to train for new jobs. But the immigrants often craved more than merely the necessities—something that stuck out to observers, who were often "surprised that amid the so-called 'slum' population there should be a people who have a high standard of ability, an intense desire to acquire knowledge, and great strength of purpose in carrying it out." The public schools were typically only open from October to February, with two-hour classes being held three evenings per week; this was simply not enough to satiate either the intellectual desires of many Jewish immigrants or their immediate need to learn English or workforce skills.[279]

Over time, more charities were established to provide more education of all varieties. In Philadelphia, in the Hebrew Education Society's Touro Hall building at Tenth and Carpenter Street, for example, one could take immigrant-friendly English courses in addition to classes on dressmaking, cigar manufacturing, stenography, millinery, and many other textile industries. Between its library, reading room, and auditorium, which could seat six hundred, it is no wonder that

---

[*] Their daughter, Minerva, on the other hand, has the longevity record of anyone on my father's side of the family. She was born in 1901 and passed away in 2005, a few months before her 104th birthday.

Touro Hall became a center of Jewish immigrant education in Philadelphia. Similar schools existed for women and girls too—something unheard of in the Pale—which taught sewing, embroidery, and cooking, in addition to general education.[280]

The Jewish immigrants, of course, found all of this incredible. Education was almost exclusively religious back in the Pale, and was generally reserved for boys. And while the Pale did have state-run schools that some Jews could have attended, few had any interest—they (correctly) anticipated that they wouldn't just be attending school, but also a Russification and de-Judaizing camp. But this wasn't the case in America. As Marcus Ravage observed:

> In New York, it appeared, education was to be got altogether without cost, by Jew and Gentile alike, by day or night. The government of America not only did not extract charges for instruction; it compelled parents to send their children to school, and it begged grown-ups to come and be educated when their day's work was over. There, in America, was my future, as well as my family's. For it would take me only a few weeks to make enough money to send for them.[281]

Soon enough, armed with an education, new skills, and the ability to freely put them to use, many immigrant Jews discovered a path to economic and social upward mobility—if not for themselves, then at least for their children. One frequent casualty along the way, though, was the loss of some of their old-world culture, religion, and tradition.

New and Old Traditions in America

New freedoms were found not only in economic and social life in America but also in religious matters. New traditions were formed and old traditions reformed in the early years by the American Jews, perhaps reaffirming the skepticism that the family and community they left behind in the Pale had about the benefits of moving to America. And to be fair, those skeptics were right, in a way.

Perhaps the most prominent tradition to be weakened was the observance of the Sabbath. To be sure, there is some evidence that strict observance of the Sabbath's prohibition of working between Friday and Saturday's sunsets had already been tested in the Pale by the increasingly terrible economic conditions toward the end of the nineteenth century—this was not a purely American or Western development. What was new, however, was the extent to which the rules were rewritten or modified. Even for the most observant Jews, Sabbath observance went from absolutely mandatory to something one would at least try their best to avoid violating.[282]

Before we concede that the skeptics were right about America, it is important to note that the rules were anything but forgotten—just adjusted. Even though industrial age's six-day work week meant that Jews were expected to work not just on Friday but on Saturday, too, most simply adjusted their behavior rather than giving up on Sabbath observance entirely. Many synagogues in the immigrant quarters moved the Sabbath's prayers even earlier on Saturday mornings, so as to allow congregants to attend before going to work. Women adjusted their schedules to do as much of their shopping as possible on Thursdays and Fridays, during which they still bought all the Sabbath's traditional matzah, candles, wine, and—if the finances could afford it, at least—brisket.[283]

If not necessarily indicative of a desire to leave Judaism behind, the adjusted Sabbath was at least indicative of a major difference between Jewish life in America and in Eastern Europe. In the Pale, the small but predominantly Jewish shtetls gave rise to a self-contained and largely self-reliant Jewish economy within (and sometimes separate from) the Pale's economy, a development effectively reinforced by the Russian Empire's endless rules and regulations regarding Jewish participation in the economy. This Jewish economy served as a bubble in which Jews were reliant on one another, not only for goods and services but also for jobs and incomes—Jews worked not only with other Jews, but often *for* other Jews. But given the Jews' frequent majority in these shtetls, separating the workplace from home—or either the workplace or home from the synagogue—was impossible. They were all connected, all parts of the shtetl's Jewish community.[284]

Things couldn't have been more different in America. Jewish immigrants, as numerous as they were, had to interact with the American economy itself—there was hardly a self-contained Jewish economy to rely on. The desperate need to earn a living, to provide for the family, and to bring remaining relatives over meant Jews—like just about all other immigrants—had to take whatever opportunities were available to them. Even the best of these opportunities, however, lacked the setting and context of Jewish life in the Pale, which itself only evolved over centuries. Without many familiar institutions and societal structures that had guaranteed a rich Jewish culture and a strong sense of Jewish community, religion and tradition faced major challenges in the United States. Outside of the shtetl, there was no difficulty in separating religious and communal matters from the workplace—in fact, this was the norm! But neither was there much difficulty in accepting religious observance as a domestic matter, one which did not matter much in the workplace.[285]

We cannot know for sure or for all, but we can only assume that most Jews did not arrive in America with the set intention of forgetting their religious identity, even if they also did not arrive here with the intent to keep it perfectly intact. Indeed, the core ethics, worldview, and religious customs proved difficult to shake off, if not entirely impossible; many continued to instill both Judaism and Jewishness in their children. For example, even if work and play had become acceptable—perhaps more so tolerated—on the Sabbath, all of my great-grandparents' households (both as children and later as parents themselves) kept kosher, as best as they could. The core Jewish holidays continued to be observed, if not always in synagogue. And even if the traditionally exuberant marking of Purim was replaced with turning Channukah into something of a Christmas equivalent, bar mitzvahs were still celebrated (and, as we will soon see, took on a whole new form) and Jewish learning still encouraged—indeed, Jacob Wexler had the Torah committed to memory, just as his father did, despite being raised almost entirely in Philadelphia. American Jews may have redefined and reformed their religion, but they did not lose their Jewishness.[286]

Sometimes the culture simply began to be expressed in different ways. Philadelphia had a particularly active Yiddish press by the early 1900s, with the *Jewish Exponent* becoming the flagship Yiddish newspaper. Over the years, the *Exponent* became a leading voice of Philadelphia's Jewish community, not least in political matters. After immigration was cut off in 1924, the editorial section of the *Jewish Exponent* was filled with articles deeply critical of not only immigration restrictionism and antisemitism—a 1925 article deplored the fact that Jews were being welcomed into Mexico "while the U.S. puts up bars"—but also of anti-Catholicism.[287] But the *Exponent* was only one of many papers keeping Philadelphia's Jews up to date with global events, political developments, and the issues of the day. Not all of them even printed in Yiddish, English, or Hebrew: before long, many of the languages of the Pale—even including Russian, unfamiliar to most Americans at the time—had their own printing presses.[288]

Yiddish, of course, was the *lingua franca* of the Jewish quarter. This was not always a result of it having been the immigrants' preferred language back in Eastern Europe, though, as many Jews in the Pale spoke the languages surrounding them—Russian, Polish, Ukrainian, and their many regional dialects. Instead, it was often something of a lowest common denominator: Jewish immigrants may have all preferred different languages, but nearly all of them were at least familiar with Yiddish. In America, Yiddish received translations of everything from the United States Constitution and the Declaration of Independence to the poetry of Keats and Shelly, Simon Dubnow's *History of the Jews in Russia and Poland*, and even Indian poetry. The Yiddish press even published entirely new and original works, including titles such as the *Yiddish Guide to the United States of America* (published in Connecticut but widely distributed in Philadelphia), *Sketches and Letters of Jewish Life in America* (a book critical of Jewish life in the cities of the New World), and the Zionist novel *The Watch Tower*. There was a clear demand for all of these kinds of books, both in Philadelphia and elsewhere.[289]

While much of the culture of the Pale went on to thrive in America, unquestionably with the assistance of the proliferation of Yiddish-language content, some parts of the culture were not so lucky. The absence of a rigid and religiously homogenous social structure left Jewish immigrants in a new world with very different rules, expectations for behavior, and societal norms, all of which required learning and getting used to. One area that sparked great excitement and interest: courtship and marriage. Those who married in America and were also immigrants themselves would have found the courtship process and marriage ceremony strange, if not outright unfamiliar (and not only due to their Christian undertones). And unlike their children, they would not be able to pick up these social cues and patterns as you and I did in school or through various forms of media (unless they were young enough to go through the school system here).

Back in the Pale, most marriages were arranged with great precision and some commercialization by town matchmakers, the *shadkhonim*. In America, however, Jews were free to marry out of romance and attraction rather than convenience and societal norms. This was not a liberty only exercised merely by a few cultural revolutionaries or secularists—the young men and women throughout the Jewish immigrant community had increasingly little interest in doing it any other way. In its discussion of the dire business conditions faced by wannabe *shadkhonim* in America, one popular English-language Jewish newspaper in 1910 welcomed their struggles "as a sign that the young men in question are repudiating the undignified method of choosing a life partner represented by the [*shadkhon*]."[290]

However eager as many were to marry on their own will and by their own choice, though, the *shadkhonim* were not as much erased from Jewish American culture as they were replaced by a deluge of newspapers, short stories, and books offering guidance. Indeed, having hardly had to contend with Western practices of courtship or modern concepts of romance, the younger members of this wave of Jewish immigration had little to no clue how to handle themselves. An immense collection of resources across all media—even the Yiddish theater, the radio, and the classroom—appeared to guide them through the unfamiliar process, commonly suggesting young couples spend time in parks and take walks through (pleasant) parts of the city together, with some even promoting the writing of love letters.[291]

Other sources offered plentiful advice on the traits of the perfect husband or wife: the ideal groom was to be tender, industrious, moral, well spoken, and well mannered, while the ideal bride needed to be healthy, adept at housekeeping, and armed with common sense. Good looks and intelligence were welcomed, of course, but neither made for a good husband or wife on its own—it was the soul that mattered most.

Though they were not considered to be make-or-break qualities for a partner, and despite having far greater freedom to choose their own partner than their parents did, intelligence, money, and social class continued to play a part in the courtship process for many young Jewish immigrants. While the pressure to marry young had largely disappeared—the consensus in America had shifted to seeing the early to mid-twenties as the prime age to marry—many young women still felt social or parental pressure to marry a successful or well-educated man, while many young men were under similar pressure to marry the daughter of a well-established businessman, or at least someone of the same social class.[292]

In the Pale, much of the success in arranging a marriage depended on the money saved by the bride's family as a gift of sorts to her future husband upon marriage: the larger the dowry, the wealthier and more prominent the possible grooms. In America, though, this was largely unfeasible due to the deep and widespread impoverishment of urban Jewish immigrant life, and all but impossible in the absence and influence of the *shadkhonim*. Yet the instinct and tradition carried on: as Louis Rubin, the scholar of Southern American literature and son of two Russian Jews, put it:

> College men, unless they're homely as all get-out, sell well in the marriage market even when they're not professional men. Doctors, lawyers, and dentists, however, rate highest with Jewish parents looking for sons-in-law.[293]

Along with the courtship process, the marriage ceremony changed dramatically too. The traditional mores around Froim Knobel's 1826 marriage to Gitla Goldflus in Chapter 2—that of an outdoor service, often away from the synagogue, centered around the religious, communal, and familial importance of marriage—did not survive long in America. The pre-wedding contract, the *ketubah*, faded into an Orthodox obscurity as American customs, from expensive engagement rings to oversized and over-the-top wedding receptions, took hold.

Unlike Froim and Gitla's wedding, New World weddings moved to reception halls and upscale hotels—and, despite the false tradition of it, the synagogue. No wedding was complete, it seemed, without fine foods one would (or could) never eat at home, fanciful place settings for hundreds of guests, and sometimes even a glamorous—and often entirely unnecessary—transport for the bride to the service. "Anything short of a white satin gown and matching shoes, two carriages, a five-piece band, and a crowded, dazzling reception constituted a 'slipshod wedding' and was to be eschewed at all costs."[294]

Max and Pearl Rabinowitz, center in the back, at their son Benjamin's wedding. Their son Harry, my great-grandfather, is seated second in from the right, next to Max's mother (Hannah) and in front of his wife, Mildred Wexler

Of my eight great-great-grandparents we've been following in this book, only Harry Waxman and Esther Tyszgarten were married before they arrived in the United States, largely a consequence of the fact that by having been born in 1875 and 1874, respectively, they were ten years older than the other six (all of whom were born in the 1880s, except for Fannie Lefcovitch). Max and Pearl Rabinowitz do not necessarily count as an American love story either, as they had met and agreed to marry each other before coming to America, back in Chernihiv.

Of the two couples remaining, Harry Shirofsky and Fannie Lefcovitch were the first to marry, although I have no idea how Harry and Fannie could have met. Fannie arrived in Philadelphia in 1893, nearly eleven years ahead of Harry—and though the Lefcovitch family had once lived just down the street from the site of Harry's future store, they moved soon after her father, Nathan, died in 1903, a year before Harry arrived in Philadelphia. And the family did not simply move nearby; they moved eighteen blocks west, to 917 South Twentieth Street.

One hint to how they may have met comes from the naturalization paperwork signed by Fannie's oldest younger brother, Max, in 1904. One witness on his papers was a furniture merchant and former neighbor of the Lefcovitches, living a few doors down from the Lefcovitches' previous home on South Second Street. Of all places, the merchant lived at 736 South Second, a building directly across the street from 735 South Second—which happened to be where Harry was living and working by 1906. Perhaps the story is of a mutual friend who introduced them; perhaps he had invited the Lefcovitches over for a dinner also attended by Harry.

Yet it is also entirely possible that the credit really belongs to Sarah, Fannie's widowed mother. Though Fannie would consistently lie about her age and underestimate it by up to a decade for the rest of her life, she was getting relatively old to be married when she met Harry. Whereas he was twenty when they married, Fannie was twenty-eight (even if she said she was twenty-one on the paperwork). One can imagine Sarah growing anxious that her only daughter was running out of time to find a suitable partner and zealously marketing her daughter to Harry at the hypothetical dinner hosted by that furniture merchant after becoming aware that he, too, was a young and single Jew. Whatever the true story is, Harry and Fannie were married in Philadelphia on October 9, 1906.

We do not know how Jacob Wexler and Esther Satalof first met. Yet whenever they did meet, it could not have taken much time for them to realize they had so much in common. In addition to living so close to each other, both had come to America in the earlier years of the migration wave, with Jacob arriving in 1893 and Esther in 1896. Though they were both only children when they came—Jacob was five and Esther six—they likely had many of the same faint memories of Bremen or Hamburg, or perhaps of the perilous journey here by sea. And by the time they were married on March 9, 1912, they would have been quite familiar with America, its society, and its customs—indeed, by then both would have had a close familiarity with the same corner of its economy, as they both had spent years working in clothing factories.

Aside from courtship and weddings, another prominent change within Jewish life was the role and importance of the bar mitzvah. The bar mitzvah itself was always a bit of an invented tradition, seemingly having originated only in the late Middle Ages, but American Jews nonetheless reformed and remade it into a new tradition in America. If you have ever been to an American bar mitzvah, its memory is likely to be defined by two of its modern core components: the calling up of family members and close friends to light candles at the reception and the grandeur of the reception itself—but these are recent additions to the ceremony, innovations made roughly one hundred years ago.

A minor rite of passage as one came of age back in the Old World, in America the bar mitzvah seemed like one of the few guaranteed opportunities to ensure the passing on of Jewish customs and religion to a new generation—a generation that had far greater freedom of religion and far less time for Torah study in adulthood. Entire schools, which the disapproving conservatives referred to as "bar mitzvah factories," popped up to prepare young Jewish boys for their "big day"—even if they often did a subpar job at best in instilling the Jewish faith in their pupils. Before long, even those who rarely attended synagogue suddenly saw the bar mitzvah as a moment of great importance. But given the weak curriculum in the bar mitzvah factories, the speeches given by the bar mitzvah boy could no longer take the traditional form of a commentary on the day's Torah portion, leading to the transformation of the speech into a formulated one full of thanks, praise, and appreciation of family, friends, and teachers—with the addition of the classic "This is the most important day of my life" or the fan-favorite: "Today I am a man."[295]

As much as it would have pained her father, a cantor (or possibly rabbi) back home, Pearl Rabinowitz was one of many who were caught up in this frenzy, as is made clear by the bar mitzvah portraits taken of her oldest son, Morris. Indeed, these portraits themselves were an innovation—so, too, was the necessity of having fine suit for both the portraits and the ceremony itself.

Pearl Rabinowitz and (I believe) her oldest son Morris, likely at his bar mitzvah.

As the bar mitzvah took on increasingly greater importance for Jewish boys, some began considering what, if anything, should be offered for Jewish girls. One early attempt at a solution was the *confirmation*, a term and procedure that correctly brings to mind the Christian ritual with the same name, which marketed itself as a ritual—something like a watered-down bar mitzvah—that both Jewish boys and girls were eligible for. While it caught on for some time in many Reform communities, confirmation unsurprisingly appealed to the girls far more than it did to the boys and ultimately failed as an equally accessible alternative. Only the bat mitzvah came to have widespread acceptance and practice, although it took some time. The first bat mitzvah in America was that of Judith Kaplan, the daughter of Rabbi Mordecai Kaplan, the founder of Reconstructionist Judaism. Her bat mitzvah in New York City on March 18, 1922, proved controversial—as she later recalled, it "was enough to shock a lot of people, including my own grandparents."[*] Shocking as it may have been to some, though, the bat mitzvah gradually became accepted in Conservative synagogues over the following few decades and was broadly accepted by all major denominations by the 1950s.[296]

As the bar mitzvah was being remade and the bat mitzvah brought into existence, these ceremonies were also put under increasing scrutiny and criticism. The increasingly common use of "bar mitzvah factories" was particularly disturbing and disappointing. Israel Goldstein, a cofounder of Brandeis University and a born-and-raised Philadelphia Jew, argued that it must be emphasized that bar mitzvah "is something earned, a something for which the child has worked, a privilege he has earned, and not an empty ceremony contingent upon a parrot-like

---

[*] Indeed, Kaplan later got himself excommunicated from Orthodox Judaism for his radical reinterpretation of Judaism; for an excellent overview, see Mel Scult, *The Radical American Judaism of Mordecai M. Kaplan*, First paperback edition, The Modern Jewish Experience (Bloomington (Ind.): Indiana University Press, 2015).

recitation of a few Hebrew passages."[297] The failure of the "bar mitzvah factories" to instill an adequate Jewish education in their students was lamented by those who were concerned by their children's disinterest in synagogue attendance or their preference for English over Yiddish. Such worry over their children's increasing distance from Jewish culture is clear in a note written by an anxious mother and attached to a draft of her son's bar mitzvah speech, part of which was to be made in Yiddish:

> Dear Rabbi: I didn't correct anything. I just copied the speech but wrote some words the way we express ourselves; instead of *u* we say *i*; *o*, we say *u*. It is very hard for Sidney to pronounce the Jewish [Yiddish] words. We talk to him [in] Jewish [Yiddish] but he answers in English. Do you think he could pronounce it right?[298]

More cynically, others felt that the bar mitzvah ceremony had become "little more than a concession to the sentimentality of parents who may have joined a liberal-progressive congregation, but who still are maudlin about this medieval puberty rite." More diplomatically, Samuel Sussman, the director of Philadelphia's Har Zion Temple's education program, felt that the "entire idea of bar-mitzvah must be toned down."[299] For these critics, the increasingly excessive receptions that came to accompany the bar and bat mitzvah were a case in point. These receptions had hardly existed back home (and were rarely anything special even when they did) and even in America were little more than a small gathering of family and close friends at home at first. Soon, however, these receptions grew into the form that many are familiar with today, complete with music, catered (and rarely Jewish) food, gift giving, dancing, and a guest count that typically went into the hundreds (many of whom, both then and now, were often completely unknown to the bar mitzvah boy!).

Many worried that the extravagance of the reception was rewarding the completion of the shoddy religious education curriculum received in the "factories" rather than any actual milestone in a young Jew's life. Even worse, some were concerned that the extravagance made the bar mitzvah boy feel "complete" in the responsibilities of his faith, whereas in their eyes it had only just begun. As Jenna Weissman Joselit put it, "No sooner did the bar mitzvah boy's parents pay the bill, it seemed, than the bar mitzvah boy dropped from sight, rarely setting foot in a synagogue again, let alone continuing his Jewish education."[300] In an attempt to fight this tendency, many clubs popped up in Philadelphia's Conservative and Reform synagogues that tried to keep young Jewish men involved in the congregation and their faith.

But at the end of the day, as sociologist Herbert Gans argued, the bar mitzvah ultimately came to "salvage from Jewish tradition only those themes, objects, and experiences which bring pleasure and at the same time never conflict with or disrupt the basically American way of life."[301] It is no wonder that the family that stayed behind in the Pale would often react in dismay or with disdain upon hearing about the new lives their children were living in America. Yet in hindsight it is hard to imagine it having happened any other way, given the sudden shock of the culture of abundance and consumerism that first- and second-generation immigrant Jews went through.[302]

Judaism and Jewishness in America

The religious reform and cultural change outlined in the section above also represent a critical development in Jewish life in America: the increasing separation and distinction between Judaism (the religion) and Jewishness (the culture). The causes and origins of this split in the Jewish world are far too complicated and disputed for me to possibly describe fairly here, but it is important to note that this was not a purely American phenomenon—these ideas were also spreading among not only Jews in Eastern Europe but also those in Western and Central Europe. In America, this distinction largely came hand in hand with the separation of the workplace, religious practice, and domestic life from each other. With domestic affairs and the workplace no longer intertwined with communal and religious matters, the home and workplace became the place where Jewish *culture* thrived; religious *practice* was left for the synagogue. This thinking was what led to the idea of the Jewish community center, something championed and greatly influenced by Rabbi Kaplan—the founder of Reconstructionist Judaism, the one whose daughter was the first to be bat mitzvah in the United States. Kaplan's aptly-titled *Judaism as a Civilization*, published in 1934, proved as influential in popularizing these ideas it was controversial.[303]

Indeed, Jewish culture has long appreciated a distinction between *Jewishness* and *Judaism*. Being Jewish and being an active member of a Jewish congregation were distinct things. Jewish immigrants struggled with how to instill Jewishness, let alone Judaism, in their children, particularly in the absence of a homogenously Jewish society. Much of the bar mitzvah's explosion in popularity and extravagance owes to the early advice of American rabbis on how parents might interest and involve their children in the Jewish faith. Another popular solution took the form of classes available at one's preferred synagogue, such as Jewish Music and Games for the Child, Jewish Arts and Crafts for the Child, or more blatantly, What to Aim at in the Upbringing of the Jewish Child. The proliferation of "Jewish toys" promised another solution in distinctly American and consumerist fashion. Philadelphia's own Bible Doll Company of America manufactured "accurately" dressed dolls of biblical characters designed "not just a religious doll" but also to "[teach] the child to be good" and "[create] happy experiences and memories which are associated with the Bible." The dolls even came with their own small vials of soil from the Holy Land.[304]

Ultimately, however, much of the responsibility to instill Jewishness fell to the mother. The reality of economic life in America meant that it was the mother's "prime function" to "safeguard her home and to make it Jewish."[305] Only the successful among the Jewish immigrants of this era were likely to have the time, energy, and desire to pass down the lessons, teachings, and ethics of their own fathers to their children.

Moreover, few women had received a formal education in such things back in the Pale. With this other new reality, American Jews hardly had a choice to grow up surrounded with more Jewishness than Judaism.

The economic and social forces described in the section above—in addition to many others—led to drastic changes within Jewish identity and religion in America. "The major way that South Philadelphia Jews identify with being Jewish is not now, nor has it ever been, synagogue attendance," notes one author.[306] For someone like the proudly religious Israel Wexler, this must have been disconcerting to say the least. Even his own son, who knew the Torah by heart, seemed to distance himself from his religion as an adult; his granddaughter (Jacob's daughter) didn't seem to think the High Holidays were important enough to merit synagogue attendance when she was married with children of her own. In fact, she threw sweet-sixteen parties for her daughters, who were never given the option of becoming bat mitzvah or going through confirmation.

This lack of interest in Judaism was not a trend particular to Philadelphia, either. A national survey in 1900 estimated that about four out of five Jews did not regularly attend synagogue; a Yiddish newspaper in New York City figured that no more than a quarter of that city's Jews did either.[307]

Of course, many began shedding elements of their Old World lives even without an economic or social reason to do so—America had attracted many reformers, religious outsiders, nonbelievers, secularists, and nonconformists, after all. But it was not always so simple. Even among those who wished to preserve every ounce of their Jewishness and Judaism in America, doing so proved difficult for far more practical reasons. First, America never appealed to the most orthodox and conservative Jews, and certainly not to many rabbis. Unsurprisingly, this meant that relatively few rabbis immigrated to America, leaving many American Jews without spiritual and communal leaders. Evidence of their general absence from spiritual and communal life can be seen in the proliferation of the Hebrew schools and bar mitzvah prep programs—the latter of which had been entirely unnecessary in the Old World—and in the startling fact that across the whole of America, there were fewer than two hundred rabbis in 1890; roughly one per every two thousand Jews.* Without sufficient rabbis and spiritual leadership, the practice and interpretation of Judaism fell to the household to manage—a household already burdened by the economic reality of life in America.[308]

In addition to the numbers problem, the same American civics that enabled Jews to practice their faith without interference also left Jewish customs to be superseded by civic ones. In the Old World, marriages and divorces were only possible through Jewish law; Jews were not entitled to the same practice of civil laws as the rest of the Russian populace. There was no option to go it your own way—you could not just start your own congregation or move to a new town and start anew because you and every ounce of your being were entirely and irrevocably Jewish from birth. Your options were to either accept—or submit—to Jewish law and your rabbi or to convert from Judaism entirely. The latter was rarely an option taken in practice, at least by choice. In America, however, neither was the case. While free to practice their religion as they wished, marriages and divorces now occurred through American civil law, for which one hardly needed a rabbi's involvement. One may have a Jewish identity, but that identity received no strict enforcement, perpetuation, or backing by civic or societal influences. The need for communal Jewish organization, at least for religious matters, was somewhat diminished.[309]

The weakening of religious organization and observance left conceptual Jewishness to outspeak Judaism; thus was born *Yiddishkeit*, of which I will have more to say in subsequent chapters.

---

* One important consequence of this was that a lot of supposedly kosher meats were all but certainly a lot less kosher than many of their consumers thought they were.

Jacob Wexler and Esther Satalof

Chapter 9
THE TRENTON CROCKERY COMPANY

◆―――――◆

With my own eyes, I saw thousands, hundreds of thousands of people, banished from the Old World, living in freedom across the ocean where they have found safety, dignity and often even prosperity—human beings who, less than fifteen or twenty years after arriving, have transformed themselves so completely that is sometimes hard to recognize them...it took very few years for [Jewish immigrants] to make the most of American tolerance and the conditions in the New World.[310]
~ Anatole Leroy-Beaulieu

The story of one of my ancestors is conspicuously absent from most of the previous chapter—that of Hersch Scherovsky. We now return to him while first noting one important change. As seen earlier, he had anglicized his name shortly after immigrating to the United States; he was already Harry Shirofsky by January 1906, when he declared his intent to become a citizen (five months before he was legally able to, but whatever). But he wasn't done. By the time of his marriage to Fannie Lefcovitch in October (nine months later), the man born in Novhorod-Siverskyi as Hersh Scherovsky had completed the transition to Harry Shiroff.*

This sort of name change is something we hardly think much of, but it was often about more than just assimilation into America. In Harry's case, in the imagination and social hierarchy of Jewish immigrants, Russian Jews were superior to Polish Jews (at least one aspect of its culture that Russia successfully got its Jews to absorb). Yet the Russians and Poles could only be regarded as beneath the more assimilated German American Jews from the point of view of those very same German American Jews, who had little interest or trust in working or dealing with their more eastern religious brethren. "Those remnants of Russian dress and manner, those loud ways and awkward gesticulations," one German Jew suggested, "are naturally repulsive and repugnant to the refined American sensibilities."[311]

With this in mind, Harry made an incredibly clever change. To boost his chances of success in America, he somewhat obscured his Eastern European origins by dropping the Polish-sounding "-sky." But to enable his wife to "marry upward" and increase his appeal to her family, he retained the "-ov" ending for its Russian sound. However, to still evade detection as an obvious Russian Jew, it would be spelled (and pronounced) "-off," blurring his surname's geographic origin enough to almost make it sound like something of English-language origin. Brilliant.

After they married in October 1906, Fannie moved into Harry's cramped apartment in the upstairs of 735 South Second Street, not too far from where she had lived between her emigration from London and her father's death a few years later. Harry had moved in there no more than a year or so earlier, perhaps after having established himself enough to move out from his uncle Harris Jacobson's apartment, where he had first lived after arriving in Philadelphia. While Harry's new

---

* This was officially recognized on January 26, 1912, which I like to refer to as International Shiroff Day.

apartment wasn't exactly close to the Jacobsons—Harry's only known relatives in the United States, aside from his cousin Mendel—it was close to the Neziner Congregation, a synagogue for immigrants from northeastern Ukraine like himself, which moved nearby to 771 South Second in 1905. Nizhyn—where the congregation got its name—was only ten miles from his cousin Mendel's hometown of Nosivka (indeed, Mendel also moved close to the synagogue), and though it was a bit far from his hometown of Novhorod-Siverskyi, it was within the same province; at the very least, Harry would have recognized Nizhyn and vaguely known where it was. In a very new, very foreign, and very unknown world, it is easy to imagine that being near—and perhaps even attending, as he was one of my more observant ancestors—the Neziner Congregation was a source of comfort for him.[312]

Surely, though, it was not just the Neziner Congregation that drew Harry to South Second Street. South Second also offered innumerable business opportunities—one of which forever changed not only his life but those of all of his descendants as well.

Capitalism and the American Dream

Like so many others in the Pale (and in my own family), Harry had been a tailor back in Novhorod-Siverskyi. But after living with his uncle, who was a tailor working out of his own home (and likely under the sweatshop conditions described in the previous two chapters), he had seen up close and personal how undesirable and unpleasant that line of work could be in America. After his certainly difficult childhood and strenuous journey to the United States, Harry wanted to make an entirely new (and hopefully more pleasant) life for himself here—he refused to submit to tirelessly tailoring away in a sweatshop as his uncle had.

As noted in the last chapter, many of the arriving Eastern European Jews brought with them the strong work ethic and sharp business intellect they had developed in the Pale, where the laborious days required to eke out a living demanded shrewd skills in strategy, pivoting in accordance with quickly changing environments, dealmaking, and accounting. Soon, Harry got to prove that, thankfully for himself and his aspirations, he was a perfect archetype of exactly that kind of immigrant. By the time Harry and Fannie had their apartment there, South Second Street had become a busy commercial street, home to stores, retailers, peddlers, and merchants selling just about anything one could imagine. It was also home to all kinds of new opportunities if one were brave, smart, and strong enough—and soon, Harry found an opening.

At around the same time Harry and Fannie married, two crockery retailers were established within 500 feet of each other on South Second Street, which, as absurd as it may sound, would go on to be as important to my family's story as the marriage. The first to open was the cleverly named Trenton Crockery Company, established at 710 South Second by two Ukrainian-born Jewish brothers, David and Hyman Shapiro.[*] The second was established by no later than 1907 on the first floor of 735 South Second by the tenant upstairs: Harry Shiroff.

Sometime between his arrival in 1904 and the opening of his own store, Harry left tailoring in favor of a new career as a chinaware merchant. After a year in business, the venture was joined by Louis Rezwine, another Ukrainian-born Jewish immigrant (who arrived only a month after Harry), who had established himself as a business agent in America, and thus the crockery company of Shiroff & Rezwine was born. Indeed, so were Harry and Fannie's first two children at this time: first came Nathan (commonly known as Ned) in 1907 and then Morris

---

[*] To this day, it is hard to find information about the Trenton Crockery Company. Any search is dominated by results pertaining to the then-booming Trenton pottery industry and chinaware in general, with nothing of the store itself; it was genius marketing.

the following year.* Both were born in the Shiroffs' apartment above the crockery store.

Fannie Lefcovitch (holding Morris Shiroff); her mother, Sarah Lefcovitch; and Harry Shiroff (holding Nathan "Ned" Shiroff), photographed circa 1909.

---

* Nathan was almost certainly named after Fannie's deceased father, while Morris may have been a tribute to her oldest brother, who was likely the first in her family to come to America.

Whereas David Shapiro of the Trenton Crockery Company is known to have been a talented crockery manufacturer and decorator, it is unclear whether either Louis Rezwine or Harry was the creative one—perhaps they both were, though both were consistently referred to as "chinaware merchants" or "chinaware dealers." In either case, Shiroff & Rezwine evidently built up a thriving business together in only a few years, as by early 1910 they had moved up the street from 735 to 710 South Second—the location of Harry and David Shapiro's Trenton Crockery Company. Shiroff & Rezwine was no more—they were now a part of, and indeed part owners of, the Trenton Crockery Company. Nor was it just the store that moved: Harry, Fannie, Fannie's mother, and their two infant children moved there, too, along with Louis Rezwine, his wife, and their two children. By contrast, neither of the Shapiro brothers lived immediately nearby, although Hyman was relatively close; David, on the other hand, had moved to the successful and wealthy West Philadelphia outskirts of Sixtieth Street, where he employed a live-in servant. Regardless of what brought Shiroff & Rezwine to the humble headquarters of the Trenton Crockery Company, the Shapiro brothers remained part owners. Perhaps they bought out Shiroff & Rezwine to further strengthen their own business, one that had already earned them a small fortune (evident in David's address and living situation), though it is also possible that Shiroff & Rezwine actually bought the Trenton Crockery Company—after all, they moved into *their* store.

Thankfully, the five members of the Shiroff family did not have to share the tight living quarters above the Trenton Crockery Company's 710 South Second location with the four-member Rezwine family for long. Likely in desperate need of more living space after the birth of their first and only daughter, Esther (commonly known as Estelle), in 1910, who, too, was born at home, the Shiroffs soon moved into an apartment of their own at 1621 South Orkney Street in 1911. A two-story row home about a mile south of the store, their new apartment could not have been much larger than their previous one—but it certainly must have felt like it. No longer would they—Harry, Fannie, Fannie's aging mother, and their three children—need to split an apartment with four or five rooms at best with an entire other family.

Their move reflected not just their need for more space but also the family's rapidly improving economic condition. This improvement seemed to have already been underway in the early days of the Shiroff & Rezwine Company, when in March 1908 a notice in the *Philadelphia Inquirer* informed readers that Harry had bought the furniture in a home a few blocks south of his store at auction. I have no idea how or why he did this or what he did with the inventory, but it is certainly striking that he already had enough capital ready for that sort of use after only four years in the United States, and after only about a year in business. The business was successful, and Harry was clearly materially benefiting from it.

But an arguably far greater advance in the family's economic situation is probably not immediately appreciated by the reader: Harry's commute to work would no longer be heading downstairs or through the living room—his work was no longer in the home. This is a luxury that is hard for us to appreciate, particularly in today's age of "working from home." As we have seen in the previous two chapters, for Jewish immigrants, "working from home" was nothing like it is today. Indeed, the ability to work "away from home" was surprisingly rare for many new immigrants, unless one had scored an office job (which was all but impossible for the newly arrived) or turned to manual labor (which, while not uncommon, was not typical). Much more common were living conditions like those described in previous chapters: overcrowded tenements that somehow doubled as a workplace. A reporter for the *Jewish Daily Forward* described a typical such tenement in 1905:

> This family of nine lives in one room, of which the front part is the father's shoemaking "business." Here he plies his trade. The single window is also the show window.

> The room is indescribably filthy. The parents look to the time when the oldest boy will be twelve and go to work.[313]

These conditions attracted the attention of the urban reformers of the twentieth century, who not only struggled to convince Jewish immigrants to spread out and move into larger living spaces but also struggled to break their tendency to work long, laborious hours in the home. In the reformers' view, men were simply not supposed to be working at home; doing so, they thought, turned "what should be a woman's world into a man's world" and brought strangers "into places where strangers should never tread."[314] But as with the overcrowding, working in the home was simply the way of life, something many had also done back in the Pale. Many children of immigrants—such as Harry and Fannie's children, Ned, Morris, and Estelle, although only in their earliest years—grew up as parents "sold stuff right out of the house," watching them persevere through "[long] hours and very little profits." It was difficult for the children, too:

> I remember the first butcher shop my father had. We lived behind the store. The store had three rooms in the back, and you got entrance into this apartment only through the store. And there was a refrigerator in the little hallway that separated the apartment from the store. Oh! I used to hate that apartment. I hated it because my parents worked so hard. And I hated to bring my friends home through that store, all the garbage—the bones and the fat—in the back, right in front of our apartment.[315]

It was not easy for anybody, though. Having grown up with her father and oldest two brothers working as tailors—at home, of course—Fannie surely could have related to the following memories of annoyance and dismay recalled by a tailor's son:

My father had been a capmaker in Galicia, and he got a job in a factory here making caps, too...and he worked at home, too: piecework he would bring home; and some of his friends would work at our house, too. There was a machine in the house, and at night I heard it going when I went to sleep. Foot operated. We had no electricity then; we had gas lights. My father's sewing machine was in the kitchen. I remember lying awake at night and wishing they would stop, already, with the machine and go to bed. I slept in the same room with my mother and father and when he finally came to bed, I always woke up, and then I couldn't go back to sleep again. I hated that sewing machine.[316]

Whether it was similar memories from her childhood that led Fannie—someone who had personally felt the bitter knife of class division in London—to push her husband to conduct his business and family matters in separate places or something else, the Shiroffs were among the lucky few to live in an entirely different building than their place of work. But Harry didn't only work away from where he lived; he was also, in effect, his own boss. He was running his own shop, or at least running it with others. Unlike Harry Waxman, who worked outside of the home as a tailor in a department store, Harry Shiroff worked on his own terms. And, importantly, the move brought them just outside of the traditional domain of the Jewish quarter, away from the crowded and bustling central core of Jewish Philadelphia, a place their oldest children could have only ever had the faintest memories of.

As the Shiroffs settled into their new home on South Orkney Street, Harry helped expand the Trenton Crockery Company's operations from merely dealing consumer-ready crockery to entering the wholesale market, manufacturing and selling chinaware to households and restaurants alike. And, perhaps having felt like it was as good a time as ever, he decided to finally complete the process to become a naturalized citizen. On the same day in October 1911, Harry and his business partner

Louis officially renounced their Russian "citizenship" and became United States citizens—both with Hyman Shapiro as a witness.* What a justified moment of pride that must have been for Harry, after having accomplished so much in so little time.

More was to come. By August 1913, Harry had had enough success with the Trenton Crockery Company that he could afford to move nearly sixty blocks west to 5905 Arch Street, a relatively new home built sometime around the turn of the century.† The home must have felt like a mansion relative to the living standards that Harry and Fannie had known at any earlier point in their lives. It would have surely been close to the kind of home Fannie had dreamed about living in when she was a young teen in London. It contained a kitchen, three bedrooms, a laundry room, a sitting room in the front, a reception hall, a porch, and one or two other rooms. For all this, Harry paid $1,850—not a huge amount of money for a city home at the time, but certainly a price that would have felt unimaginable only a few years earlier. And it must have been especially gratifying for Harry that he was now living not too far from David Shapiro, who only a few years earlier must have seemed far wealthier than him.

The home's West Philadelphia location confirms that Harry was doing quite well, at least relative to the majority of his peers. Just as the West End became *the* place to be for successful Londoners, even Jews, West Philadelphia had become a top destination for many successful immigrants, particularly successful Jews who had previously lived in South Philadelphia. Whereas many of their former neighbors only moved to the suburbs of West or Northeast Philadelphia between the

---

* Along with Myer Mitkin, a mysterious figure who cannot be found elsewhere. I know nothing of him.

† Harry later purchased 5907 Arch Street as well. Even though I do not have any record of him living there, the 1917 City Directory lists Harry at 5909 Arch Street. I have no idea what was going on.

late 1920s and 1940s, Harry was able to move his family out to the much more open and far less crowded West Philadelphia. And although there were some other successful Eastern European Jews in West Philadelphia, they made up nowhere near the same share of the population as they did in the Jewish quarter.

It is easy to imagine that the choice to move westward may have been somewhat of a compromise between Harry and Fannie: perhaps Harry longed for the calm, peaceful, and quiet scenes of his remote hometown of Novhorod-Siverskyi, whereas Fannie felt more at home in any chaos and noise that reminded her of London and preferred the more cosmopolitan feel of the city. West Philadelphia was indeed newer, quieter, and more sparsely populated than South Philadelphia, but thanks to the construction of Sixtieth Street Station in 1907, it was still only a relatively short subway or trolley ride from Center City. An additional piece of evidence suggesting that Harry wanted to get away from the city is his purchase of a plot of land in Beechwood, an up-and-coming—both literally and figuratively—new suburb further west of Philadelphia, northwest of Cobb's Creek Park. The exact date of this purchase is unknown, but it almost certainly came after Beechwood officially "opened" in 1907. Harry presumably invested in the plot of land with the hope to one day have a home built there—a home out in the much calmer and quieter suburbs, exactly as the Beechwood properties were advertised in the paper.[317]

Such a home, had it ever been built, would have certainly brought Harry closer to the familiar feeling of the quiet, rustic living of his hometown. But aside from indicating a desire to return to a more serene environment, the purchase also serves as another indicator of his financial well-being. We do not know what he paid for it, but buying land like this—which didn't even have a house built on it yet!—was a luxury only affordable for the middle class at best; it likely cost at least a thousand dollars, possibly as much as the home he had just bought on Arch Street. Moreover, the finished Beechwood home would have been one of modern engineering, design, and technological features, complete with electricity and heating. As close to the serenity of Novhorod-Siverskyi as the location might have brought him, such a house would have also been a long way from the quality of life back home.

About nine months after the family moved into their new and much larger home on Arch Street, Harry and Fannie had a fourth child, Victor, born at home at three in the morning on April 18, 1914. The family's choice of the name "Victor" is an interesting one. Victor is not a biblical name; its origins are in Latin, and its popularity stems from its usage by early Christians, including three popes. It is anything *but* a Jewish name, unlike those given to all of Victor's siblings: Nathan, Morris, Esther, and, later, Joseph and David. It may well have stemmed from the Old Testament name Avigdor, but Victor's name was explicitly Victor, not Avigdor or Vigdor/Figdor, the Eastern European Jewish adaptation. Where did the name Victor come from?

This stumped me for a long time, until a scan of the census record listing Harry's family back in Novhorod-Siverskyi from 1882—at least a year before he was born—was uploaded onto JewishGen's website. From it I learned that the name of Harry's oldest brother was none other than Victor. Whether his name was really Victor or if it was actually Vigdor and simply misrecorded by the census taker is anyone's guess, but it is hard to imagine Harry wasn't thinking of his older brother when he proposed the name. This was, of course, a relative Harry hadn't seen in almost exactly a decade—indeed, I have no idea if his brother was even still alive by this point.* That Harry named his son after his brother suggests that they were close, that Harry had looked up to him, and

---

* In fact, Ashkenazi Jewish tradition is to not name children after living relatives. Harry and Fannie's first child, for example, was named Nathan in honor of Fannie's father, who had passed away a few years earlier. While this could suggest that Harry was aware of his brother's passing, this rule was never followed too closely in either America or the Pale.

perhaps even after a decade in America, that Harry still missed him and his family back home.

While the name honored Harry's family back home, "Victor" also perfectly fit this moment in Harry's new life in the United States: he had every right to feel victorious. In every imaginable sense—physically, materially, financially, socially—Harry had come an incredibly long way from his childhood and early adolescence back in Novhorod-Siverskyi. Even if he ever had moments of nostalgia thinking back on summers spent in the pristine natural beauty of his riverside hometown or remembering the silence that surrounded the shtetl after snowfall, it is hard to imagine he would have traded his new life for his old one.

Harry Shiroff and Fannie Lefcovitch.

Victor's birth came just three months short of the ten-year anniversary of his coming into port in the United States. Despite having arrived here with no company other than his cousin and with no known family here except his aunt and uncle and their kids (all of whom he appears to have fallen out of touch with after the move to West Philadelphia), Harry managed to build an entirely new life of his own—one of success, comfort, and joy. His home was not just a home to his four children, a happy wife, and his supportive mother-in-law—it was also emblematic of the relative luxuries that his hard work, business acumen, and perseverance had earned him.

To be clear, it is not as if Harry was an incredibly wealthy man, or even a member of the upper class—and he probably knew this. Yet this was part of the pride and gratitude: he had all of those material and financial comforts, all of his success, with there *still* being so much room to go further. Harry's relative success with the crockery company was small in comparison to what was possible in America—limits some lucky immigrant Jews were beginning to explore—but yet still so many times larger than anything he could have ever dreamed of back in the Pale. And as hard as life was back in the remote shtetl of Novhorod-Siverskyi, going through the physical and emotional struggle of coming to America was no easy accomplishment either, to say nothing of running his own business in the difficult immigrant economy with a growing family at home.

Yet Harry did indeed emerge victorious after having fought throughout his life, not only to survive the harshness and unpleasantries of life in the Pale but also to make it both to and in America. His business achievements, even if modest by our standards, made him a relatively successful man, no doubt helping him feel much more comfortable and at peace. Almost certainly unlike his childhood, in America, Harry was free of hunger, fear, and oppression—and he had earned this not only for himself but for his family as well. He was quite victorious in that sense.

However, as with many immigrants, Harry most certainly had moments where he felt a knot in his stomach at the thought of the family he left behind. Yet despite the guilt he may have felt for leaving his parents, siblings, extended family (if, indeed they were still alive when he left), and friends behind in the cruel, dangerous, and impoverished world of the Pale, the fact that he had opened a new world of opportunities for his own posterity must have offered great solace. We can imagine Harry and Fannie sitting by the fireplace in the living room of 5905 Arch Street, maybe joined by Fannie's mother, Sarah, after the children had been put to bed. Harry may have confessed to the occasional pangs of guilt he felt for having left people behind back home, feelings that may have been augmented with survivor's guilt after the pogrom in Novhorod-Siverskyi in 1905, which he missed by only a year. Indeed, these were common feelings. Many immigrants would never forget the violence, fear, poverty, and hunger that defined their childhood or adulthood back in the Pale:

> I do remember as a child that the soldiers would come into the house and just commandeer the entire house...I remember stories my mother and father told me about when I was an infant. There were times when they had to run and hide...and I remember my father telling stories. In fact, all his life he would wake up with nightmares—screaming—they were "killing him!" Waking up just screaming...he had those nightmares all his life.[318]

Another Russian immigrant, born many years after Harry and shortly before the Russian Revolution, recalled her mother's nightmares centered around her memories of Russian soldiers killing her parents:

> For many years I couldn't remember all of this. My mother throughout her lifetime in America always had nightmares. And we as children were so accustomed to it: when she had a nightmare it was like standard procedure to walk in and wake her up because she would scream. And one night in the process of waking her up, it is the tendency that when you dream about something and you are awakened you will talk about it. "Mama! Mama! What is the matter?" And she woke up and described this scene [of watching her parents, the narrator's grandparents, being shot by Russian soldiers]

to me that I thought that I had dreamed—that I didn't actually think I had lived through.[319]

Many immigrants old enough to have memories of the Pale endured lifelong psychological anguish. Nightmares were frequent, and despite not having words or phrases such as PTSD, chronic anxiety, depression, and the like, they suffered from those symptoms while trying to build a new life here. Similarly, those who were too young or never lived there were likely to encounter the mental torment of those who did on a daily basis. Indeed, they all had encountered more than their fair share of trauma. Yet as unfortunate and heartbreaking as it all was, there were plenty of reasons to have plenty of optimism about the future.

Not only were their children getting an education, Fannie would be able to assure Harry, but they would do so without the pressure to drop out of school to enter the workforce and earn the household extra money. Indeed, Harry and Fannie were the only two of my eight Jewish great-great-grandparents who did not need to put that pressure on their children. They were lucky: the success of the business meant that their children would be able to graduate high school and perhaps even head off to college, an unimaginable privilege for anyone at the time. And with college degrees, their children would go on to earn far greater fortunes for themselves, money that would allow Harry and Fannie to grow old without needing to worry about their finances or work until the ends of their lives. All the struggle, hard work, and emotional turmoil was worth it, not only for the material comfort it had already earned them but also for the enhanced opportunities that would now be available to their children, grandchildren, and all posterity.

In addition to their children benefiting from a strong secular education, they would also be able to grow up without needing to fear Christian holidays, men in uniform, or their neighbors suddenly turning to violence. Unlike if Harry were raising his kids back home in Ukraine or if Fannie were in Poland, the two were able to raise their children in the Jewish faith with comfort and peace of mind, which parents in the

Pale could have only dreamed of. Whether it was Fannie's responsibility, as we saw earlier was common at the time, or both hers and Harry's, their children were raised in a Jewish household and received at least some extent of a Jewish education. They attended the Hebrew school at Lenas Hazedek, a synagogue that opened in 1919 at 5944 Larchwood Avenue, a fifteen-minute walk from their Arch Street home, a walk easily imagined happily made together as a family. There, the family likely gathered in June 1921 (or rather, just Harry, Fannie, Grandmother Sarah, and all but one of their children) to watch Morris, the second-oldest son at age twelve, perform in a sketch to close out the Hebrew schoolyear in June. The family seems to have been involved in the congregation, but whether Morris's performance was a hint of the performer gene evident in Fannie's youngest two brothers who performed in a Vaudeville troupe or was a compulsory performance is less clear.

The household also taught their children Yiddish, something that was almost a given in any other Jewish immigrant household, but this was not so in the Shiroffs', as Fannie and her mother, Sarah, were fluent in English. Furthermore, Fannie may not have known the Yiddish language well at all—when her brother Abraham met Rose Kurtz, the woman he would later marry, they had a language barrier to forge, as he spoke only English, and she was only learning the language.* Additionally, there was no longer an unavoidable Yiddish-speaking community surrounding the family once they were out in West Philadelphia. There must have been an intentional choice to speak Yiddish to their children, perhaps to help in passing on the Jewish identity that Harry and Fannie wanted instilled in them, which would make sense. It was unquestionably a kosher household: some—at least their oldest son, Ned—strictly kept kosher for their entire lives.

---

* Another thank you to Dick Altman for preserving this life story!

As impressive as Harry's accomplishments were, his wife was undoubtedly a crucial component of his success. As he grew distant from the few extended family members he knew here, Fannie and her brothers built his immediate and extended families. Indeed, Harry and Fannie's children and grandchildren remained close with their Lefcovitch and Lazarus cousins but never knew of any of Harry's family.

True to the spirit of many immigrant Jews of their age, their marriage was evidently a happy and unforced one. In the early years, when Harry would come upstairs after what were likely very long, socially exhausting, and physically tiring days running his own shop and then the Trenton Crockery Company, it must have been a great comfort to have a loving and supportive wife waiting for him. Her presence in his life was also a tremendous positive influence for another critical reason: the English language. Fannie had spent her entire life in an English-speaking country. Additionally, she benefited from the extraordinary opportunity to attend an English-language school back in England. She was likely able to read and write English before she came to Philadelphia. So by the time she married Harry thirteen years after her arrival here, she must have had a nearly native level of fluency with the English language, an incredible benefit for any immigrant to the United States. Not only could she help Harry learn the language himself—which she must have done, as it is unlikely he had the time to attend any English education programs—but she could also review his business contracts and documents as a fluent English speaker and allow them to venture more confidently out of the Jewish immigrant world on their own.

Harry did learn the language, of course. Only a few short years after his eyes likely first ever set sight upon the Latin alphabet, which was probably along his journey to Bremen, he knew enough to be signing his own name in his own handwriting—and in carefully written cursive, not print. His financial activities further reveal his mastery of the English language and keen understanding of business matters. This is evident in the thoughtful design of a loan he renegotiated on behalf of the man who bought his 1621 South Orkney Street home and had fallen behind in payments and in the business scheming of Harry's real estate transactions at the end of the 1910s.

He must have been a bright, sharp, and intelligent man. As rich as the cultural and religious education that Harry probably got as a child, I cannot imagine that the curriculum at the *yeshiva* or *heder* of Novhorod-Siverskyi included personal finance and accounting.

From the American Dream to "Nervous and Melancholy"

When the United States joined the First World War and subsequently expanded its draft to include everyone from eighteen to forty-five in 1918, Harry, like millions of American men, had to register for the draft. But for many of America's recent Jewish immigrants, the draft resembled conscription into the Russian Army just a bit too much for comfort. Harry needed a way out. Rather than dodging the draft entirely, he seems to have taken some time away from the Trenton Crockery Company to work as an inspector at the Midvale Steel and Ordnance Company, a steel venture based out of Nicetown (in North Philadelphia), though Harry worked at their plant in Eddystone (in far South Philadelphia) during the war. Midvale Steel manufactured armor and various steel parts to support the war effort, so by listing his employment there, any probability of being drafted was likely eliminated. It is hard to detect Harry's motives and reasoning, or even how he would have known about Midvale Steel in the first place, but it certainly is clear that his business management skills—some of which he must have been born with, while the rest he developed on the job with Trenton Crockery—helped him land the job.

In any case, Harry returned to Trenton Crockery after the war, at which point he and his family moved one final time to 5917 Christian Street, exactly one mile south of their previous home on Arch Street.

The family welcomed a set of twins in early October of that year, which suggests that the move was, once again, to have more space. The new home featured an additional four hundred square feet on each floor, in addition to being an even newer construction than their last. It was certainly not a cheap home either: at roughly $5,500, it cost nearly three times as much as their previous home on Arch Street. West Philadelphia was becoming the place to be; a few years later, Hyman Shapiro joined both his brother David and Harry in West Philadelphia and moved just one block past Harry, to 6012 Christian Street.

Then, after more than a decade with the Trenton Crockery Company, Harry decided to move on. The reader's guess as to why he left such a successful business is as good as mine. Trenton Crockery underwent a massive transition and expansion around this time. At some point in 1921 or early 1922, Trenton Crockery relocated from its original 710 South Second Street location to the Old City area of Philadelphia, at 106 North Second Street.* Over the next few years, the company also picked up 104 North Second along with 205, 207, 209, and 211 Arch Street, with 205 Arch Street serving as the company's headquarters for the next sixty years. Harry seems to have left the Crockery Company around the time of its move north to Old City. As Trenton Crockery began acquiring an entire chunk of the 200 block of Arch Street, in December 1919, Harry purchased a property of his own: 720 North Second, a three-story building three-quarters of a mile north of Trenton Crockery's new hub. This was the first time (as far as I'm aware, at least) that he had purchased a property not for residential use but for business.

At the time of Harry's purchase, the building was primarily leased by Back & Weiner, a joint household goods venture owned by

---

* The Trenton Crockery Company remained centered at the northwest corner of North Second and Arch Street for over sixty years. Today, the building across the street from 106 North Second has been turned into "The Pottery Building" apartments. Trenton Crockery's original painting on the exterior of the building is still there.

established manufacturers and wholesale retailers Felix Back and Benjamin Weiner. In addition to his venture with Back, Weiner also had a manufacturing firm of his own, the Weiner Manufacturing Company, at 41 North Second Street—just down the street from the Crockery Company's new location.

It did not take Harry long to become close with his tenants—and neighbors, as Back & Weiner also owned or rented a number of other properties in the area. Indeed, Harry was actually a good match for both Felix Back and Benjamin Weiner. And it is entirely likely that Felix and Harry had gotten used to getting each other's mail in the previous decade, when both men were running chinaware manufacturing/retail companies: Harry's at 710 *South* Second and Felix's at 710 *North* Second. Perhaps with this peculiarity in mind, Felix and Harry soon became particularly close. By no later than 1923, Harry joined Felix's new venture—F. Back & Company, Inc., household furnishings manufacturers—as the firm's vice president, with Felix as president and treasurer and some H. Samuel Hausman as secretary.

F. Back & Company soon acquired 711 North Second for use as a manufacturing and warehousing facility along with 238 Arch Street, which they made into a part-retail, part-office space. Readers with a sharp knowledge of the Old City neighborhood of Philadelphia may realize that F. Back & Company's headquarters were directly across the street from the Betsy Ross House, where the first American flag was supposedly designed and sewn, and the Atwater Kent building, where radios were being manufactured, but those were not the only noteworthy nearby buildings. Less than five hundred feet to the east was the Trenton Crockery Company's new headquarters, on the other side of the street. One can only imagine that Harry ran into his former partners—the Shapiro brothers—at least once in those years.

It is truly incredible to remember that this is the same Hersh Scherovsky who had been born just short of four decades earlier in the remote shtetl of Novhorod-Siverskyi and who arrived in America with next to nothing twenty years earlier. Harry had lived up to the ideas and imagery surrounding America—freedom, wealth, opportunity, hope—in the imagination of the Pale explored in Chapter 4. Harry, who almost certainly hardly studied secular matters beyond basic arithmetic in school, was now the vice president of a household furnishings manufacturing company with great potential. As the second decade of his life in America was wrapping up, he would have had a lot to be proud of. He had triumphed over unimaginable difficulties to establish a wonderful life in America—and not only for himself but for his entire family. His children were perfectly positioned to attend the finest universities, from where they would set off for even better opportunities and earn fortunes of their own. He and his family lived a very comfortable life—complete with at least one maid taking care of the housework by 1920.

As fate would have it, any celebration of victory against an unjust and cruel world would have been premature. For unclear reasons, Harry cut ties with F. Back & Company in early 1924, with a legal notice appearing in the *Philadelphia Inquirer* on January 7 informing the reader that "From this date" he was "no longer connected with the firm of F. Back & Company."[320] This succinct notice—which is also the only record of my great-great-grandparents written in the first person—reveals no immediate reasoning for his departure, but it does offer a few clues. First, the notice is signed from 42 North Second: directly across the street from Benjamin Weiner's manufacturing plant. Second, not only was 42 North Second across the street from Weiner's manufacturing facility, but according to the 1924 Philadelphia Business Directory, it was also the home of the H. Shiroff Crockery Company. One further development just over a month after his split from Felix Back also helps fill in what happened: on February 11, Harry sold his business—perhaps one of them or perhaps all of them; this is unclear—to Benjamin for $17,000, a relatively large sum for the time. It is also possible that the desire to break ties had to do with Felix joining the dodgy Security Financing Corporation, which was also based out of 238 Arch, as its vice president at around the same time Harry left.

Whatever happened, my guess is that Harry walked away from F. Back & Company and established the H. Shiroff Company at 42 North Second with the cash from the sale of his share of the company. He may have been getting ready to move further west out of the city and into the new suburbs; indeed, by this point he had already purchased that plot of land in Beechwood for a new home to be built. Even though Harry would have been taking the Elevated from Sixtieth and Market into Old City for over a decade by this point, the trip from Beechwood might have seemed too far; surely he could find a new job out in West Philadelphia, closer to home. Perhaps realizing that his neighbor across the street was ready to leave Old City's household goods manufacturing industry, Benjamin Weiner made him an offer to buy him out, which Harry accepted. These are all hypotheticals. No one knows what really happened.

Unfortunately, as the story passed down by Harry's son Victor to my grandfather and his sisters maintains, it turned out to be a tragic decision: Weiner attempted to steal Harry's company out from under him. He never paid Harry a penny.

"Nervous and melancholy." That was how Harry's family described him in the months following the sale of the business to Weiner. Of course, there was plenty for Harry to be nervous about. He certainly had bills and debts coming due—a mortgage and six children, a wife, and an elderly mother-in-law to feed, at the very least—while a business partner was refusing to pay up the monumental $17,000 sum he had contractually agreed to hand over in return for the business. But as unimaginably stressful as this dreadful situation must have been for

Harry, as if the world was closing in on him, I still cannot entirely understand or comprehend what happened next.

Nearly a decade after Harry's saga with Weiner, a brief article appeared on the second page of the *Philadelphia Inquirer* reporting on the tragic story of a Philadelphia jeweler whose business had fallen on hard times, leaving him "with only $1.49 left in the world." "I am too proud to beg; I couldn't obtain work and I have come down in the world," a letter sent by the jeweler to a friend read. "And so when you receive this letter I will be dead."[321] The jeweler's body was subsequently found dead in his apartment; he'd ended his life via gas a day earlier. Harry, both nervous *and* melancholy, ultimately fell into a similar mindset.

Friday, June 20, 1924, was Harry's thirty-eighth birthday.* Around noon on the preceding Wednesday, June 18, he went out for a walk. Despite the proximity to his birthday, by this day all the stress, anxiety, and worry had caught up to him; apparently overwhelming him and putting him into a depression from which he would never recover. Friday should have been a day of celebration, a day to spend with his six children, his wife, his mother-and-law, and his wife's brothers and their families. But perhaps Harry had tried to keep the family's impending financial collapse a secret, one that was becoming harder to keep. Forget the bills, debts, and mortgages. How would he be able to attend his birthday celebration, with all the focus on him as the beloved husband and father he was, without breaking under the weight of the truth of the impending future? Only so recently, Harry had every reason to be full of pride; indeed, he must have been overjoyed with the prospect of selling his own business for such a grand total as $17,000. He had worked so hard and achieved so much in his twenty years in the United States, both for himself and for his family, allowing them to enjoy many things that few of their peers did. Neither Harry's cousin Mendel nor

---

* Or possibly his forty-first, depending on which birth year one believes. I'm inclined toward 1886.

their Jacobson cousins had maids to take care of the housework, but the Shiroffs did.

Yet now it appeared that Harry would need to break the news to them that it seemed likely all this would soon be over. How could he do that? The immediate practicalities must have been nauseating to him. Would he have to force his children out of school and into the workforce, as most other immigrants did? This would have been a heart-wrenching thought: like most Jews, Harry and Fannie certainly valued schooling. And in any case, Harry had worked so hard to earn the privilege of allowing their kids the education—and life—that he never could have had back in the Pale. One can only imagine that many of Harry's uncountable long days and weeks during his ascent from immigrant corner storekeeper to a corporate vice president were justified with the future benefits for his children in mind. But now, this future for him and his family was being stolen from him. Had all of the work, stress, travel, turmoil, and triumph of his entire life really led to such a fate? Would it all wind up having been in vain? Had he truly failed to ensure that his family would not face the same struggles of poverty that he grew up with back home? Was he responsible for having made this mistake? Had everything, all the way back to that weeklong train journey from Novhorod-Siverskyi to Bremen, been for nothing?

Perhaps these were the thoughts echoing inside Harry's head along his half-hour walk north to Vine Street, then west to Sixty-Fifth Street, where it ended at a water-filled quarry in Cobbs Creek Park, one well known to locals as a hazard—two boys had drowned in it just two weeks earlier.

That afternoon, on June 18, 1924, two park guards discovered a coat and hat lying on the bank of the quarry, alongside a trail of footsteps leading to the water. A boat was sent out, and Harry's body was soon recovered from the water. He had been dead for about an hour.

On June 20, 1924, instead of enjoying a happy family gathering at home to celebrate Harry's thirty-eighth birthday, the Shiroff family gathered at Mount Lebanon Cemetery to bury their husband and father. The funeral had been conducted earlier in the day at home.

The death could only have been a shock to everyone. The family told the *Philadelphia Inquirer* the day after his suicide that he had seemed "nervous and melancholy" after leaving the furniture business a few months prior, but his suicide must have been as unexpected as it had been earth-shattering.

With her oldest child only seventeen years old, Fannie now had to figure out how she and her seven family members were going to get by without her husband's income. One small initial victory was likely a life insurance policy. The initial death certificate for Harry cited suicide by drowning as the cause of death, but this would not qualify for a life insurance payout at the time. However, according to the law back then, a suicide may or may not be an accident—if the deceased had lost control over their mind, if they had gone insane, or something similar, it was therefore an accident, as in the death was likely "unintended." Since Fannie would only receive a life insurance payout if it was ruled that Harry had been mentally unwell at the time of his death, a revised death certificate was issued in August, adding "temporary insanity" to the claim that Harry died in "a suicide by drowning near 65th and Vine while temporarily deranged." Perhaps that was what Harry expected would happen. Why go through all the trouble to kill oneself if there was no benefit in doing so in the form of life insurance?[322]

Once the life insurance issue had been settled, Fannie proved her mettle as a strong woman and moved to take up the fight over the money that had been owed to her husband—which was now owed to her, as in the absence of a will she took over Harry's estate. As early as 1925, she was reworking old contracts and negotiating a new one with Weiner. Yet no portion of the $17,000 debt was paid off until Weiner finally turned over $7,455 a few years later, almost exactly four-ninths of the total sale price. I have no idea why he paid such an oddly specific and incomplete portion of the full sum—perhaps Fannie had some personal stake in

Harry's business. Regardless, the remaining five-ninths of the debt was not paid off until 1930, when a series of lawsuits escalated all the way to the Supreme Court of Pennsylvania, which ruled in Fannie's favor in *Shiroff, Admr. v. Weiner* (1930). The case's opinion made it clear that Weiner was indubitably trying to rob Fannie of what she was obviously rightfully owed, claiming for those six intermediate years that Fannie had no right to even sue him, nor did she have any right to the payment owed to her husband's estate.[323]

Even in this victory, though, there must have been great pain for Fannie. The court's ruling does not refer to Harry Shiroff; there is only "Harry Shiroff, deceased." In addition to having to face the emotional toll of losing a perfect and beloved partner who brought her from the world of the poor Jewish quarter of Philadelphia to the upper-middle-class world of West Philadelphia, Fannie spent six years facing constant reminders of her husband's death, thanks to what should have been entirely unnecessary litigation. This must have been an unimaginably difficult thing to endure—and not just for Fannie but for the entire family. None of her children would come out unscarred.

Unfortunately, these soon became even more difficult years for Fannie. On June 28, 1927, almost exactly three years after Harry's death, Fannie's oldest brother Morris—her only Polish-born sibling—entered the men's room of a movie theater a few blocks away from his home and shot himself in the head. He had already died by the time he was delivered to the hospital. His thinking is entirely unknown except for a note found in his jacket, in which he had written that he "had to do this" and "could not stand it any longer."[324] I have no idea if he had been close to Harry, though it is certainly possible—perhaps even likely, although he did not live near the Shiroffs.

This was, to be sure, a very strange way to go out. While it is well within the realm of possibility that Morris's death was truly one of desperation, its peculiarity hints at other possibilities—perhaps even the mob. Ever since the early twentieth century, the "Jew Mob" had been active in Philadelphia, offering many young immigrant men an alternative to working the traditional jobs available to fresh immigrants: tailoring, cigarmaking, etc. Men like Max "Boo Boo" Hoff managed to start successful gambling rings in Society Hill in the 1910s. But when Prohibition hit in 1919, bootlegging became too profitable to ignore, and Philadelphia was at the center of it—in fact, the city was considered "as wet as the Atlantic" in the 1920s.[325]

Many had good motives—a common one was to earn enough money to one day send their own children to college—but the means were not always so harmless. As notorious Jewish mob affiliate Izzy Lavner once put it, if you didn't follow through with what the mob wanted, "you'd probably wind up floating face down in a creek on the outskirts of town."[326]

Though it wasn't a creek (but a quarry), that threat might be eerily similar to Harry's fate. Indeed, there are some possible connections between Harry's business activities and that of the Mob. After all, it was the crockery industry that made whiskey jugs in the early days of Prohibition until glass became the favorite. Everywhere Harry had a business or owned property was in the middle of a hub of bootlegging activity. The favored means of smuggling booze throughout the city and beyond was to use legitimate stores as fronts, and in the back, crates labeled "perfume," "furniture," or even "crockery" were actually filled with smuggled alcohol. Even non-alcohol-related mob activity brushed the sleeves of Harry's business world: Izzy Lavner reported how mobster Stumpy Orman knew who to pay off with "a fat envelope of cash to look the other way during a burglary" of the Atwater Kent manufacturing company, which was directly across the street from F. Back & Company's main building at 238 Arch.[327] Then there is the question of how Fannie got someone to change a death certificate.

So was Harry involved? This is an impossible question to answer with certainty. It is interesting, of course, that Harry put his notice about leaving F. Back and Company in the *Philadelphia Inquirer* on the same day that Philadelphia swore in a new police commissioner, one who vowed to go to great lengths to enforce prohibition. Also, one can't help but wonder why he did not pursue legal action against Weiner the way his widow wound up doing. But there is no definitive link between either Harry or Fannie's brother Morris and the Mob, and there is (at least in Harry's case) plenty of reason to believe that he may have had nothing to do with it whatsoever. The reader's guess is as good as mine—we'll never know the answers, and the truth doesn't change the fact that these events clearly left deep emotional scars on all who went through them.

In any case, fate tragically had one final emotional shock in store for Fannie. Almost exactly a year after the State Supreme Court handed down its verdict in Fannie's favor, her mother, Sarah, died, on January 4, 1931.

Sarah's viewpoint of her family's story is one I particularly regret being unable to see from. Her seventy-nine years of life began in a Polish countryside shtetl and then took her to London, the largest city on the planet at the time, and then to Philadelphia; she effectively lived in three different worlds. Incredibly, she spent long enough in each place to know it like the back of her hand—indeed, by the end of her life, she was a Jewish Polish woman with a British accent living in Philadelphia. Furthermore, by having lived with her daughter and son-in-law's family since even before Ned was born, perhaps nobody else but Harry and Fannie themselves ever knew the family's story as well as Sarah did. She would have known how Harry and Fannie met; she likely cared for each of their children when they were young and would have been able to describe each family member's personality with great precision. She must have spent countless days doing miscellaneous errands and household chores with—or for—her daughter. She would have been there when Fannie heard the news about her husband; she would have supported her daughter in her emotionally charged six-year legal fight and been relieved by the final verdict; she really saw it all. Sarah's life seems like so many different lives all packed into one lifespan. Surely not every moment of it was pleasant, but one can only aspire to live as many lives in one as she did—and, if we are lucky enough, with more joy and a little less hardship. May her soul be bound in the bundle of life.

Picking Up the Pieces

None of Harry and Fannie's six children ever got the opportunity to properly process their father's sudden and shocking death, at least certainly not as children or young adults. Life had to go on—and there were urgent needs that had to be met. In the six years before Fannie was able to financially avenge her husband's death, there was still food, utilities, and presumably a mortgage to be paid for. Fannie, a middle-aged woman who likely hadn't worked in at least twenty years, was not going to be able to find good employment, if any employment at all. In fact, she was already working full time in caring for the twins, who turned five only two months after Harry's death. Moreover, her mother was aging, and she was certainly not going to be returning to work—she likely had not even worked since the family lived in London, if she even did then!

There was hardly any option but for one of Fannie's oldest sons to step up to the plate and become the man of the household at far too young of an age and in far too tragic a circumstance. Unfortunately, this would not be so easy. Whether it was recognized at the time or not—and it almost certainly wasn't—all of Harry and Fannie's six children experienced their father's suicide at just about the most psychologically and developmentally vulnerable time imaginable. Today, psychologists recognize the death of a parent (especially a non-accidental death) as an adverse childhood event (ACE), a traumatic event in the first seventeen years of a child's life that puts them at a higher risk for physical and psychological health consequences as an adult. Whether they realized it or not, all of the Shiroff children would struggle to deal with their father's death for the rest of their lives, each in their own way.[328]

Next Year in America

Because he was the oldest child, at seventeen, there was every reasonable expectation that Ned would be able to earn enough money to provide at least the bare minimum for his family of eight living at 5917 Christian Street, at least for the time being before they could figure out what they could do next. But the death of his father had taken too large of a toll on Ned for him to be able to do this, as he was soon overwhelmed and overridden by a reclusive and angry depression that kept him from working just about any proper job for a long time. The impact of his father's suicide showed up in other places too. Until the day he died, sixty-three years after his father, Ned lived at 5917 Christian Street—the home he had lived in since he was nine years old. Ned remained there despite the "white flight" from the area in the 1960s.

The home must have been a very complicated emotional space for him. This was the home he and his family had once celebrated holidays and enjoyed family dinners in; it was the place where he had almost certainly last seen his father alive; it was the emotional obelisk marking the complex knot that tied the nostalgia of the good days of his youth together with the trauma of the adulthood that came all too soon. But as family photos show, the home was already devoid of family mementos and photographs by the time he was raising his children—two adopted boys—in the same place he had been raised. All that remained were a few pieces of art, including an artisan-made clock and a seemingly Japanese-styled painting, which had probably been acquired by his parents. Surely the most personal family artifacts were kept away in a safe place, where Ned could revisit the painful, heartwarming past on his own terms; having them out in the open, though, for all to see and for them to constantly remind or haunt him, was too much.

But the house was still his childhood home. He went to bed each night in the same bedroom his parents had used many years earlier; he must have imagined his father's thoughts or feelings at least once while coming home and walking through the front door; he must have at least once sat in the kitchen on a Sunday morning and seen, in his memory, his mother cooking as his father read the paper and his younger siblings ran around the living room. And how could he have never thought about the last time he saw his father alive while saying goodbye to his family before heading out in the morning? How could that whole house not have been entirely haunted and ruined by the memories created and trapped within it? Ned's choice to remain there until the end reveals a parasitic emotional attachment to his family core. There is no doubt that remaining at 5917 Christian did absolutely nothing to ease his depression or alleviate his anger or increasing oddness, but it clearly meant too much for him to let go, regardless of how it must have hurt him to wake up every day in that same home.

Needless to say, with his emotional well-being so deeply thrown off course, Ned was effectively out of the picture, at least for the time being (eventually, he opened a paint store nearby). Of course, Ned's inability to work and provide for the family was—and remains—an unfortunately common outcome for a child after losing a parent to suicide. It was still the case, though, that the family needed an income—and if Ned couldn't provide it, that meant that his younger siblings had to step up in his place. Naturally, this created tensions between Ned and his siblings.

With Estelle still only fourteen and Victor and the twins even younger than that, there was only one other person at the time who could ensure that the Shiroffs would not go hungry, destitute, or without a roof over their heads: sixteen-year-old Morris, the second oldest. And indeed, with great sacrifices and hard work, Morris was able to keep the ship afloat. It took him dropping out of high school, as Victor did later, and forgetting his plans to attend college—an extraordinary privilege at the time, and one that would have almost certainly rewarded him with an extraordinarily wealthy life, and a missed opportunity and sacrifice that meant something to him for the rest of his life.[*] After bouncing

---

[*] He would one day establish a scholarship fund at Temple University for Philadelphia's Central High School graduates.

around a few jobs, he ultimately settled at the Electric and Lighting Company in downtown Philadelphia, where he worked as a salesman, a skill doubtlessly inherited from his father—and one also inherited by at least Victor and Estelle too.

Supposedly, upon joining the company, he found himself one Morris out of too many. As there was already enough confusion, his boss asked him if he wouldn't mind using his middle name instead; Morris obliged, and from there on, he was more commonly known as Harry. But not only is Harry *not* listed as the middle name on his birth certificate; there is in fact *no* name listed at all. Harry and Fannie declined to submit a legal middle name. Perhaps it had always been his unofficial, family-designated middle name; perhaps it was a name he wished to identify with and that had particular meaning to him. Either way, for the rest of his life, Morris was known as Harry to everyone, including his family. It was, in a way, fitting: he had stepped up to effectively become the family's paternal figure in the aftermath of losing their father, Harry.

After giving up so much to ensure that his family would make it through one of the most tragic and devasting things that could happen to a family (and all while doubtlessly suffering emotionally), Morris—who I will continue to refer to as Morris to avoid confusion amid too many Harrys—and Ned struggled to get along. Though a man of reportedly indisputable virtue and ethics (again, one can only imagine where that came from if not his father), Morris would forever have a complicated and strained relationship with his oldest brother. But Morris was not the only one who had a problem with Ned—they all did. Soon enough, Ned was effectively exiled from the family. Of the seemingly endless photographs shared with me by Morris's son's family, Ned appears in not a single one. By comparison, every other sibling, their spouses—even Samuel Tabbey, who had a multidecade extramarital affair with Estelle—and their children all appear in at least one photo.

Even after Ned was cruelly beaten into a coma while walking home from the humble and sleazy paint store he ran roughly thirty years later, none of his siblings came to check on him—either in the hospital or later at his home. Only the youngest, the twins, David and Joseph, had reliably, yet still not consistently, decent relations with him, perhaps as they only would have had faint memories of their oldest brother's behavior immediately after their father's death. Estelle visited Ned, but only with a great reluctance and visible disinterest; both were clear enough to be among the first things that came to mind about Estelle by Ned's adopted son some fifty years after he probably last saw her (he also recalled her great elegance and kindness to him). Victor occasionally made the trip out to visit his brother's paint store, sometimes even with my grandfather—at least before Victor followed much the same way—but he was still no big fan of his oldest brother. Later, during his own bouts of severe depression, Victor never let his family forget that Ned was responsible for everything having gone wrong. "Ned didn't want to support the family." "Ned didn't care about us." "We're poor again after having such a luxurious childhood all because of Ned." So on and so on.

Ironically, both Victor and Morris held Ned in contempt for the same reason that Ned was unable to provide for the family: the trauma of losing their father to suicide as children or young adults. One of the most common behavioral tendencies seen among those who have lost a parent to suicide as a child—one that often lasts for life—is a habitual tendency to blame things on others.[329] Even if this statement makes my great-grandfather roll in his grave, Victor was much like his oldest brother. Indeed, most of their differences can be explained by the variance in their ages at the time of their father's death. As he experienced it at an older, more mature age, Ned became increasingly reclusive and angry over time, something that only worsened after the beating-induced coma. At a younger, more delicate age when his father died, but still old enough to understand what was going on in the moment, Victor's emotional scars took the form of emotional instability, most clearly seen in his bipolar episodes and occasional periods of psychosis some years later. Yet their greatest similarity is why Victor eventually faced the same fate in the family circle as Ned: simply put, both men were seriously mentally ill, with both suffering from depression (Victor's illness eventually developed into what was diagnosed as bipolar disorder in his forties). Victor and Ned's mutual depressions led them to drastically underperform what both men would have been capable of had they been spared the trauma of their childhood or had they had access to modern therapy and medication. Moreover, their depression led them to not merely underperform but to hardly get by at all. It may be nothing short of a miracle that Ned—who became so antisocial by the middle of his life that he immediately hid upstairs if his wife had company over when he came from work, only coming down for dinner once they left—was able to keep his paint store going until the day he died. After a visit to the paint store, when my grandfather was very young, he once asked his father why the paint cans in Ned's store were covered in dust. Victor's half-sarcastic, half-truthful response was that "Uncle Ned doesn't sell much paint."

Victor only had a marginally different fate than his brother and for much the same reason. As he was only ten when his father died, the external, real-world effects of his father's death did not impact him until he was a teenager. At that time, Victor—once an outstanding student, particularly gifted in mathematics, likely a trace of his father's intelligence—needed to drop out of high school to help support the family, never to attend formal schooling ever again. Other big changes were afoot then too: this would have been at about the same time that Fannie's mother, Sarah, died in 1930 and around the same time that Fannie finally won the remainder of the money owed to her by Benjamin Weiner. Clearly, even though the household was yet again reduced in size and despite the six-years-delayed receipt of about $8,000, things were still not in great shape for the Shiroffs at 5917 Christian Street. Otherwise, one would imagine Victor would have at least completed high school, but he did not. Instead, he followed his older brother Morris, by then the de facto man of the household, into working as a salesman, as did Estelle—again, all clearly inherited their father's sociability and charisma, with some of their mother's Lefcovitch showmanship and confidence mixed in.

Remarkably, through all these unimaginable trials in the decade after her beloved husband's death, Fannie managed to remain true to herself, never losing her character or her noble-like matriarchal position in the family. When Victor's wife called Fannie to say she was pregnant with her first grandchild-to-be in 1935, Fannie was almost *disappointed*—claiming that she was "too young to be a grandmother".* Unfortunately, however, Fannie would never become "old enough" to be a grandmother. Shortly after the news of her impending grandchild, and two years after Victor's marriage, Fannie began treatment for stomach cancer, even undergoing a very risky surgical attempt to stop its spread. Ultimately, the cancer could not be stopped, and Fannie died on December 11, 1937. But even her death certificate takes after her style: though it indicates she was fifty, she was instead fifty-nine with certainty.†

The fact that she lived twenty fewer years than her mother but still lived a life as full and dense as her mother's is truly incredible. In fifty-nine years, two countries, and two continents, Fannie went from rags to relative riches in London, back to rags in Philadelphia, then to riches, then back to rags before returning to some level of comfort shortly before the end of her life. Not only that, but she enjoyed and endured some of the greatest emotional joys and pains of life on Earth. She beat the arguably comedically small odds that she—the daughter of Polish Jews born in London—could meet and marry what one could say was a soulmate—the son of almost entirely unknown poor Ukrainian Jews

---

* Unfortunately, like Ned's child, Victor's first child was stillborn in 1936.

† Her death certificate was filled out by William Nitzberg, who seems to have been the family's lawyer, as he represented both Fannie and later Ned in their respective legal ordeals. Curiously, Nitzberg is buried across from Fannie and Ned at Roosevelt Cemetery.

born in an almost unimaginably remote shtetl—here in America, in Philadelphia. If you change any one small little part of either her story or Harry's story, those odds almost certainly go from being very small to being nonexistent. Though they enjoyed a little short of eighteen years of marriage together, their story does not have a happy ending, but it can remind us of at least two things: first, that life is too fragile for us not to enjoy each moment to the fullest extent possible, as if it were a gift—because it may well be—and second, that though terrible, tragic things are an unfortunate feature of life, to the best of our ability, we should not allow such things to make us ungrateful for or unappreciative of all that previously made us joyful.

Indeed, through it all, Fannie held loved ones close. She had three things still in her possession when she died: the house, her wedding band, and a diamond ring. Thirteen years of emotional and financial stress after her husband's premature death, she still held on to the jewelry he had bought her. It could simply never be given away; the emotions in the memories provoked by the wedding band and the diamond ring were too vivid, too tangible, and too sensitive for her to let go of them. She could have sold them—and she certainly could have used the money—but she did not want to. They were too important to her.

A worker in front of the kiln at 710 South Second Street in 1921. By this point, the building was used by the Acme China Company.[330]

Chapter 10
AMERIKANE KINDER

The days fly by so fast that often I feel as though I were leaping over a whole generation. At times I even see myself an old man, like my grandfather, but without his confidence, without his faith.[331]
~ Isaac Raboy

It is difficult to understate the extent of religious, cultural, and social change within America's Jewish population between 1880 and 1950. In the seventy years since the *Illinois* became the first immigrant steamship carrying Jewish refugees to dock in Philadelphia on February 23, 1882, the world of Jewish Philadelphia underwent many transformations of unimaginable scale and scope. As we will see over the course of this chapter, many of the Jewish immigrants' children gradually left the factories and sweatshops, as well as the small, self-owned grocery stores, cigar shops, and butcheries, behind in favor of less-grueling and better-paying jobs in the lower-middle class. At the same time, the same forces we have already seen lead to assimilation and reform within the immigrant generation continued to influence their children and grandchildren, perhaps even more so. Indeed, as we will see in this chapter, the younger generations often fell under even greater pressure, as unlike their parents, they went through the American school system. There were important geographic changes, too, as the Jewish quarter grew from a few blocks between South Street and Washington Avenue to the majority of southeast Philadelphia east of Eighth Street by the 1920s—but by the end of the 1950s, it had all but disappeared as its residents moved away, mostly to North Philadelphia.

Remarkably, all these changes did not lead to the complete loss of Jewishness among the younger generations, or even necessarily of Judaism. To be sure, this was not because the Jewish immigrants had no intentions to assimilate—most were at least somewhat eager to assimilate, and if not for themselves then for their children. Even those who would have otherwise resisted the pressure to assimilate often had no choice in the matter, as participation in the American economy often required adjustments to religious and cultural practices; we have already seen this in the work-related declines of Shabbat observance and synagogue attendance, for example. But despite the steady process of assimilation over their first few decades in America, the immigrants' children nonetheless managed to inherit their parents' Jewishness—even if they modified and reformed it, occasionally even cutting out bits they felt were best left behind.

Their parents' Judaism, on the other hand, proved not as easily passed down. One reason is that as the process of assimilation and acculturation continued, the immigrants' children and grandchildren found increasing appeal in Reform Judaism—a denomination that, as the reader might recall, few immigrants had any interest in, considering it a lesser, foreign, and specifically German variant of their religion. But despite these immigrants' best wishes, Reform Judaism went on to become the predominant denomination by the latter half of the twentieth century, beating out Conservative, Reconstructionist, and Orthodox Judaism. With an increasingly reformed and lenient approach to religious life and many still subjected to the same practical obstacles to observance faced by their parents, synagogue attendance remained poor, while qualified rabbis remained scarce, and traditional religious observance continued to slip away.

These opposing trends—the success of passing down Jewishness, but difficulties in passing down Judaism—led to widespread interest in what some have called secular Judaism. In the words of some of its early American proponents, secular Judaism sought "to foster Jewish concepts and ideals—ideals that are reflected in Jewish literature, in Jewish history, and in all emanations of Jewish culture" and to establish "a new Jewish culture grounded in democracy and humanistic values."[332] It was, in a sense, an attempt to adapt the broader Jewish world for life in the modern, Western, and industrialized world. But this must be understood to be distinct from encouraging assimilation, as one might be tempted to describe it at first. Jewish secularism instead sought to emphasize (or perhaps even propose) Jewishness, rather than Judaism, as the primary feature of Jewish life. Indeed, rather than encouraging universal usage of the English language, the secular movement saw the continued usage of Yiddish (or, less frequently, Hebrew) as critical for maintaining the sense of shared civilization. *Yiddishkeit*—the adaptation of Eastern European Jewish civilization for life in America—was thus born.[333]

While many of their children and grandchildren took after this new secular Jewish tradition, many of the Jewish immigrants themselves—particularly those who were already adults by the time they came to America—found it concerning. It must have reminded them, understandably, of the warnings of their home shtetls' rabbi and elders before they left: that America was an unclean, an unkosher land, where Jews gave up fasting on Yom Kippur and worked on the Sabbath. Most would have understood the pressure to accommodate religious life for life in America as they, too, had experienced the same obstacles, but Jewish secularism was something different—it openly accepted the decline of religious life in favor of continued cultural traditions. Their anxieties were clear in one commentator's story on the tensions between (perhaps even only relatively) religious parents and their more secularly minded *Amerikane kinder* ("American children"):

"Why don't you say your evening prayer, my son?" asks his mother in Yiddish. "Ah, what yer givin' us!" replies, in English, the little American-Israelite as he makes a beeline for the street. The boys not only talk together of picnics, of the crimes of which they read in the English newspapers, of prizefights, of budding business propositions, but they gradually quit going to synagogue, give up *cheder* when they are thirteen years old, avoid the Yiddish theaters…they even refuse sometimes to be present at supper on Friday evenings…"*Amerikane kinder, Amerikane kinder!*" wails the old father, shaking his head. The trend of things is indeed too strong for the old man of the eternal Talmud and ceremony.[334]

The Rise of Jewish Secularism

How is it that the younger generations managed to retain their Jewishness while their religious observance simultaneously became increasingly lax? One critical part of the answer is that even as the younger generations took less interest in religious observance, they were nonetheless surrounded by an effectively Jewish world in the Jewish quarter. Even the most secularly minded of the immigrants' children would have likely related to writer Vivian Gornick's childhood recollections: "The dominating characteristic of the streets on which I grew was Jewishness in all its rich variety…we did not have to be 'observing' Jews to know that we were Jews."[335] The prominence of kosher butchers and restaurants, Yiddish and Hebrew bookstores, and street vendors selling Jewish variations of street food maintained a distinctly Jewish atmosphere—it kept the Jewish quarter distinctly Jewish, rather than just being an immigrant quarter. This was especially the case on the Sabbath and even more so on holidays, when the Orthodox Jews' continued vibrant in-synagogue religious observance reminded their more secularly inclined neighbors of their ancestors' religious customs.

The continued exposure to Jewish culture, even in the partial (or complete) absence of exposure to Judaism itself, helps explain why even those who hardly ever attended synagogue in America nonetheless continued to mark many holidays (especially Rosh Hashanah, Yom Kippur, Passover, and, with newfound importance, Hannukah) at home. It also helps to explain how the bar (and bat) mitzvah became a default feature of a Jewish upbringing, as we saw in Chapter 8; it helps us understand why *shivah*, the "memorial week" of mourning after a death in the family, was perhaps even observed with greater interest than back in the Pale; and it makes clear why for many decades to come, Jews often continued to live around other Jews in Jewish communities rather than in isolation in gentile neighborhoods.[336]

The guarantee of exposure to Jewish life in the neighborhood also contrasts the increasing infrequency and irregularity in synagogue attendance. As we have already seen, the demands of the American economy—which often required particularly long workdays, often on weekends too—made consistent synagogue attendance difficult if not entirely impossible. With many unable to bring their children into the religion through a lifetime of synagogue attendance from birth, some hoped that sending their children to the "bar mitzvah factories" would serve as something of a replacement, hopefully instilling at least some understanding of the religion in them. Unfortunately, as we saw in Chapter 8, such an outcome would have been the exception and certainly not the rule; a far more common outcome was for the bar mitzvah boy to never again step foot into a synagogue, or at least not until the next major life event. The younger generations simply had little to no understanding of Judaism as practiced in the Old World.

Between the obstacles keeping the religiously inclined away from the synagogue and the religious inexperience and disinterest among the younger generations, less than a quarter of American Jews regularly attended a synagogue they were affiliated with by 1920. Synagogues themselves were even becoming scarce, with only one synagogue for every 1,309 Jews in 1926; the equivalent statistic for churches stood at one per 220. The situation had hardly improved by the time the immigrants' children began having children of their own: only about only about 11 percent of boys and 7 percent of girls in New York regularly showed up for services in 1935.[337]

Perhaps Jewish secularism's greatest victory was its insistence that religious observance was a private matter. Rather than practicing their religion in a synagogue (or, for the rapidly growing number of Reform Jews, in a temple), many opted to instead do so in the comfort of their own home, where they could do so however they wished, to whatever extent they felt obligated.

Moreover, the decline of the synagogue was matched by the rapid and widespread rise of associations of Jewish immigrants from the same hometown, *landsmanshaften*. Even though subscribed to secular thought, their efforts to avoid religious infighting in favor of creating a sense of Jewish community and fraternity with their shared culture and origins often wound up effectively promoting many of the ideals of Jewish secularism. Indeed, their belief that "religious practice was less critical to Jewish preservation than shared experiences and values" sounds just like what the secular movement was saying. But the *landsmanshaften* must not be confused as secularists. Even if many of their members came to sympathize with secularism, many others came to respect the idea of *Yiddishkeit* while still insisting on the primacy of Judaism and Jewish law. The *landsmanshaften*, after all, were responsible for building the vast majority of the Eastern European Jews' synagogues in America. But at the end of the day, so, too, were they responsible for offering an alternative form of Jewish community—one that needed not necessarily be centered around the practice of Judaism but rather on Jewish culture.[338]

The American public school system—and the ideals promoted within it—are another important part of the story. As anyone with a Jewish upbringing likely knows well, education is among the most venerable, respected, and encouraged pursuits. This tradition within the Jewish world goes back centuries, if not millennia, and is evident in how the

NEXT YEAR IN AMERICA

Jewish immigrants raised their children. Both parents and children alike—most children, at least—were incredibly eager to get into the classroom and learn. Any reader familiar with Mary Antin's memoirs is likely to recall the pride, joy, amazement, and gratitude Antin and her father had for the public school system; coming from the Pale, it was truly something to marvel at. "Jewish children attend the public schools in large numbers," wrote one observer in Philadelphia in the first decade of the twentieth century. "No nationality down-town is more appreciative of the public school system," he claimed.[339] Out of the roughly 17,000 students living and attending school in or around the Jewish quarter at the start of the twentieth century, half were Jewish.[340]

The secularly minded American school system stood in stark contrast to the *yeshivas* and *heders* attended by many men raised in the Pale of Settlement. Thanks to the classroom, even children who had entered school with hardly any knowledge of the English language came out more than just fluent and, broadly speaking, Americanized. This was not by accident—it was part of the plan. "You cannot catch your new citizen too early in order to make him a good citizen," one early twentieth-century education expert argued; "The kindergarten age marks our earliest opportunity to catch the little Russian, the little Italian, the little German, Pole, Syrian, and the rest and begin to make good American citizens of them."[341] Perhaps it is unsurprising that these tactics instilled Jewish children with a love for celebrating Memorial Day and the Fourth of July, two holidays that achieved nearly religious-level importance for some. A natural tension rose between the immigrants and their children:

> Given Jewish devotion to schooling and the fact that American schools were secular, Jewish students were going to be drawn away from the traditions of their parents, no matter what their teachers did and did not do, simply by the process of education itself. The more time the immigrant child spent reading the central texts

of Western civilization, the less time he or she spent reading Talmud; the more the child came to respect the secular leadership of the country, the less need he or she had for a rabbi's judgement.[342]

The Wexler family (and others) at the Jersey Shore, Memorial Day 1934. Mildred Wexler is on the far right.

Interestingly, as valid as the quote above is, the school system's other main concern suggests that this religion-school trade-off might not have always been as it seemed. For example, Philadelphia's school principals noted that attendance around the High Holidays and the Sabbath was quite often poor, suggesting that the schools did not always stand in the way of maintaining religious practice. More damning for their observance was employment: hardly anything of significant consequence followed from missing a day of school, but skipping work came with a much larger penalty. Indeed, as we have already seen in the case of Jacob Wexler and Harry Rabinowitz, the difficult economic realities of life in the Jewish quarter often took children out of the classroom altogether at too young of an age.

In any case, by and large, Jewish children generally did well in school and were well regarded by their teachers. A survey of principals of southeast Philadelphia schools from the turn of the century almost universally found that Jewish children had a "lively interest in American history and institutions," as one principal put it, and benefitted from their parents' "active" encouragement of education; many even showed up to school events and exhibitions. One Philadelphia school principal even went as far as to say, "Of all foreign children, the Jews are preferred as citizens of the future."[343] A common concern, however, was that sons were far more likely than their sisters to continue attending school as they got older. One principal noted that while parents were eager to encourage their boys to continue pursuing education, "less interest is shown in the girls [, who] leave at an earlier age." We have already seen this happen with Pauline Waxman, and we will continue to see it happen in later generations too. Even still, it appears that most Jewish immigrant children at least attended kindergarten and a few years of early grade school, all but guaranteeing that they would have a decent proficiency in the English language—even if their parents never would.[344]

Aside from education, another important factor that guaranteed a trend toward an increasingly religiously disinterested Jewish secularism was the rapidly changing nature of the American economy in the interwar years. By the time the last of the immigrants' children were entering into the workforce in the 1920s and 1930s, economic progress and urban development meant that many of the Jewish quarter's inhabitants slowly shifted away from industries traditionally dominated by immigrant Jews—which were often occupations brought over from the Pale, like tailoring—into more religiously and culturally heterogeneous occupations. Many became salespeople, quite often in department stores frequented by city dwellers of any imaginable origin, though all kinds of careers were on the table: luggage manufacturing, mail carrying, chinaware manufacturing, shipbuilding—and for the very lucky, careers that required college degrees, such as dentistry or law, were soon within reach.

In these new jobs, customers, coworkers, and bosses were increasingly likely to be gentile. One would have to get used to eating lunch with, or at least around, coworkers who did not keep kosher and who came from entirely different cultural backgrounds. Gentile bosses were far less likely to sympathize with requests to avoid working on the Sabbath or on days of fasting. And, of course, one certainly could not count on everyone knowing Yiddish!

No matter how much one might have resisted, for most there was simply hardly any choice *but* to enter mainstream American society, participate in its economy, and slowly absorb its culture. This was not because the American government was forcing it, like Russia had more or less tried to do, but rather a direct consequence of the opportunities available in America—even including the twists and turns that came along with these opportunities.

The Shiroffs show how inevitable this process was, even for those who truly wanted to keep their Jewish identity. Unlike any of the other families in this narrative, the Shiroffs were free—at least before Harry's death in 1924—from the immediate pressure to quit school and enter the workforce or the need to work seemingly never-ending shifts, weekends included. They were, therefore, free from many of the obligations that prevented others from being able to continue to observe their religion as fully as they had back in the Pale. Perhaps this helps explain why Harry and Fannie's children went to Hebrew school and appear to have *enjoyed* it. Moreover, to whatever extent they made it an obligation, it does not appear to have been aimed at making up for the near or complete lack of religious activity at home. They kept a kosher household, as most of their children did when they had families of their own. They also successfully managed to teach their children Yiddish, with some keeping the language in active use for the rest of their lives.

Their father's tragic and premature death, however, left them with hardly any choice *but* to enter into the mainstream American workforce and economy, simply as a matter of urgency and need. They would not have the luxury of choosing a boss who was perfectly willing to accommodate Shabbat and the Jewish holidays, nor of picking a workplace where the employees were of Jewish descent. They would just have to go out there, find a job, and do well in it. This did not mean that they would need to abandon their faith or identity—and they didn't. It did mean, however, that they got far more exposure to American society and customs than they would have had they grown up in the Jewish quarter or even had they continued on their lives in their own little bubble in West Philadelphia. They were submerged into American life much faster and further than they likely would have been had their father not lost his life.

While their story was one of tragedy, similar stories unfolded just about everywhere. Nearly everybody faced the same requirement to figure out a way to put food on the table, and just about nobody lived in a comfortable-enough state that this need could ever feel anything but pressing. Jewish secularism was understandably appealing to those during these kinds of experiences. It validated their increasing distance from religious practice and their selective observance thereof while also offering a way to maintain one's identity, to "honor thy parents," and to retain the values instilled within them from a young age, for example, without religion being front and center. The thinking of Mordecai Kaplan, the founder of Reconstructionist Judaism who held the inaugural bat mitzvah for his daughter, resonated with many American Jews, even if it was taboo in some circles (Kaplan had been excommunicated by the Orthodox, after all). His formulation of Judaism revolved around the idea of reconstruction: examining each and every tenet of Judaism, reassessing its originally intended use and purpose, and reimagining how that same aim could be achieved in modern society. Kaplan's approach to Judaism offered many American Jews of this generation (and those after it) a way to maintain their Jewish identity even as they adapted Judaism's ancient religious customs to their modern American life.[345]

The circumstances became even more conducive to secularism's appeal when, just as many of the immigrants' children were marrying and starting families of their own, the United States suffered through the most severe economic catastrophe of its entire history: the Great Depression. Those who had settled down into stable jobs in the preceding decades now faced sudden unemployment, and those just now entering the labor force had to make do with whatever job they could find with even more urgency than ever before. Whatever remaining cases of flexibility one might have once had to choose between a Jewish or gentile employer certainly only became rarer as the unemployment rate skyrocketed, businesses closed, and work became scarce.

Things were made more difficult by the continued observance of the biblical command to "be fruitful and multiply"; there were many more children to house and feed than most families have today. While having plenty of children meant that one also had plenty of additional sources of income, this obviously only worked if the children could find work in the first place. Many of these children were left with miserable childhood memories of being forced out of school and into work, which stuck with them for life; those who were too young to work or whose families were unable to secure work were left with memories of poverty, hunger, and material discomfort. The immigrants' youngest children, however, were relatively lucky: without any children, they did not yet face the problem of enlarged grocery bills; unsurprisingly, many of them then opted to have fewer kids. Between the four of them, my father's grandparents had five children in total—yet each of my father's grandparents had at least four siblings!

The Waxman family is a good example. Harry Waxman was a bit of a Jewish anomaly in that he was never much of a believer in the value of education for his children, but his motives were relatively normal for the time: they needed to work, and the family couldn't afford to have them in a classroom when they could be working instead. He had already pulled his oldest children out of school long before the Great

NEXT YEAR IN AMERICA

Depression began, but soon, in the middle of the Depression, the need for extra income became all the more dire after Harry's unanticipated death on September 6, 1934.[*] In addition to the shock to the family's emotional well-being—he was adored by his children—Harry's death meant that finding work to support the family was all but mandatory for his children; his wife, Esther, after all, was certainly not going to be able to earn an income to support the family. She had not worked for decades by the time her husband passed away, and she was sixty-two, a year older than her husband had been. Moreover, she knew hardly any English—as more than one of her descendants recalled her explaining to them, she never bothered learning English because she already knew Yiddish, German, Polish, and Russian and was sure that whoever she'd encounter (in the Jewish quarter, at least) would speak at least one of those!

Thankfully, most of Esther's older children were already working. But Esther's oldest son, Jacob, had firmly established himself in New York after first moving there about twenty years earlier to live with his uncle (Esther's brother Frank), and would not be coming back to Philadelphia. The next oldest, Frank, was already out of school and working in the clothing industry, but while he eventually became extraordinarily successful, this only came after many years, with plenty of failures along the way. Except for their youngest, Isadore, the rest of Esther's children were girls; given the implications of their gender for their income and the jobs available to them, they all needed to work to supplement the family's income and support their mother.

One way "out" of this arrangement, whether intentionally or not, was to marry. While two of Esther's three daughters, Fanny and Celia, had already married by the time of their father's death—in 1928 and

---

[*] Pauline told her children that he died of leukemia, which is perfectly reasonable, but his death certificate says heart failure. Pauline's daughter told me that her mother said that Harry suddenly fell dead in front of Jefferson Hospital in Philadelphia.

1931, respectively—Pauline had not. And thus, it was Pauline who remained with her mother after her father's death. In fact, Pauline did not move away from her mother for nearly an entire decade after she married.

Politics, Religion, and the Road to the Suburbs

Whether it was a result of the civic virtues instilled in the American classroom, a consequence of their experiences in or around the sweatshops that dominated the immigrant quarter, or both, Jewish immigrants and their children quickly became both interested and involved in politics. While their exact political ideology could go in just about any direction, there were a few common threads. Perhaps most prominently and least surprisingly was a strong endorsement of immigration, especially after the closing of immigration in 1924. For many, the immigrant experience had been a formative one, the memories of which—the horrors and discomfort of immigrating and of the old life back home—would never be forgotten, not even by the children of immigrants.

A second tendency, especially during and after the Great Depression and particularly among the immigrants' children, was a general support of the Democratic Party. This was especially the case during the New Deal era: Franklin Delano Roosevelt won over three-quarters of Philadelphia's Jewish vote—not quite as unanimous as the 97.1 percent majority won by Roosevelt in Chicago's most Jewish precincts, but significant nonetheless. But their simultaneous support for Roosevelt, an isolationist who sought to keep America from getting involved in the rapidly darkening situation in Europe, often conflicted with their advocacy for restored immigration rights. Many were deeply disappointed by Roosevelt's failure to allow their relatives still in Eastern Europe to come to America and escape the imminent arrival of the Nazis.[346]

Participation in unions and other forms of organized labor was common, too, especially in the early years in America, when most immigrants were working in the horrendous conditions of the sweatshop. Like so many other features of the industrial era, unions and labor politics were relatively late arrivals in the Russian Empire, which saw its earliest unions and organized labor parties only in the last decade of the nineteenth century. Interestingly, it was Russia's Jews who first experimented with organized labor politics, founding the Marxist-aligned Jewish Labor Bund in 1897. Many were driven to Marxism and the broader labor movement as a direct result of the government's increasingly oppressive and discriminatory policies toward the Jews, but some were genuinely interested in the goals and ideas movement itself after having tried out working in Russia's miserable early industrial factories.[347]

One must not forget, though, that the average demographics of a Jewish immigrant in this era—relatively younger and typically with light-industrial work experience at best—meant that most immigrants were either too young or too far away to have gotten a dose of the revolutionary spirit that was slowly spreading throughout Russia's industrial centers. Thus most were only radicalized by their experience in America's sweatshops or by the speeches of those spreading the gospel of union membership and working class solidarity in the urban education centers described earlier. Unsurprisingly, given their experiences in both Russia and America, many immigrants were easily energized by the late nineteenth and early twentieth centuries' calls for workers' rights, organized labor, and sometimes even socialism, communism, or outright anarchism.

Philadelphia's joint shirtwaist and dressmaker strike in 1906—quite possibly joined by the Waxmans, Wexlers, and Satalofs—serves as a demonstration of the influence of these ideas on Jewish immigrants. The vast majority of the community, from conservatives to reformers to radicals alike, stood in solidarity and participated in the strike. But though they demonstrated that they could effectively organize as workers to demand better and safer working conditions for themselves, relatively few were actively interested in politics much more radical than that, aside from a small number of anarchists and utopian socialists. Broadly speaking, far-left politics never truly took off within Philadelphia's Jewish community as much as it did in some other major cities, even if it did lead many of the second-generation to lean toward the political left.[348]

As noted above and as we have already seen many times so far, the experience of working in the modern American economy not only influenced American Jews' politics but their religion too. One incredibly important part of the story that is crucial for understanding the seemingly rapid increase in the pace of assimilation and the spread of secularism as the twentieth century went on was the Jewish community's geographic shift. In a process that began shortly after the end of the First World War and accelerated with the opening of the north-south Broad Street Line on September 1, 1928, Philadelphia's Jewish quarter gradually lost its Jewishness as its inhabitants moved out, most often to the north but occasionally west too. The east-west Market-Frankford Line, which was mostly opened by 1906 but only finally completed in its modern form in 1922, had already introduced the average Philadelphian to the wonders of the subway—and they loved it. In the coming decades, most of the Jewish quarter's residents found new homes in the neighborhoods around the Broad Street Line's northern terminus, such as Olney and Logan.[349]

The highly attentive reader might recall that this was not the first time Philadelphia's Jews were living in the city's more northern reaches: some seventy-five years earlier, advances in transportation and living standards after the Civil War allowed the German Jewish population's center to shift a good bit north from its original location around Franklin Square to just south of where Temple University stands today. Though few Eastern European Jews lived in this area until the period I am now describing, the German Jews nonetheless paved the way for them to eventually settle further north. There they started their own businesses, opened their own charities, and, starting with the first in 1871, established their own synagogues—though they were more often temples rather than synagogues, owing to the German tendency toward Reform Judaism.[350]

However, as we saw in Chapter 7, the German Jews did not always feel the sense of fraternity with their Eastern European peers that we might expect; even after a generation or two in the United States, there were still many differences between the two groups. To start, even in the second quarter of the twentieth century—by which point, as we know, the general liberalizing of Jewish religious observance was already well underway—relatively few Eastern European Jews embraced the Reform Judaism favored by most of the Germans, favoring just about any other denomination instead. Their customs were different, too, perhaps most easily seen in the preference of many Eastern Europeans to use Yiddish (though, as the *Amerikane kinder* quote earlier in the chapter hinted at, Yiddish was often a hard language to sell to the younger generations). And at any rate, the vast majority of Eastern Europeans had thus far opted to live their lives almost entirely within their own Jewish quarter, where opportunities for employment at Jewish-owned or majority Jewish-staffed tailoring shops, textile factories, and other typical industries were plentiful. While some got to know their German peers through the businesses they owned on South Street, there weren't always many opportunities for the two groups to get to know each other—and their preferences for different synagogues certainly didn't help that.

All this meant that the Eastern Europeans arriving from the Jewish quarter, in short, needed to bring all of the Jewish quarter's attributes and amenities with them. From the kosher delis and Hebrew schools to the synagogues and Yiddish theaters, all the features of the Eastern European-centered Jewish quarter needed to be transplanted in hitherto German-dominated North Philadelphia, where the same institutions were likely to differ too much for the Eastern Europeans' tastes, if they existed at all. This was, of course, a momentous task. The Jewish quarter had all of these things in the first place only because of the large numbers in which the Jews arrived, the density in which they settled, and the limited economic opportunities immediately available to them as recent arrivals. If one had been a butcher back home (and didn't hate it too much), for example, why not carry on as one in America?

Needless to say, a complete set of all the institutions that helped to preserve the cultural and religious aspects of life in the Pale brought over by the immigrants could not possibly be immediately rebuilt in Philadelphia's northern suburbs, nor could such a thing ever truly be done. In the meantime, the new Jewish communities of North Philadelphia would decide what parts of the Jewish quarter would stay and which ones would go. In the absence of reliably kosher food, some began to experiment with non-kosher diets; at first, however, kosher rules were most likely to be broken outside of the house than inside of it. Synagogue attendance, which we have already seen be challenged by the demands of the American economy, the relative scarcity of rabbis (a problem no less acute in North Philadelphia's newer Jewish communities), and the rise of secular Judaism, remained infrequent, with most opting to perform their acts of religious observance at home. Some mainstays in the Jewish quarter were never truly re-created outside of it. Its Yiddish theaters, for example, which had thrived in something of a golden age only a few decades earlier, were one such casualty; the younger generations, the *Amerikane kinder*, never took as much interest in it as their parents and grandparents did.

The same thing had happened when their parents and grandparents first arrived in the United States, of course. When the immigrant generation arrived, they built and opened institutions as an expression and continuation of their culture from home; most accepted this as inevitable and natural, something that many immigrant groups have done in many countries. But they too left behind or transformed many of the religious and cultural traditions and customs of the Pale, as we saw in Chapter 8. The second generation did the same thing, except that their transformed and renegotiated Jewish identity meant that the institutions that they built up or took over from their parents reflected *their* culture and traditions, neither of which were necessarily the same as their parents'. Again, whether they followed Mordecai Kaplan's Reconstructionist way of thinking or not, this was very much in line with it.

Inevitably, the Jewish atmosphere brought to North Philadelphia was not as religious as the Jewish quarter had been. What kept any semblance of a Jewish atmosphere around whatsoever was, aside from the weakened contribution of religious institutions, the *Jewishness* of the Jewish quarter—*Yiddishkeit*. In North Philadelphia—and, indeed, in many of the suburbs Jews across the United States relocated to—Jewish life was increasingly secular, with the virtues of American democracy and good citizenship mixed in, along with warm feelings toward capitalism and education (and baseball). It cannot be emphasized enough, however, that this was not typically one and the same with assimilation. While it was true that synagogue attendance was hardly ever any better in the suburbs, most of the suburbs' new Jewish residents nonetheless kept kosher households, cooked many of the same dishes as their parents had, and observed select holidays, in their own way, at home; some even continued to use the Yiddish language, even if only for a few words or phrases.

The Decline of the Jewish quarter

Like the vast majority of the Jewish immigrants' children, my great-grandparents all opted to start families of their own in North Philadelphia rather than in the Jewish quarter. We'll get to that part, but let's not get too far ahead of ourselves yet—they have to meet each other first!

While I know how my father's maternal grandparents met, I have only a guess for his paternal grandparents. Both sides, however, tell a similar story that helps us both literally and figuratively propel Philadelphia's Jewish immigrants and their descendants out of the

Jewish quarter. Often, it was simply the search for a better place to raise a family and better economic opportunities to support one's family that led them out of the Jewish quarter—but it often accelerated the Americanization process and the renegotiation of Jewish identity, too, for the reasons outlined in the section above.

My grandmother's parents met just as so many Jewish (and indeed gentile) couples did around this time: at a dance. As my grandmother tells me, her mother—Mildred Wexler—used to love to go dancing with her little brother, Albert. Well, so, too, did my great-grandfather Harry Rabinowitz, and one night they met; next thing you know, they wound up married for just shy of sixty years. They almost certainly must have been dancing somewhere up in North Philadelphia, as by the time of their marriage in 1939, Harry had already been living in North Philadelphia for at least a decade. At some point in the 1920s, his parents had moved their family—including Harry, his two brothers, and his father's brother David—into 534 Marwood Road in Olney. Curiously, however, the Wexlers lived nowhere near Olney in 1930; that year's Census suggests that Mildred's father, Jacob, made it out of South Philadelphia's shipbuilding steelyards and into a job as an automobile mechanic, a job that temporarily kept him tied to South Philadelphia. By 1940, however, the situation had changed. In addition to the easier transportation offered by the Broad Street Line, Jacob suddenly found himself out of work, likely as a result of the Depression. The financial distress must have been severe, as his wife, Esther, returned to work as a dressmaker after more than two decades out of the workforce. Desperate for work and new economic opportunities, Jacob brought his family to North Philadelphia. They moved into 4602 Marvine Street, just southeast of Olney, by no later than 1939, when his daughter Mildred married Harry Rabinowitz.

My grandmother's parents, Harry Rabinowitz and Mildred Wexler, on their wedding day

Harry moved in with the Wexlers, as still remained customary. But their plans to start a family of their own meant that they would need a place of their own—after all, 4602 Marvine Street wasn't so big, and Mildred's younger brother, Albert, was living there too. Thus Harry and Mildred moved to 4632 Marvine Street, 250 feet up the block from Mildred's parents. It was here that my grandmother and her sister grew up—but let us save that for the next chapter.

Taylor Shiroff

In many ways, some for the better and some for the worse, the Shiroffs had a very different experience growing up in America than the Wexlers and Rabinowitzes—or the children of most Jewish immigrants, for that matter. Harry and Fannie's six children all spent the bulk (or entirety) of their childhoods in West Philadelphia, where they lived in greater comfort than most of their peers in the Jewish quarter—at least before their father's suicide in 1924. After that, as we saw in the previous chapter, their oldest children urgently needed to enter the workforce to keep the family's finances afloat. Aside from Ned, who remained in the Shiroffs' West Philadelphia home until his death in 1987, the urgency to work brought the other five children back east. Morris and Joe both found employment at an electrical equipment supply company in downtown Philadelphia and lived together for some time in an apartment just outside the northwest corner of the Jewish quarter. Joe's twin brother, David, moved to Northeast Philadelphia, where he opened a paint store, just as his emotionally damaged oldest brother Ned did. Estelle worked as a salesperson before taking up a job as a secretary in a law office, where she met Samuel Tabbey, a lawyer a dozen years her senior with a family of his own, with whom she had an affair (and a child).

Victor, on the other hand, wound up back in the Jewish quarter. I am not sure exactly why he went there—all of the Lefcovitch uncles on his mother's side were in either Logan or Olney, and all of his siblings were in Center City or somewhere north or northeast of it. I am almost certain, however, that his choice to move further south and into the Jewish quarter is the only reason he ever met his wife, Pauline Waxman.

Though I also do not know the story of how Victor and Pauline, my grandfather's parents, met, their children at least have some faint recollections that suggest it might have had something to do with a shared hobby: tennis. Tennis had become one of the de facto favorite pastimes among both first- and second-generation Jewish immigrants—it was, by all odds, one of the few sports most immigrant Jews found much interest in playing! Indeed, Victor's late father, Harry, had played it, as did his children; one of Victor's many exaggerated stories of his youth was that there was a tennis court at the "mansion" where he grew up in. (There was not, but there were—and still are—tennis courts a few blocks west on Christian Street, next to Cobb Creek Park.) Whether or not this is how they met, it is surely a clear sign that this first generation of American-born children of Jewish immigrants were fitting in with their American peers a little more easily than their parents had.

Even if they shared a love for tennis, Pauline and Victor admittedly still seem like an odd match. Whereas Victor's parents shed much of whatever attachment they had to the "old world" of Eastern European Judaism behind—in fact, Fannie, his mother, was not even born in Eastern Europe—Pauline's parents were a different story. Her beloved father remained a tailor until his death in 1934, presumably the same occupation he held back in Staszów; her mother, who argued that being fluent in Yiddish, Polish, German, and Russian had to be "good enough" to get around, never learned much English, if any at all. When Pauline cooked, she kept kosher; Victor, at that point, did not.* Pauline's household was one of foreign languages, which Pauline would continue to use with her siblings throughout her entire life; Victor had learned Yiddish from his parents but ultimately preferred to stick with English, likely owing to his parents' English fluency (indeed, his parents likely encouraged him to use English). Pauline's parents pulled her out of school at a young age, not understanding the point of educating a woman beyond elementary school; Victor, though a high school dropout, was once a gifted, motivated, and encouraged student.

---

* Essentially all of the Jewish recipes that remain in my family are passed down from Pauline.

Perhaps their greatest difference was where they grew up. Though Victor did not grow up in the mansion that he later claimed that he did, he grew up in a relatively affluent, middle- to upper-middle-class neighborhood of West Philadelphia. For roughly the first twenty years of his life, he lived in newly built homes; every home he had ever lived in had had modern electricity and plumbing, and 5917 Christian Street even had marble bathrooms. Meanwhile, 444 Jackson Street, where Pauline lived for the first fifty years of her life, had none of these things. In the heart of the old Jewish core of Philadelphia, 444 Jackson was valued at about half the valuation of 5917 Christian in 1930. If that year's Census is to be trusted, the Shiroffs had a radio set, while the Waxmans did not. Pauline's closest encounters with the kinds of wealth that her husband's family had once enjoyed were thanks to her older brother, Frank, who had made a fortune by legally questionable means in the clothing industry during the Second World War, but this was only after she married. Yet somehow, they made for a good couple—and they truly did love each other.

Shortly after their marriage, Victor moved in with his wife's family— her mother, Esther, and younger brother, Isadore—at 444 Jackson Street. Victor and Pauline opened a clothing store in around 1937, financed by Pauline's older brother, Frank, who by then had built up at least enough wealth to do such a thing. Just like so many first-generation Jewish immigrants to Philadelphia, they opened their clothing store on South Street; unlike the entrepreneurs of their parents' generation, however, it was somewhat further west, around Eighth or Ninth and South Street. It was, unfortunately, terrible timing. The Great Depression was still ongoing, and though things had improved somewhat in the mid-1930s, the economic situation dramatically weakened once again later in the decade. The business failed early in the 1940s, and Victor ultimately found a job as an insurance collector at a small Philadelphia insurance company.

Left: Pauline holding Florence, her and Victor's oldest daughter, outside of their home at 444 Jackson Street sometime in the early 1940s. Right: Pauline in 1945.

He was assigned a route whereby, on a regular schedule much like a postman, he went through to collect insurance payments from subscribers to the company's policies (at the time, this was a weekly or biweekly occurrence). It was a good match at first, one that let him exercise both of his greatest characteristics: his friendly sociability and his mathematical ability. The regular and rapid tabulation of entire lists of two-, three-, or four-digit numbers soon came with ease, and became a skill that each of his three children would separately attest to six decades later. Owing to his charisma and natural salesmanship (both surely inherited from his father), Victor enjoyed and perhaps even thrived in this kind of work—it brought him into people's homes, where he got to know not just the subscriber but often the entire family. It also let him offer to others the same kind of insurance which all but certainly kept his mother from having to sell their comfortable, middle-class home and return to the near-slums of the Jewish quarter after his father's death. Indeed, before long he was doing well enough in his job to move his family from the Jewish quarter to Oxford Circle in Northeast Philadelphia, just east of Olney, in the late 1940s.

His employer primarily sold life or "sick and accident" insurance policies, designed to help protect a family's income in the event that the primary earner fell sick, was incapacitated, or died—the impact of which Victor understood all too well. It hardly took any time at all, however, for him to notice that just about all of the families on his route had one thing in common: they were typically low-income Black families living in impoverished, likely redlined, neighborhoods. It wasn't the setting that bothered him, or the people: he built relationships with many of the families on his route through conversations in their kitchens and living rooms. He developed a deep and genuine sense of sympathy and empathy for their situations: families struggling to pay bills, often equally struggling to put food on the table, families who just had some terrible thing happen to them—their beloved father and husband, their favorite daughter or son, a wonderful mother and loving wife—who suddenly really needed something to work out for them, else they face hunger or eviction.

What bothered him was instead how these people in such precarious financial situations, who were all but guaranteed to already be dealing with racism and all kinds of discrimination, were essentially being robbed by his employer. Over time, Victor noticed how often his employer failed—or, more accurately, refused—to properly pay out claims that were rightfully owed to beneficiaries. This must have stung him terribly: how similar it was to the traumatic events of his childhood! His own father took his life after being denied the sum of money rightfully owed to him, leaving himself, his five siblings, his mother, and his grandmother at the mercy of their father's life insurance policy being duly paid out. Indeed, they had come quite close to such a moment of panic: were it not for the revised death certificate that was issued for Harry two months after his death, the family quite likely would have been given nothing. Surely Victor had taken pride in offering that sort of peace of mind to other families, especially financially vulnerable ones, as many of the customers on his route were.

The simultaneous feelings of worry, anxiety, and heartbreak these people felt must have not only reminded Victor of the death of his father in his childhood, but also of his father, Harry, himself. It would have been out of character and atypical for Harry, as a child of the Pale and its Jewish education and culture, to have not one time gone on and on at a family dinner about how one ought and ought not to behave. After all, Harry had surely been subjected to these monologues, whose lessons—to care for the poor and take part in charity certainly among them—must have been reinforced by his own lived experience, both of growing up in complete poverty in an obscure corner of the Russian Empire and as an immigrant Jew in America. When Harry did become successful, he became a member of the Brith Achim Beneficial Association, a brotherhood of sorts that was tasked with collecting funds to take care of widows and children who lost their fathers, among other things. Victor and his siblings, especially his brother, Morris (as reported to me by Morris' son), clearly absorbed these lessons from their charismatic and impassioned father over the dinner table.

But as it turns out, Victor was effectively duping his customers into contributing to his employer's profits rather than to their own insurance. The nature of his job—going door to door, selling policies, and collecting money from families that were often already struggling to put food on the table for a whole variety of reasons that often included racism or discrimination—too severely conflicted with his conscience. Nearly seven decades later, my grandfather can still "vividly" recall "how bitter" his father was once he became aware of how terribly his customers were treated when claims were made on their policies. Overcome with frustration, depression, and envy of the fortune that his brother-in-law Frank had built up during the war, Victor became miserably unhappy with the job and quit (or was quite possibly fired from) the insurance industry for good around 1952 or 1953. By this point, he had already moved the family to Oxford Circle, another up-and-coming community of first- and second-generation Jewish immigrants located just to the east of Olney in Northeast Philadelphia.

Victor's experience working in these neighborhoods stayed with him, though. Like most first- and second- generation Jewish immigrants, Victor held a lifelong allegiance to the Democratic Party and was a staunch supporter of President Roosevelt, particularly of his welfare reforms.[*] He kept a close eye on current events both at home and abroad, seemingly always eager to come across an issue where he could somehow make a difference. Later in life, Victor became actively and passionately involved in a North Philadelphia business program that sought to connect Black business owners with their white peers, where he volunteered business advice, training, and support on his own time, for no compensation.

I have offered the details of Victor's employment and his frustrations with it as an up-close example of what adapting to the American economy and renegotiating one's Jewish identity looked like in practice; I do not reasonably expect that the story is particularly fascinating to anyone outside of my family. One can hardly imagine Victor, naturally gifted with numbers, growing up aware of his father's business ventures and yet wanting to have a job completely unlike his father's. He certainly had little interest in working for someone else; even with his intelligence aside, Victor preferred being in the driver's seat much more than being

---

[*] This qualification applies to most Jews' allegiance to FDR as well. As was mentioned above, despite their near-universal support and vocal endorsement of FDR's economic relief programs during the Depression, many Jews were particularly disappointed in Roosevelt's "isolationist" foreign and immigration policy and unwillingness to shift American policy on immigration. They were right to oppose these—the same laws and logic that kept many Jews (and people of all nationalities) from bringing friends and family over to America after 1924 later led Roosevelt to direct ships full of refugees fleeing the Nazis and the Holocaust to turn around and sail back to Europe.

yet another employee. But unfortunately, his childhood trauma damaged him too much and left him with no choice but to enter the workforce. One might imagine that Victor would have made for an outstanding actuary or engineer; indeed, Milton Friedman, the Nobel Prize-winning twentieth-century economist and child of two Eastern European Jews who fled Russia in the late nineteenth century, first attended Rutgers University (my alma mater) with the intent of becoming an actuary. But there lay Victor's other problem: the urgent need to find an income source left him without the freedom to spend a few years in school earning a degree—he did not finish high school for exactly the same reason. Regardless, even if higher education were a possibility, he did not have the funds to afford a college degree anyway.

Many, perhaps most, second-generation Jewish immigrants were under similar pressures and circumstances—the need for work superseded "luxuries" like a college education even if it could have improved their economic condition. It was only the postwar generation—the third- and fourth-generation Jewish immigrants, if we can even call them such a thing—that would finally be largely free of those pressures.

Let us return one last time to the Jewish quarter before we leave it behind for the rest of the book. Needless to say, the migration of Philadelphia's Jews out of the Jewish quarter and into North, Northeast, or West Philadelphia led to a drastic change in the character of the Jewish quarter. The Jewish quarter had grown significantly in size from its humble beginnings when mass immigration began in the early 1880s; it had transformed from only a few blocks within Society Hill to almost the entirety of southeast Philadelphia. At its height, it stretched from Lombard Street in the north all the way to Oregon Avenue in the south, and from Eighth Street in the west to Front Street in the east—and were it not for the Delaware River, it would have surely gone further east.

But by 1930, its territory was definitively shrinking. Those who had enough money to leave and could find or transport themselves to jobs elsewhere did.

To some extent, this was inevitable. The Jewish quarter, after all, did not become the Jewish quarter because all the arriving Jews *wanted* to live there or on account of its loveliness. It was instead simply what was available, where fellow Jews lived, and where the typical immigrant could find a job and afford to live. Before the arrival of the Jews in Philadelphia, Society Hill was a poor, dilapidated corner of the city; the area to the south between Washington Avenue and Oregon Avenue was hardly anything better. The inflow of Jewish immigrants was just too strong: in the years before 1924, for every Jewish family that moved out of the Jewish quarter, there was at least one family—often many more—entering the United States through the Washington Avenue Immigration Station or arriving to Philadelphia by train after having already entered through Ellis Island or Baltimore.

But as immigrant families and their children began earning enough to move out of the Jewish quarter, there was no longer another immigrant family—or two or three—moving into their old apartment. This was, of course, a consequence of the 1924 Immigration Act, which cut off practically all immigration into the United States. The act came in the middle of a decade of general prosperity, and despite the fact that Jewish immigrants, like most immigrants, did not always benefit as uniformly or even as much as their native-born (and specifically white) American counterparts did, they benefited nonetheless. Work became more stable; wages rose. With immigration effectively impossible, there was no longer a need to save money to spend on bringing a seemingly never-ending list of relatives over from Europe. There was at least a little more money around—so why not move somewhere better?

As it turns out, progressively fewer and fewer Jewish families living in the Jewish quarter were able to provide an answer to that question in the interwar years, until just about everybody was leaving—or had already left—by the 1950s. Even by the time Victor Shiroff moved into the Waxman family residence at 444 Jackson Street in the mid-1930s, only a few blocks from where Victor's own father had first lived after first arriving in America thirty years earlier, this transition was already well underway. In 1920, the 400 block of Jackson Street was practically entirely inhabited by immigrants—most often Jewish, but not necessarily—from places like Russia, Poland, or Romania. By 1940, it was more of a fifty-fifty split between Eastern European immigrants (including second-generation ones) and non-Jewish native-born Americans. By 1950, all except for a very small number of first- and second-generation Eastern European Jewish immigrants were American-born.

The area around 2213 South Front Street, the Rabinowitzes' 1920 residence just to the east down Jackson Street, tells a similar story. When the Rabinowitzes lived there, almost all of their neighbors were immigrants—mostly from Eastern Europe, but also from Germany, Finland, and Ireland. This is about what we would expect—the next-door dockyards offered many low-skill new immigrants a laborious but stable source of income. Only ten years later, though, very few immigrants from Eastern Europe remained; many of them had moved away, like Max and Pearl and their family, and were replaced by poor (and almost always gentile) working-class immigrants from Central or Western Europe and native-born Americans alike. By 1940, native Pennsylvanians with Central or Western European-sounding surnames occupied almost the entirety of the surrounding blocks. In 1950, only five people living in the 2200 block of South Front Street were foreign born; three were older than fifty, and one was eighty-six.

To be fair, these were homes that had always been on the outskirts of the Jewish quarter, even at its height. But the same story can be told about homes in the center of Jewish quarter. A particularly strong example is 226 Monroe Street, the Waxman family's first recorded residence in Philadelphia. In 1910, its prime location within the Jewish quarter meant that just about every single resident on the 200 block of Monroe Street was either an Eastern European Jewish immigrant or the child of two of them. By 1950, however, the same block was home to overwhelmingly more "immigrants" from other American states than from other countries. Whereas the Morganstein, Rosen, Waxman, Arbeiter, Berkowitz, and Rezin families occupied the four floors of 226 Monroe Street in 1910, it was the Wright, Davis, Seldon, and Young families who called 226 Monroe Street home in 1950. Almost all of the very few Eastern European Jewish immigrants or their children who remained were older than fifty.

Just as the customs of the Jewish immigrants and their children did not change overnight, neither did the Jewish quarter. Over a prolonged period of slow and gradual change, its Jewish inhabitants began to move away—to better neighborhoods, to new jobs, to college, for military service, or sometimes just even to a new adventure. The lack of any inflow of new Jewish immigrants meant that nobody would take their place, therefore leaving the Jewish quarter to inevitably dry up of Jewish residents.

It was yet another lapse of recursion in the Jewish Diaspora. Just like the Russian Empire and its Pale of Settlement, Philadelphia's Jewish quarter—like most Jewish quarters throughout the United States, with the partial exception of Brooklyn's—would not be the forever home of its Jewish inhabitants. And just as the Jewish religion and its culture and traditions changed when the Diaspora brought one batch of Jews into Central and Eastern Europe and made them into so-called Ashkenazi Jews, and just as it did again when the Diaspora led millions of Ashkenazi Jews into the Pale of Settlement, and it did yet again when the Diaspora brought these Jews to the United States, so, too, did the Jewish religion, culture, and tradition change as Philadelphia's Jews dispersed outside of the Jewish quarter.

My great-grandfather, Harry Rabinowitz, outside of his family home at 4632 Marvine Street sometime in the early or mid-1950s.

Chapter 11
INTO OUR WORLD

✦━━━━━━━━━✦

Most American Jews [by the 1960s] were to be found neither among the very rich nor among the very poor, but rather in the "middle" middle class. It was a respectable status; as "typical" American businessmen they had come a long way. Hardly more than a century had passed since their parents and grandparents had arrived at Ellis Island with just the clothes on their back and little more. No immigrant people had ever responded to opportunity with more willingness or resourcefulness; no ethnic group had ever proved itself less "likely to become a public charge."[351]
~Howard Morley Sachar

In the wake of the migration out of Philadelphia's Jewish quarter, merely 15,000 Jews called it home in 1958; by 1980, that number had dwindled to only about 4,000. This remarkable geographic transformation—over 100,000 Jews lived in the Jewish quarter before the First World War—occurred, by no coincidence, in tandem with social and cultural transformations within the Jewish community, religion, and home. The previous chapters explored these changes as the immigrant generation passed the torch to the next generation, who by and large brought it to new and increasingly secular Jewish communities in Philadelphia's northern and northeastern suburbs. Now, having already brought the Jewish immigrant out of Eastern Europe and onto American (Philadelphian) shores, into the Jewish quarter and then out of it, we are—both literally and figuratively—onto the final chapter in this story.

America's greatest and most remarkable talent is its miraculous ability to take any stranger from any strange land and, hardly a few decades after first welcoming them in, turn them into an American just as any other. Of course, it is not really that simple: this often involves some transformation within both the immigrant and the native populations as well as years or even decades of difficult work, physically or socially, on the part of the immigrant, as we have seen. But the process works—and has worked for centuries, since even before the United States came into existence. The second part of this book has, among other things, argued that the main channels through which the Eastern European Jewish immigrants were Americanized were participation in the economy and workforce, the public school system, and the collective pressures that culminated in the spread of secular Judaism. Our task is to now complete the circle; to do so, we must turn to the grandchildren of the immigrant generation.

Passing Down the Immigrant Experience

> *Cultures are slow to die; when they do, they bequeath large deposits of custom and value to their successors; and sometimes they survive long after their more self-conscious members suppose them to have vanished.*[352]
> ~Irving Howe

Old habits die hard, even cultural or traditional habits. In the Pale—indeed, throughout most of the Jewish world—Torah study had been a practice generally reserved for men and their boys; even in America, acceptance of the bat mitzvah proved controversial and only came with time. Even as immigrant parents began favoring—or at least implicitly endorsing—secular education over religious education, the education of their sons always took priority over the education of their daughters.

Let us return to the story of the Wexler family. Jacob Wexler and Esther Satalof had their first child, Ethel, shortly after they married at the end of 1912, followed by a second daughter, Mildred, in 1916, and a son, Albert, in 1918. Much like all of my great-grandparents' families, the Wexlers were a firmly working-class family. Jacob was constantly switching jobs and moving the family around wherever he could find work; at one point, presumably for economic reasons, he opted to take a job at the Maybaum Hosiery Company, a five-mile commute from his residence at the time. In their childhood, Jacob's children would have known him as a shipbuilder, a hosiery knitter, and a car mechanic.

Even as Jacob tried out all kinds of jobs, the family's ever-precarious financial situation never seemed to improve. When Jacob lost his job in the early years of the Great Depression, not only did his wife have to reenter the workforce, but he also pulled his daughters out of school so that they could work too. But while all three of the women in the Wexler household went to work as dressmakers, the story was very different for Albert, the youngest child. Whereas his older sisters were pulled out of high school at the age of fifteen, Albert completed high school. And though he, too, soon entered the workforce, his job at a law firm had little in common with dressmaking.

After a few years, Albert then moved on to college. But as they so greatly valued education (for boys, at least), his family financed their son's education by any means necessary—even if it meant that their daughters would need to work in the same line of work as their parents, in only marginally better conditions than they did, and for only slightly better wages. The girls did not get a chance to continue their own education, even though those who knew them felt they were just as intelligent and equally capable. They only had the misfortune of being born the "wrong" gender.

As an intelligent, well-read woman (as she proved to be throughout her life), dropping out of high school years before graduation just so she could help bring in income to pay for her younger brother's education was certainly not the outcome Mildred wanted for herself. But what was she to do? Her parents, Jacob and Esther, were seemingly dead set on their son completing high school—and that was just the bare minimum. After all, not only were they clearly infected with the same adoration of public schools and education that most first- and second-generation Jewish immigrants held, but they may have felt like they had some distance to make up for. Jacob never received a university education himself—instead, as we saw a few chapters earlier, he left school around the age of twelve. Both of his younger brothers, on the other hand, not only graduated high school but went on to obtain degrees from the University of Pennsylvania. While Jacob was laboriously bolting together sheets of metal in the dockyards of South Philadelphia in the mid-1920s, his younger brother was studying abroad in England, France, and Germany. This must have stung at least a little bit.

With this experience in mind, it is not too surprising that Jacob set out to send his son to college, regardless of what it cost him or his family. His daughters did not get the same opportunity, but this, too, is unsurprising in the light of Jacob's childhood. Whereas the boys, except for Jacob, went all the way to the University of Pennsylvania, his two sisters went no further than middle school. All Jacob had ever known was the prioritization of the sons' education; his daughters would just have to figure out a way to help out.

On the one hand, he got what he wanted: Albert went to college and became magnificently successful and enormously wealthy indeed. On the other hand, however, this came at a great cost to the family. The family's record in the 1940 Census, taken just one year after Mildred married Harry Rabinowitz, my great-grandfather, looks like it could have been from decades earlier. Both Mildred and her mother, Esther, were dressmakers, the classic trade for immigrant Jewish women, while my great-grandfather Harry worked in a leather bag factory. The only giveaway that this was truly a record from 1940, aside from their residency in North Philadelphia, is Albert's status. At twenty-one years old, he was clerking in a law office, where he earned nearly double his mother's annual pay and just under my great-grandfather's. This must have made for uncomfortable or awkward family dinners.

Family relations were even more strained by the fact that, unfortunately, Albert was not always thankful and appreciative for the opportunity his family had sacrificed so much to give him. One particularly poignant anecdote passed down to me says it all. At one point, many years later, when his involvement in a medical supplies company had already made him at least a millionaire, Albert was preparing to move into a new home and offered his sister and brother-in-law a spare dinnerware set that he did not want (or need) to bring with him to his new home. It would have been a kind gesture, except for the fact that he charged them a few hundred dollars for it! Mildred and Harry took the deal regardless, even though they were still in the lower-middle class; their relationship with Albert, however, deteriorated.

One might guess that this experience would have led Mildred and Harry to raise their family differently, especially as they had no sons but two daughters: Carole, born May 17, 1942, and Barbara—my grandmother—born December 15, 1943.[*] However, just as one would be wrong to assume that Jacob's childhood would have led him to be different to his own children, the same would be true for Jacob's grandchildren.

As both my grandmother and her sister have put it to me, their parents "would have preferred to have had boys." This was particularly true for my great-grandfather. Not only did he comfortably embody the second-generation immigrant working-class experience, but he took far greater interest in sports—particularly baseball, which he (supposedly) came close to making a career out of as a catcher—than he did in

---

[*] I cannot be certain, but I believe that the name Carole came from Mildred's maternal grandmother, Clara, who had died a few years earlier in 1936.

education.* It is hard to blame him for this: together with his two brothers, his father, and his uncle, men outnumbered women five to one in his childhood home, and he had grown up without any sisters. Moreover, having dropped out of school after the eighth grade to enter the workforce, the world of higher education was entirely unknown to him; his closest exposure to it was through his brother-in-law, Albert, who it is hard to imagine he had a great impression of. There would be no dream of college for his children, even if they would at least graduate high school, and without being able to bond with his daughters over a shared adoration of baseball, bonding with them at all proved difficult.

Indeed, they were not particularly affectionate parents, either. I would be mistaken not to also mention their version of timeout. The punishment for letting one's mouth run a little bit too far or any other act of misbehaving was the greatly dreaded coal bin in the basement—I will never forget the way my grandmother and Carole's faces lit up recalling the frequent, though not necessarily always undeserved, stints they served in the coal bin.

Regardless of their parents' preferences and personalities, my grandmother grew up in a household quite similar to most other households led by working-class or lower-middle-class second-generation Jewish immigrants. Theirs was one quite like increasingly many others in that their practice of the Jewish religion was relatively lax—even despite the fact that Mildred's father knew the Torah by heart, itself likely a result of his own father's piety and occupation as a Hebrew school teacher. Moreover, one of her husband's grandfathers and one of his great-grandfathers had been rabbis. But regardless of the piety in both of their pedigrees, their household was one that nonetheless

---

* The family lore has it that he was offered a position on the minor league team the Philadelphia A's, but he couldn't take it because he would have had to pay his own way to the training, and as this was during the Great Depression, the family was in no position to be able to afford the loss of his contribution to the household's income.

followed a relatively liberal interpretation of Jewish secularism. As my grandmother and her sister recall it, the extent of their family's observance of the Jewish religion hardly went further than a modest Passover seder and the lighting of candles on Hannukah; synagogue attendance was essentially unheard of. To some extent, this may have been because Mildred and Harry were still not too far removed from the same economic and social factors that led to significant transformations in Jewish life overall; they were, after all, closer to the working class than the average second-generation Jewish immigrant was. "They gave us nothing," my grandmother once told me, "but, truth be told, they had nothing to give."

My grandmother with her grandmother, Esther Satalof; her mother, Mildred Wexler; and her sister, sometime in the mid-1950s.

But as was often the case in secular Jewish households, there were many aspects of Jewish life that did not change within their home at 4632 Marvine Street. Even if Mildred and Harry would have likely had to stop for a second to remember the last time they had stepped foot into a synagogue, they kept kosher—most certainly within the house and almost always on the rare occasions that they ate elsewhere. The second set of dishes, the separate sink, and the separate counter to ensure that the kosher dietary laws could be properly observed are a wonderful symbol of the evolution within Jewish life in the suburbs of the 1950s and onward. From an outsider's perspective, I understand entirely—and have some inclination to agree—if it seems somewhat odd that one would continue to bother with maintaining a kitchen that met God's standards (not always an easy task!) when they otherwise hardly ever engaged with the Jewish faith. While it may seem strange, one must remember that such a thing must have been natural to them, at least in their place, time, and life experiences. Few people sit down and design an entirely new identity for themselves, deliberately and explicitly picking and choosing which of their parents' customs and traditions to carry on, which to reform, and which to leave behind. Instead, this process occurs largely subconsciously and in the context of what made sense to them at the time.

Kosher cooking may have been a matter of comfort and preference, but it was at least equally an internalized norm. After having spent your entire life thus far without ever eating pork and always hearing your mother's voice preemptively scolding you before you had the chance to inadvertently mix meat and dairy, it is understandable to feel uncomfortable violating these rules—even if one hardly fears punishment from God nearly as much as they fear their parents' judgement. Mary Antin—anything but Orthodox herself—offered a vivid recollection of her reaction to seeing (and eating) pork for the first time, during her first experience in a gentile household; it was likely representative for many of her generation.

All went well, until a platter was passed with a kind of meat that was strange to me. Some mischievous instinct told me that it was ham—forbidden food; and I, the liberal, the free, was afraid to touch it! I had a terrible moment of surprise, mortification, self-contempt; but I helped myself to a slice of ham, nevertheless, and hung my head over my plate to hide my confusion. I was furious with myself for my weakness. I to be afraid of a pink piece of pig's flesh, who had defied at least two religions in defense of free thought! And I began to reduce my ham to indivisible atoms, determined to eat more of it than anybody at the table...I ate, but only a newly abnegated Jew can understand with what squirming, what protesting of the inner man, what exquisite abhorrence of myself. That Spartan boy who allowed the stolen fox hidden in his bosom to consume his vitals rather than be detected in the theft, showed no such miracle of self-control as did I, sitting there at my friend's tea-table, eating un-Jewish meat.[353]

Throughout his entire life, my great-grandfather, Harry, would not mix beef and dairy—not even for a Philadelphia cheesesteak. His children, however, were not so opposed. Carole, the oldest, eventually managed to talk her mother into allowing a bacon pot: one pot, only one, with the exclusive use to cook bacon. Her mother never ate it, even if her father did when Mildred wasn't looking.*

My grandfather's upbringing was not too dissimilar, at least at first. My grandfather was born on February 25, 1942, the middle of Victor and Pauline's three children: his older sister, Florence, was born in 1940 and his younger sister, Joyce, in 1948. Victor may have been somewhat

---

* My grandmother and Carole would be disappointed in me if I did not also include the fact that Mildred was, by all accounts, a terrible cook—except when it came to brisket, as my father tells me.

lax as far as his adherence to a kosher diet went, but at least within the house, Pauline kept their kitchen and everything made within it strictly kosher. Thankfully for my grandfather and his siblings, and unlike his future mother-in-law, by all accounts, Pauline was a spectacular cook. Sweet and sour meatballs, apple kugel, potato kugel, potato knishes, liver knishes, strudels made with spare knish dough—it is no wonder that my father often skipped Hebrew school in favor of going to his grandmother's apartment just across the street; all of our traditional recipes are owed to her. Pauline doubtlessly learned how to cook from her parents, and almost certainly from her mother, Esther. Esther supposedly so favored Pauline's cooking over any of her other children's that once she was confined to a nursing home in her later years, she refused to eat anyone else's food but Pauline's—and thus a rotating crew of Pauline, my grandfather, and his older sister, Florence, needed to be on-call to stop by with a lifesaving meal.

Whereas the Rabinowitz household was relatively laxer than the average second-generation Jewish immigrant household, the Shiroff household was closer to the average, perhaps even slightly less lax. In addition to keeping kosher, my grandfather—but neither of his sisters—attended Hebrew school and became bar mitzvah. Pauline attended synagogue with some regularity, and, at least later in life, joined a Conservative congregation—like mother, like daughter. Esther had, after all, been at least lower-case-c conservative throughout her life, attending synagogue each Shabbat until she was physically unable to do so. Like many Jewish homes, the Shiroffs kept a *pushke* box or can in which they collected spare change to be donated to whatever cause or charity needed it at the time.* Supposedly, some of this money was sent off to Israel to support the Tyszgarten and Waxman relatives who miraculously

---

* פושקע in Yiddish. The etymology is disputed, but certainly Eastern European. They often took the form of a small tin can or box much like a tip jar.

survived the Holocaust; I have unfortunately never been able to find these relatives.

Though Victor and Pauline were certainly not wealthy, they were definitely at least in the lower-middle class by 1950. As discussed in the previous chapter, Victor's job as an insurance collector had worked out well enough for him to relocate his family from 444 Jackson Street in the remnants of the Jewish quarter and into the rapidly growing Northeast Philadelphia suburbs. They first moved onto Passmore Street, into a home with a warm-air heating system—which, as modern readers likely know, generates heat by a furnace and then distributes it throughout the home with ducts and vents. Such a system, however, could not be mastered by Pauline; while Victor surely grew up with this kind of heating in 5917 Christian Street, Pauline, at either 226 Monroe Street or 444 Jackson Street, certainly did not. Her inability to adapt to it actually forced the family to relocate.

Before long, the Shiroffs moved yet again to 1126 Gilham Street, a radiator-heated home just around the corner from the house on Passmore. Pauline felt she could handle radiator heat, so this was the house my grandfather grew up in.

Even though Victor and Pauline had moved out of the Jewish quarter, their neighbors on Gilham Street serve as a reminder that the rest of the Jewish quarter had moved, too, and often to the same place. Though there were essentially no first-generation immigrants on their street, their neighbors' surnames—Rosenberg, Meyer, Tushinsky, Rasinsky, and Shaffers (who were actually born in Russia)—hardly obscure their origin.

As was told in the previous chapter, Victor became disillusioned with his insurance job and left—or was fired—sometime around 1952 or 1953, shortly after their move to Northeast Philadelphia. Sympathetic, but surely also fed up with Victor's incessant complaining about his job, Pauline asked her brother, Frank, who had already helped put him in business once over a decade earlier, to find a menswear store suitable for them to take over and run. Frank did indeed find something but also came back with an idea: Pauline's youngest sibling, Isadore—Itz, as he was known—should come on board as well. After all, Itz had spent the last several years working for his older brother Frank's gigantean clothing store in Chester, Pennsylvania, other than the two years he spent overseas in the army during the Second World War, and had become an outstanding retail salesman with a strong work ethic, excellent purchasing instincts, and a keen sense of fashion trends. With Itz making a fortune for both himself and his brother, it is hard to imagine why he would have been willing to leave—except for the fact that Gloria, the girl of his dreams, would only marry him on the condition that he started his own shop. Itz had been reluctant to do so, as though his talent as a retailer was undeniable, his academic talents were far less pronounced. Unable to read or write at a sufficient level and even less able to do the basic math that retail management requires, Itz would have failed on his own; Frank would not let him do that to himself.

    Luckily, Victor made for an excellent counterpart and partner to Itz—the math, legal contracts, and financial matters that inevitably came up for a retailer were no challenge for Victor, armed with his father's genetics, a decade's worth of experience in retail sales, and yet another decade's worth of experience in tabulating numbers and handling contracts. Moreover, the lapses in Victor's work ethic that soon became something much more serious were counteracted by Itz's hardworking nature, and their common charisma and sales abilities made them a powerful partnership. And he and Itz were not strangers. As the youngest son and a bachelor until after the war, Itz lived at home—444 Jackson Street—until at least 1950 and may have worked in the first shop Victor and Pauline tried to open on South Street shortly before the Second World War. Indeed, when he returned home from the war, he would have found out pretty quickly that he now had an almost four-year-old roommate: my grandfather. Itz's youth, at least from my grandfather's perspective, quickly made him into the beloved Uncle Itz.

All the stars having aligned, Victor and Pauline welcomed Uncle Itz into the plan and, with Frank's financial support, purchased the Allen's Men's Shop menswear store sometime in the early 1950s. Unlike the first shop Victor and Pauline opened about fifteen years earlier on South Street, the Allen's Men's Shop was not just outside of the Jewish quarter: at 43 South Broad Street in Woodbury, New Jersey, it was entirely outside of the city of Philadelphia itself. Over the next few years, Victor, Itz, and Pauline (when she was not raising her three children, at least) cleaned up and triumphantly reestablished the Allen's Men's Shop as a fine menswear store in the rapidly developing New Jersey suburbs.

The partnership between Victor and Itz had indeed worked out well. Victor, having clearly inherited his father's brain, handled all of the store's financial and banking matters, in addition to the marketing and advertising; Itz, on the other hand, put his keen eye for men's fashion to use as the primary buyer, stocker, and store designer. Before long, the store was earning a tremendous income, and all seemed well. The Shiroffs were yet another example of the tendency toward family-owned-and-operated businesses among second-generation immigration Jews.

The Cycle Repeats

Just as it proved difficult for Harry and Mildred Rabinowitz to avoid raising their children in the same way they had been raised, the Shiroffs soon found it difficult to avoid giving their children an uncomfortable dose of the difficult circumstances in which they were raised by their own parents, the immigrant generation.

The first cracks began to appear shortly after the Allen's Men's Shop takeover. Just as Mildred and Harry were unable to resist the instincts instilled by their own parents and life experiences with regard to education and thus kept the immigrant experience alive for their own children, Victor and Pauline had my grandfather working—without pay, starting from when he was only ten years old—at the family store, just as many immigrant children had done decades earlier. Granted, my grandfather did not need to drop out of school in order to do such a thing, and thanks to the movie theater right next door, he did at least get *something* out of the many Saturday evenings spent cleaning up the shop. On its own, this may have just been a sign of the times, a leftover relic from the immigrant generation. Unfortunately, however, it was, in hindsight, likely the first sign of a brewing problem at home.

Beginning around when he turned forty in the early 1950s, Victor began showing symptoms of severe depression. While at first one might be able to blame his depression on his dissatisfaction with his insurance collector job, forty just so happened to be about the same age his father had been when the financial wrongdoing around his business led him to suicide. Whether the two were connected or not, the late but very serious onset is certainly linked to his childhood trauma of losing his father. At first, the depression was somewhat manageable; his working hours became shorter, less reliable, and occasionally unpredictable, but he was still himself at work. But by the late 1950s, it had progressed to a point where Victor was essentially unable to work for weeks or months at a time—time that he would spend laying on the sofa, hardly getting up for days, and if he did get up, it was more often to anxiously pace the halls of his home than to groom himself or fix something to eat. Things were hardly made any better by a fire in November 1954 that left much of his shop in need of rebuilding just ahead of the busy Christmas shopping season.

It soon became clear that this was not merely depression but bipolar disorder. When the periods of mania came, they were anything but a relief; as is often the case with bipolar disorder, they were usually even worse than the periods of depression. If you were lucky, you might only get a well-intended but absurdly overzealous rant offering unsolicited advice to Martin Luther King Jr. in his pursuit for civil rights. Or if you were his brother, David, who lived and owned a paint store (yes, another one) nearby, you might have the pleasure of him bursting in at any odd hour of the day to offer, for certainly not the first (or last) time, his latest and greatest business idea to tear down the wall between your store and your neighbor's and build a paint empire.

But more often, Victor's mania had a dangerous paranoia attached to it, and indeed it is within his paranoia that we can see the traces of what had disturbed him so deeply in the first place. His paranoia would make him obsessively anxious that his business partners were plotting against him, that they were aiming to steal his interest in the store out from under him, and that he was not being paid the true amount that had been owed to him—all things that had happened to his father. He was worried that what had happened to his father would happen to him. This is the most tragic thing about Victor's story: he was a brilliant, charismatic, and compassionate man who had the great misfortune of undergoing a significant trauma at a young age and never dealing with it appropriately, leaving him struggling to cope with his childhood trauma for the rest of his life.

Unfortunately, Victor's mania led him to share these thoughts, with all the overconfidence and self-pity of a manic man, with whoever was around to hear. Even more unfortunately, the business partners he would so greatly fear were none other than his wife and his brother-in-law. Needless to say, this took a toll on his marriage, the success of the business, and his relationship with my grandfather, who certainly had nothing against either of his parents, and even less against his Uncle Itz.

As his condition continued to worsen, in 1960, Victor anointed my grandfather, then eighteen and a senior in high school, with the title of salesman and gave him additional stocking duties, a job my grandfather would worked on the weekends in addition to an after-school job at grocery store. Again, if it were not for the circumstances, this might not have been such a bad thing; after all, my grandfather learned a lot on the job from both his father and uncle. But the reality was that his father's mental health was spiraling out of control, and without my grandfather's help, the store could hardly operate—and then how would the family survive?

Victor Shiroff, 1960

It is a terribly tragic and truly unfair thing that Victor's entire life was defined by the trauma of his childhood. It is utterly heart wrenching to imagine him, only ten years and two months into his life, standing by his father's gravesite, on his father's own birthday, watching, heartbroken, as the coffin containing his beloved father descended into the Earth—and I was not even there. I cannot even begin to imagine the mental burden Victor carried with him through his entire life; it is impossible to blame him for his subsequent illness. But even though his illness was anything but his fault, and even though we really should feel sorry for him, Victor is not excused for failing—later outright refusing—to take his medication (of lithium, as was common at the time), craving instead the impossible combination of all the good things his mania gave him (the confidence, drive, and energy) without any of the downsides.

Almost inevitably, as his illness worsened, it slowly began cutting off those closest to him. First went his siblings. Victor had remained close with his siblings, even if they were all (except for Ned) probably closer to each other than they were to him. Nonetheless they held monthly gatherings well into the 1960s, dubbed the "Cousins Club," where they all got together at Fried's Restaurant or one of the siblings' homes, put on a baseball or football game, and enjoyed each other's company. In fact, my grandfather and his cousins were not the only cousins that attended the Cousins Clubs—Victor and his siblings' cousins, through their mother's side, attended too. Despite the fact that their mother had died over twenty years earlier and the fact that they unlikely saw their Lefcovitch—now Leftwich—cousins that often as children, they still kept in close touch with them; some, such as Morris, kept in touch with them for life.

But as fun as the Cousins Club could be, Victor's mental decline was problematic for his siblings. After all, they had seen most of this before in their oldest brother, Ned, after their father's death, and, likely as a result of that experience, they had little desire, energy, or interest in looking after Victor. To be fair, of course, by this point they all had their own families, careers, and personal lives to look after. Attempting to take care of an out-of-control man, who by this point was already refusing to take the medication offered to him, was not only the last thing they needed put onto their plate, but something they reasonably had no responsibility to deal with. Accordingly, Morris—who was still and would always remain the family's stand-in father figure—eventually told my grandfather the deal at some point in the early 1960s. "I've already dealt with this before," the conversation essentially went, "and I can't deal with it again. He's your father." (Victor's funeral three decades later attracted few attendees; among them were very, very few Shiroffs.)

After losing his siblings, next came his marriage. The unfortunate reality of Victor's trauma-inspired paranoia was that he was in business with his wife and his brother-in-law. If Itz were anyone other than his wife's brother, he could, in theory, tear his relationship with him to shreds with little consequence; instead, he was Pauline's beloved baby brother—there was no getting away with that. Nonetheless, Victor came to accuse many other relatives and in-laws of conspiring against him over time. On one occasion, Pauline's brother Frank—who had generously put him into business not once but twice—was visited by a severely manic Victor, who threated to report Frank to the IRS for cheating on his taxes. To be fair, Frank was indeed cheating on his taxes, but threatening a man who had done tremendous favors for Victor and who had lent him large sums of money was entirely uncalled for.[*]

Not even Pauline could avoid Victor's accusations of conspiring against him. But how could you share a dinner table with a man who thought you were out to steal everything from him, particularly when you still loved him dearly? And, of course, Pauline and their three children knew better than anyone else that Victor was more likely to destroy the business himself by abandoning it in favor of laying on the couch all day than he was to have it stolen from him. His marriage inevitably fell apart, and after Victor first moved out of the home during a manic period around 1963, Victor and Pauline were officially divorced during yet another manic period in February 1966.

As his relationship with his wife began to fall apart, Victor's relationship with his son became increasingly difficult. A divorce is never easy for any children involved, and it is certainly no easier when you are an employee of your father, who is the one suing for divorce, as part of a business collectively owned by your parents and uncle. Victor's illness, however, made any working relationship between him and my grandfather impossible. Their relationship hit a new low point when my grandfather expressed his disagreement with some stance his father had taken during the divorce process. Appalled, Victor demanded his son take it back, apologize, and go home for the day; confused, my

---

[*] Frank conducted a cash-only business specifically so he could report nonsense revenue numbers on his taxes. This was not the only way in which he had bent the law, nor was it probably the most serious offense—he made his fortune during the Second World War by skirting clothing rations at his store in Chester, which at the time was near a major navy base and dockyards.

grandfather refused. Likely feeling betrayed and as if his paranoia had been justified, Victor threatened to call the cops and report my grandfather for trespassing; my grandfather stood his ground. Unfortunately, Victor was serious, and to this day this remains the only occasion my grandfather was escorted to a police station. Needless to say, he hardly spent any time there. This incident, however, particularly after having already spent an entire decade living with his father's illness, marked the beginning of the end of my grandfather's relationship with his father. Victor was allowed to meet my father, his first-born grandson, and my next-oldest uncle on one occasion, when both were too young to remember it, but after that, never again.

In a clever move by Victor's lawyer to slip a clause into the divorce settlement that effectively entitled him to a considerable payout of his share of the Allen's Men's Shop he co-owned with Pauline and Itz, Victor managed to profit greatly from his divorce. He subsequently squandered the entirety of the proceeds nonetheless. Now living in Bustleton, six miles north of his ex-wife and children on Gilham Street, he appears to have used the money to establish the wryly named Victor-Allen men's clothing store in February 1968; Samuel Tabbey, his sister Estelle's longtime partner with a family of his own, signed off as solicitor on the registration. Perhaps because of Victor's comfort working in poor Black neighborhoods going back to his days as an insurance collector or out of his now-signature cash-strapped recklessness—or both—Victor-Allen opened in Kensington—a particularly impoverished neighborhood of Philadelphia. Whether due to a lack of customers or of proper management, Victor-Allen only made it eighteen months before Victor declared bankruptcy and Victor-Allen's inventory was sold at auction. Just to add to the chaos, Victor, likely in another manic period, remarried only a few months before the bankruptcy—to another Pauline, no less. This Pauline owned a card and gift shop in Feltonville, a neighborhood immediately south of Olney; the shop gave Victor, as my grandfather put it, "a place to spend a few hours 'being the boss,' and someone to live with."

It seems that Victor's condition stabilized somewhat for at least a few years in the 1970s, during which he managed to become the president of the Feltonville Business Association. In a display of who he really was at heart, Victor became closely involved with the Entrepreneurial Development Training Center, a North Philadelphia organization established to help train minority (mostly Black) business owners in the art of running a business.[354] Without charge, Victor gave twice-weekly lectures on self-owned businesses at the EDTC. An article in the *Jewish Exponent* said that he "looks forward to the day when white and black businessmen can work side by side in all neighborhoods," and tells of how he generously stepped in when a Black-owned store in the EDTC's training complex became short-staffed ahead of Easter.[355]

Before long, however, Victor entered another period of instability, which cost him his marriage yet again. He consequently fell into a period of poor health until his brother David—who had similarly looked after Ned, the other excommunicated member of the family—found him dead in his apartment on January 8, 1991. Victor lived a truly unfair, unfortunate, and tragic life, all stemming from the terrible hand he was dealt at only ten years of age. At the same time, while he truly did deserve better, he still should have taken better care of himself, if only for his family's sake. I hope that my telling of his life does him sufficient justice; may his soul be bound in the bundle of life.

On to the Third Generation

To some extent, many second-generation Jewish immigrants wound up raising their children under many of the same conditions in which they themselves had been raised by their immigrant parents. In one way or another, they typically managed to instill some aspects of the immigrant experience—which they had known quite well through their own upbringings—into the next generation's lives. Of course, this much more commonly resembled the parenting style of my grandmother's parents,

Mildred and Harry, than the psychiatric problems that tore Victor's life apart. But all essentially had the same effect: the children of many second-generation Jewish immigrants would still grow up in the immigrant world.

We should be careful, however, not to conflate the "immigrant world," which the second half of this book is concerned with, with the world the Jewish immigrants left behind in the Pale, the topic of the first half. The immigrant world I refer to here is the world described over the previous four chapters, the world that, at least for Philadelphia's immigrant Jews, was in peak form between 1890 and 1925. But even if many immigrants kept one foot firmly set in each world, they were certainly not the same. Life in the Pale was unimaginably different from life in the Jewish quarter, even if many of the quarter's inhabitants could not help but notice the somewhat similar living conditions. Even at its peak, with more than one hundred synagogues, one hundred thousand residents, and uncountable other Jewish institutions of all varieties, the Jewish quarter was not a pocket enclave of the Jewish Eastern Europe in Philadelphia. In this way, Philadelphia was quite unlike London. As discussed in Chapter 4, London's Jewish community, while absolutely massive, largely kept to itself. From clothing to religious observance, London's Jewish immigrants generally preferred to retain their customs from home. Contemporary observers often felt as if they were in a foreign country; as David Englander put it, "Immigrant Jews, it seemed, lived within English society but were not part of it."[356] While contemporary Philadelphians could surely tell the Jewish quarter apart from any other part of Philadelphia, it never felt as "foreign" to non-Jewish contemporaries as London's Jewish quarter did. With its capitalistic work ethic, deification of the public school (even if more for their sons than their daughters), and the democratic, cosmopolitan, industrialized, and modern society that surrounded it, the Jewish quarter was quite unlike the world many of its inhabitants had been born into but quite like the typical urban environment in early twentieth-century America.

The economic and societal traits of the immigrant world more or less dictated behavior within it. It was the immigrant world's impoverishment and adoration of education that forced many daughters, and sometimes sons, out of school and into the workforce, often before they even reached high school; it was the immigrant world's difficult economic realities that led to overworked parents who were neither home nor energized enough to find the time to transmit to their children the entirety of the Jewish world that had been passed down to them by their own parents. It was not necessarily the case that the immigrants wanted these kinds of outcomes for their children—there was just hardly any other way. Work also left the immigrant generation with hardly any choice but to accept dramatic reforms to the practice of their religion. Working on the Sabbath became normalized; synagogue attendance declined dramatically, and most children received hardly any of the religious education their parents (at least their fathers) had. Many renegotiated their identity through a secular approach to Judaism, whereby they could continue to enjoy the familiar cultural comforts and feel a sense of community with their Jewish peers, but without necessarily being tied down to the religious requirements of Judaism.

For their children, however, experiences from within the immigrant world were often carried with them for life; indeed, many set them up for nearly inescapable predetermined futures. Those who had been forced out of school and into work, for example, often remained in working- or lower-middle-class occupations for life—as Jacob Wexler can attest—and only the lucky married out of their class. For the vast majority without college degrees, white-collar jobs were typically (though not always) out of reach; not until after the Second World War did this change. Accordingly, the long hours that defined work for the first-generation immigrants continued for many of their children. At the same time, however, their nearly incessant exposure to Jewish culture growing up in the Jewish quarter meant that while many grew up without the same religious devotion as their parents or grandparents, they still carried an attachment to Jewishness—*Yiddishkeit*—with them for life. For many in this generation, it wasn't abnormal to rarely attend synagogue but still keep a kosher kitchen at home.

In many ways, while the second-generation immigrants had taken a step out of the immigrant world, the immigrant child experience still remained deeply engrained within them. Thus they, too, inevitably passed on their experiences down to their children, the immigrant generation's grandchildren. This was the case even though my grandparents grew up far outside of the Jewish quarter, despite the fact that their parents were perfectly fluent in the English language and they personally knew relatively few members of the first generation.* Even though they never knew the immigrant world themselves, the immigrant generation's grandchildren were very much raised and shaped under its influence.

Perhaps a beautiful example of the hold of the immigrant world on the second generation can be found in the reason the first time my grandfather stepped foot inside a zoo didn't happen until he was in his sixties. My parents were taking my sister and me to the Philadelphia Zoo and invited my grandparents to come along. They did, but with some hesitation from my grandfather because, as he explained, his mother, Pauline, had told him he should never go to the zoo. As a good, obedient boy, he never questioned her, hence no zoo trips, even with his own sons when they were little. As an adult, he was too busy to think about why

---

* While my grandmother knew all four of her grandparents, only one of my grandfather's grandparents, Pauline's mother, Esther, was alive by the time of his birth. My grandfather knew her relatively well and cared for her as she grew old. I still find it amazing that my grandfather, who I know well, knew his grandmother well—a woman who almost certainly knew her grandfather, Froim Rubin Knobel, born way back in Staszów in 1806.

she had put in the command, but in a conversation with my great-aunt Joyce when I was an adult, I learned the "rationale" behind the reason.

It seems Pauline's oldest daughter, Florence, had gone to the zoo on a school trip and a few days later she came down with scarlet fever. The whole house was put in quarantine—with an uncle delivering kosher meat in secret so Pauline could still continue to cook for her family. In Pauline's old-world view, one where the question of which animals were "clean" or "unclean" was an extremely serious spiritual matter, of course a zoo filled with exotic animals could be the cause of scarlet fever. She blamed Florence's illness on that field trip and forbade her other two children to ever step foot in the zoo. The family had dabbled in that American thing, and, well, it didn't work out. No need to try it again.

While holding onto old fears and beliefs, it was also exactly this extension and legacy of the immigrant experience that essentially confirmed the changes and transformations within Judaism and Jewish life that came with immigration. Since it had largely been the realities of immigrant life that had led to such evolution in the first place, it is no surprise that the second generation, still stuck in the immigrant world in many ways, not only carried on with the adaptations their parents had made but also continued to make adaptations themselves. Even if they had loosened up their observation of Shabbat, for example, it is impossible to imagine the Wexlers allowing Mildred a bacon pot even though Mildred kept one in her home for her children many years later. But Mildred was still not out of the woods yet herself: after all, the bacon pot was the exception to her otherwise-kosher household, and, like many Jewish immigrant mothers, likely including her own, she was not particularly affectionate toward her children.

But as each generation stood on more solid financial ground than the one before it, over time many parents found themselves more able (and perhaps willing) to attend synagogue and to provide their children with a Jewish education. An intense wave of synagogue building, motivated in part by the need to populate the newly settled suburbs with places of worship and communal gathering, took place just after the end of the Second World War, during which came improvements in synagogue membership and attendance. The number of children receiving any kind of a Jewish education, once a miserable statistic in the 1920s and '30s, doubled to more than half a million students over the course of the 1950s.

This rediscovered interest in Jewish religious life had its limits, however. Even though synagogue attendance was up, *regular* attendance was not—one 1950s survey of Detroit found that only 26 percent of Jews attended weekly services, compared to 69 percent of Catholics. This was not, however, a trend exclusive to more lax denominations, namely Reform Judaism. Another survey from the same decade found that only a quarter of Orthodox children wished to remain Orthodox and that half planned to turn Conservative (which, by the 1970s, had indeed occurred). In lieu of synagogue attendance but nonetheless inspired by the greater number of synagogues and an increased likelihood of having received anything of a Jewish education, many households came to look like the ones my grandparents grew up in. Hannukah candles would be lit and Passover observed, and the High Holidays were marked in at least some way, but careful observance of the Sabbath and of the kosher dietary laws slipped away (the bacon pot!). Despite all the new synagogues, most truly preferred to conduct their religious affairs at home, something they likely had become accustomed to in their own upbringing.

The dramatic increase in the uptake of Jewish education was not necessarily a sign of a revival of Jewish life either. With higher enrollment need not come higher quality, and many of the educations received in this era weren't all too much better than those offered by the bar mitzvah factories in Chapter 8. Moreover, in another example of how strong the hold of the immigrant world—and, indeed, the influence of their parents' and grandparents' lives in the Pale—remained even in this era, religious education generally continued to be a privilege reserved for boys. While my grandfather was among the hundreds of thousands of young Jews attending Hebrew school in the 1950s, neither of his two sisters, my grandmother, her sister, or many millions of Jewish girls were. The bat mitzvah, then about three decades old, evidently still had some distance to go in terms of acceptance and prevalence.

Even the movement of secular Judaism was challenged in this period. Whatever organized structure the movement had built up in the preceding decades soon collapsed after a number of significant hits to the validity of its ideology and messaging. First and perhaps most dramatically was the shock of the Nazis and the Holocaust, which naturally inspired many questions about the nature of mankind, specifically mankind without the guidance of God or a religious code of ethics and morality. Then came disturbing news from the flagrantly atheist Soviet Union of purges and persecution targeted toward its Jews, many of whom suffered greatly under Stalin and his Gulags; the association of the Soviet Union with secularism, coupled with the then-recent evidence from Nazi Germany of how badly Jews suffered in allegedly secular states, did significant damage to the secular movement. Then, with the onset of McCarthyism in the 1950s, the very usage of the world "secular" could attract unwanted attention, given its associations with the Soviet Union. The ideas of the movement, of course, remained subconsciously popular, but most organized efforts at propelling it forward struggled in the second half of the century.[357]

This was a world in which many of the ideas of secular Judaism were accepted by many suburban Jews even as they continued to build new synagogues seemingly without end; where the rules around the Sabbath could be bent on demand even as more Jewish parents than ever saw providing their children with a Jewish education, presumably one that taught their children about the laws surrounding the Sabbath, as crucial. This was the world in which Jews, once among the least likely to marry outside of their own faith, soon became among the most likely, even as many, especially after the Six-Day War in 1967, felt an increased attachment to the Jewish community, now including Israel. This was a world in which many Jewish households began to let go of the kosher dietary laws in favor of placing increased importance upon the core Jewish holidays—quite possibly doing more than they had ever seen their own parents do—and who gave a whole new life to Hannukah, in part to ensure that their children would have something to hold on to from a young age.

This was a world that, quite evidently, remained quite influenced by the experience of life in the Jewish quarter and of life in Eastern Europe.

It was also the world in which my grandparents and their Jewish peers grew up. Even though by this time, most, including my grandparents, grew up nowhere near the Jewish quarter, their parents' minds were, to some extent, still trapped within it, quite like many others in their generation. The process of intergenerational cultural transmission and evolution continued accordingly. Like so many of their generation, my grandparents inherited their parents' Jewishness as well as their rendition of Judaism: the holidays were always celebrated, and their three sons each attended Hebrew school and became bar mitzvah, while so much of the culture—particularly the food—is still enjoyed to this day.

At the same time, the first date my grandfather took my grandmother on is as representative of our imagination of the 1960s as it is representative of the continuing transformation of Jewish life in America: they went to a burger joint after a movie, where they both ordered bacon cheeseburgers—just about the most non-kosher thing one could eat!

Despite her difficult upbringing and all the chaos in her family's life in the 1950s and 1960s, Pauline was, by all accounts, an outstanding grandmother.

Victor adjusted well into the grandfather role, until his illness got too out of control.

Left: my great-grandfather, Harry Rabinowitz, and my dad.
Right: Mildred Wexler holding my dad (her grandson), next to her father, Jacob.
Both photos from around 1970.

AFTERWORD

A century on from the end of the mass-migration era, where do the descendants of Jewish immigrants from Eastern Europe stand in America? Were those opposed to emigration in the first part of this book correct? Did America turn out to be the place where Judaism and Jewishness disappeared?

In 2020, a survey conducted by the Pew Research Center found that America was home to approximately 5.8 million Jews, roughly two-thirds of whom—about four million—consider themselves Ashkenazi.[358] While not all Ashkenazi Jews living in the United States are descendants of the two million immigrants who fled from Eastern Europe as seen in the first part of this book, the vast majority of them undoubtedly are. Not included in these figures, however, are 2.8 million Americans who had at least one Jewish parent or some sort of a Jewish upbringing but do not identify as Jewish—or perhaps as uniquely Jewish—today, as well as another 1.4 million who had neither Jewish parents nor a Jewish upbringing but still identify as Jewish in some way, even if not religiously. Even when excluding these two groups, America today is home to more Jews than the Russian Empire ever was.

It should go without saying that America has also been an unimaginably better place for Jews to live than the Russian Empire was, or indeed the Soviet Union was during the entire course of its existence. There are so many reasons for this, many of which we have explored in the second half of this book; perhaps they can be summarized as the combination of America's Western, capitalist, democratic, open, and (at least formerly) cosmopolitan values and nature. America was a place where an immigrant from an obscure shtetl in northeastern Ukraine could go from rags to riches in less than a decade; it was a place where the religious were welcome to practice as they saw fit, even if the economic demands got in the way; it was a place where even if discrimination still occurred and antisemitism could still be found, the threat of physical violence of the sort seen in the pogroms in Eastern Europe was all but nonexistent. It was a place where Jews could—and did—become involved in community and civic life, and not only in Jewish communities but in the nation at large.

With all this, of course, came what one might call the *renegotiation* (or, more provocatively, the *reconstruction*) of Jewish identity in America, which was the main theme of the second half of this book. The new economic, social, and cultural setting of America meant new constraints for Jewish life and identity to exist within. It was also true that many of the constraints that kept Jewish life intact in Eastern Europe were also no longer in place in America. Given the new setting and its coexisting new freedoms and constraints, over the course of the first half of the twentieth century, many American Jews came to accept the separation of Judaism and Jewishness as valid. Many turned toward secular Judaism, preferring to center their identity on their parents' and ancestors' cultural customs and traditions rather than their religion. But rather than dropping Judaism entirely, most continued to find a place in their lives for at least some aspects of the Jewish faith. Many of the core holidays were still marked, many of the life cycle events—bar mitzvahs, weddings, *shivah*—still observed, and many of the traditional recipes still cooked in kitchens with two sinks and two sets of dishes.

I would like to conclude this book with three comments. The first concerns the facts summarized so far. Far from having abandoned the civilization of their Eastern European ancestors, American Jews have successfully continued to keep Jewish life and culture alive and well. There are, of course, those who regret what they see as the transition of Jewish American identity into a much more mainstream American one, perhaps because American Jews today work with too many non-Jewish peers, marry non-Jewish partners, or send their children to secular schools. They might not necessarily mind secular Judaism all too much, but they certainly see these things as proof that it has gone too far; as a result, they worry that Judaism and Jewish life in as a whole in America is doomed to disappear.

What these people might not realize, however, is that even though these trends are all present and perhaps even prominent in modern Jewish American life, the median Jew regularly attending synagogue is younger than the median regular churchgoer, and the majority of synagogues today are either growing or maintaining their membership.[359] Especially in the digital age, where somehow we all feel less connected even though it is easier to connect with each other than ever before, my sense is that many long for the feeling of Jewish community that, in some sense, has had a hard time fully reestablishing itself in the suburbs in most cases. While it is certainly true that the rise of institutions like the Jewish Community Centers—which, as we saw earlier, were already deemed necessary early in the twentieth century, long before Jews moved into the suburbs—has provided crucial support to local Jewish communities, these institutions have not proved themselves to be sufficient replacements as the center of local Jewish life. This might not be all too surprising in a world where bar mitzvah factories still exist (in some sense at least) and where some parents seemingly feel as if sending their children off to a nominally Jewish summer camp or to Israel on birthright will provide them with a sufficient dose of Jewishness to feel properly and immutably Jewish.

The reality, however, is that culture is lived, not sampled. My genuine sense, somewhat backed by the Pew Research poll referenced above, is that the rise in synagogue attendance among younger generations can be at least partially attributed to a desire for those who consider themselves Jewish to any extent to complete what feels like an incomplete revelation of the Jewish civilization within them. To the extent that Jewish secularism has "gone too far" or has doomed American Judaism to disappear, it is true that some of secularism's adherents may have very well forgotten that while it may be perfectly valid to emphasize the importance of culture over religion, one must still actually emphasize the importance of culture. But the very fact that those who at least try to do so still send their children to Hebrew school—yes, quite often factories more than genuine learning environments—in preparation of bar or bat mitzvahs is proof that modern American Judaism is interested in preserving its own existence. As our human search for community grows more important in an increasingly online and isolated world, I would not be surprised if we see a revitalization of Jewish communal life, one truly centered around the preservation of Jewish civilization—indeed, I think this is already ongoing, given the growing synagogue membership mentioned above.

My second comment is that we should not necessarily regard the story of the transformation of Jewish life in America as unique or without precedent in Jewish history. While this book began in Eastern Europe and then followed the ways in which Jewish life took on new forms in America, had I written this book two centuries ago, I very well might have set its beginning in Germany or the Ottoman Empire and then traced the ways in which Jewish life evolved in Poland-Lithuania or the Russian Empire. I could have also begun it five centuries ago in Spain and Portugal and then watched as the descendants of those exiled from the Iberian peninsula rediscovered and sometimes reinvented their ancestors' religion in Amsterdam or in the colonial New World. Indeed, I could have started with an exposition of life in Jerusalem two millennia ago and then watched as the Jewish people narrowly escaped from the aftermath of the destruction of the Second Temple, which began the Diaspora that has ever since defined Jewish history.

On each of these occasions, things changed. To borrow yet again from the thinking of Rabbi Mordecai Kaplan, whose daughter we saw (quite controversially) become the first bat mitzvah in the United States, it is important to note that it was human beings themselves—the Jewish people—who "made history," so to speak.

Every time the Jewish people first arrived somewhere new, whether it was Spain, Amsterdam, Poland-Lithuania, or anywhere else, they inevitably adapted to their new environment. After all, what else would have inspired early Reform Jews in Germany to bring the organ into the synagogue? Why else would Ashkenazi cooking have much more in common with Eastern European cuisine than with Sephardic cooking? The attributes of the Jewish faith and the interpretations of its laws were not immune to this process either and could vary greatly from place to place. This was true even in Europe: one of the reasons behind the proliferation of country-specific and often even town-specific synagogues in the United States was to ensure everyone could find a service performed as they were used to back home.

It is important to note that this is not a new or original point, nor is it a realization that came only with the establishment of Eastern European Jewish life in America. Ahad Ha'am (born Asher Hirsch Ginsberg just southwest of Kyiv in 1856), a great influence on Mordecai Kaplan, saw nothing inherently wrong with Jews engaging with and adapting to the culture around them. Rather than this always taking the form of Jews assimilating to the world around them, Ha'am saw many cases in Jewish history in which Jews not just adapted local customs and ideas but actually Judaized them and made them their own. He gave one example of how the Egyptian Jews of Alexandria absorbed and transformed Greek thought but didn't assimilate:

> Long before the Hellenists in Palestine tried to substitute Greek Culture for Judaism, the Jews of Egypt had come into close contact with the Greeks—with their life, their spirit, and their philosophy—yet we do not find

among them any pronounced movement toward assimilation. On the contrary, they employed their Greek knowledge as an instrument for revealing the essential spirit of Judaism, for showing the world its beauty, and vindicating it against the proud philosophy of Greece.[360]

Rather than being unique to Jewish American history, this sort of evolution and change has always been a feature of Jewish life, and our understanding of Jewish life must accept that. This is usually dangerous territory for mere mortals to wander around in, but if we absolutely must think about what it means to be Jewish, the answer should reflect the immutable essence underlying Judaism, the innermost attributes that have sustained the Jewish people for several millennia. Rather than specifying a particular style of observance and religious practice—which quite likely are much newer traditions than you might think—one might, for example, consider the ethical and moral codes, the vast majority of which are exactly as applicable and relevant today as when they were written down centuries—or millennia—ago. As was consistently made clear by Kaplan, to whom much of this way of thinking is owed, this is not at all suggesting that there is no role for religious observance in Jewish life today. I only suggest that we should expect and respect the fact that religious observance and the practice of Judaism might look very different to different people. Arguments about who are "good Jews" or "bad Jews" are not only futile but counterproductive, harmful, and often nonsensical in historical context.

I see this as going hand in hand with my previous point about the importance of genuinely emphasizing the importance of Jewish civilization. One of the most remarkable things about the Jewish people is that even after thousands of years of persecution in a nearly constant state of Diaspora, they have nonetheless survived. Some part of this must be attributed to their unique, beautiful, and sometimes even revolutionary thinking about the world and humanity's place within it. We have a lot to learn from Judaism's several thousand years of writings.

My final remark is that American Jews should not forget that they are the descendants of immigrants, the vast majority of whom were refugees fleeing deep poverty and ethnic or political violence. They should not forget that most Americans, at the time of their ancestors' arrival, would have likely considered them "undesirable" for one reason or another, or that practically none knew the English language or had any modern industrial skills and that they brought what was seen as a very foreign culture along with them. They should not forget that their parents and grandparents only ever existed because their parents were lucky enough to come to America before immigration was closed off; had they waited too long or never left at all, most of our ancestors would have been additional victims in any one of the numerous atrocities committed in the twentieth century in Eastern Europe.

Time and time again, the Torah implores its readers to treat foreigners living within their country kindly, as the Jews had once been foreigners in Egypt. We must remember to do this today, when immigration to the United States has once again become extraordinary difficult and, at the same time, a topic of intense and often nonsensical political debate. This is unfortunate for everyone. Many fleeing violence, poverty, and persecution today—including those hoping to escape the war in Ukraine—find many more barriers in the way than my—and likely your—ancestors did a century ago. In some cases, even seeking refuge in America is impossible. While a combined two and a half million immigrants were let into America in 1906 and 1907 (about 3 percent of the nation's total population at the time), between 2019 and 2021, America's foreign-born population increased by about a third of a million—about a tenth of a percent of the population then. And while the total number of immigrants living in the United States has grown quite a bit, from about fifteen million in 1920 to forty-five million in

2021, the foreign-born share of the total population remains below its 1890–1910 peak.[361]

This is not the first time we have taken a restrictive approach to immigration policy; as we saw in Chapter 6, America followed a similar approach of seeking neutrality and avoiding an inflow of "undesirable," "dangerous," or "poor" immigrants in the years leading up to the Second World War. Strict adherence to this policy meant that ships full of Jewish refugees fleeing Nazi Germany were sent right back to Germany, where few were lucky enough to get another chance to escape. On the other hand, natives of the destination country miss out too. Jewish immigrants, as we have seen, were eager to get involved in the American economic machine, both as workers and entrepreneurs. With time, some immigrants (or their descendants) became extraordinarily influential in the public sphere, ranging from politicians (Bernie Sanders, Joe Lieberman) to scientists (J. Robert Oppenheimer, Carl Sagan) to economists (Milton Friedman, Paul Krugman). I deliberately said nothing about them in the text, as my goal was to keep this a story about "ordinary" immigrants, but a number of Jews became prominent and well known in the Hollywood film industry. Could you imagine American popular culture today without Warner Bros. Studios, founded by the children of Jewish immigrants from Poland? What about without the contributions of Jerry Seinfeld, Larry David, or the Zucker brothers—all descendants of Eastern European Jews who came to America!

In a country with a population density that is less than a third of France's and only a sixth of Germany's, we can surely afford to take in more people from all over the world. It will always be the case that those born in countries other than our own will be different from us. But this was no different a century ago. What's more important is that both now and then, we already have so much in common. Indeed, regardless of differing countries of origin, religion, or ethnicity, those yearning to come to America today are motivated by the same thing that inspired our own ancestors to head out on their incredible journeys over a century ago: the search for a better, safer, and more comfortable life—and not just for themselves but for their posterity too.

Acknowledgments

As a non-historian and as someone too young to have known the vast majority of the people in this book, I am deeply thankful for so many who helped make this work possible.

First and foremost, I must thank my grandparents for opening up and sharing so many invaluable stories about their childhoods and their parents, many of which I had never heard before. I am beyond grateful to have had so many long conversations with them in the course of writing this book.

I must also thank their siblings—Joyce, Florence, and Carole—for sharing their memories with me, as well as my father's cousin Beth, with whom I was able to (somewhat deviously!) recover a number of photos of Victor and Pauline Shiroff.

Special thanks go to Herb and Andrea Shiroff for providing me with truly invaluable photographs of Harry and Fannie Shiroff (the only ones I am aware of) and for their hospitality during a visit in March 2023, as well as to Robert and Angie Shiroff for sharing a wealth of family photographs and genealogical notes.

I am very grateful for all the stories about the Rabinowitz-Schusterman family shared by Pat and Shelley (along with my grandmother and her sister Carole) at a Mother's Day gathering in 2022, especially as Shelley—my grandmother's first cousin—passed away only a few months later. May her memory be a blessing.

I owe many thanks to a number of distant relatives I only know thanks to the wonders of DNA testing. Ron James generously provided me with a number of wonderful anecdotes on the Waxman-Tyszgarten family and also put me in touch with Lawrence Brown, who passed along fascinating information about the Waxman relatives who went to the United Kingdom (of whom he is a descendant) rather than America. I must also thank Sylvia and Kathy, two DNA matches without whom I would have never been able to link the Lefcovitch family to Gąbin, nor would I have ever known about the Lazarus family.

As every Jewish genealogist finds out relatively quickly, records from the Old World are not always so easy to come by—in fact, their existence and availability is often the exception rather than the rule. I would have absolutely no precise information about my family's origins in Eastern Europe without the incredible work done by JewishGen and JRI-Poland, which have preserved, digitally archived, and indexed millions of Jewish records from all over the world (and continue to do so at a truly admirable pace). In addition to their many volunteers, I must thank Jean-Pierre Stroweis at JRI-Poland for assisting me in obtaining copies of a few records that were indexed on their website but were without accompanying scans. He coordinated with a volunteer who went to the archives in Sandomierz, Poland, just to scan these documents for me (without which I could not have confirmed the parents of Leizer Tyszgarten, Eva Knobel's husband).

This book also benefited greatly from a number of records stored in Philadelphia's City Archives, where I received incredible assistance from Kenneth Rice. A number of records obtained from City Hall also proved indispensable: the tragic detail of Fannie's wedding bands being among her few remaining possessions at the time of her death is only known to me thanks to probate records (nearly a century old!) dug up by City Hall. I am also grateful for the research assistance provided by the staff at the Pennsylvania State Archives, who exhausted every last possibility to help me find records pertaining to Fannie's Pennsylvania Supreme Court case.

Many thanks go to several friends and colleagues who took interest in this work and with whom I am grateful to have had many conversations that helped me think more clearly about many of the ideas and stories that went into this book. I am especially grateful for the very thoughtful comments and useful feedback provided by Jason Meyer, who so kindly offered to read a draft copy of this book. His perspective was invaluable in ensuring this could be something anyone could read and get something out of, and I am very thankful for him sharing it with me.

Of course, the most special thanks go to my family, who have put up with my tireless research and perpetual question-asking at every family gathering since I started my research. I've said it already, but I can't say it enough: this book would have been impossible without the hours and hours of conversations my grandparents so generously had with me.

This book also benefited greatly from the advice and editing of my mother, whose comments and suggestions have made it much more clean, focused, and polished than it ever could have been otherwise. I am also immensely grateful to my father, who made sure I would know and forever remember my great-grandfather thanks to our weekly visits (and for setting such a great example, through those trips and as always).

I must also offer posthumous thanks to my great-grandfather, whose fascinating stories and anecdotes from his life inspired my interest in genealogy as a child. May his memory be a blessing.

Finally, last but certainly not least, I thank Jenna for not only tolerating my obsessive work on this book for two years but also for engaging with it and encouraging me along the way. Talking through my early thoughts on many of the points and arguments in this book with her kept so many of them from being entirely unclear, pointless, incoherent, or boring. I cannot imagine having completed this book without her endless support.

ABOUT THE AUTHOR

Taylor Shiroff is an economic research analyst and an avid armchair historian. Taylor's interest in his family's history began when he was a small child listening to the stories his great-grandfather told over Sunday lunches. Years later, as an adult, he had questions about his ancestors, but with the passing of his great-grandfather, he discovered his living relatives couldn't answer them. So he began researching for the answers himself.

He is a graduate of Rutgers University (New Brunswick) and currently lives in Cleveland, Ohio, where he spends his free time playing drums and guitar (and, of course, doing genealogical research).

You can learn more about him and his research at http://www.TaylorShiroff.com.

NOTES AND REFERENCES

Introduction

[1] "American Jewish Year Book: 1925-1926," American Jewish Yearbook (American Jewish Committee, 1924), https://ajcarchives.org/AJC_DATA/Files/1925_1926_7_Statistics.pdf.

[2] Mary Antin and Werner Sollors, *The Promised Land*, Penguin Classics (New York: Peguin Books, 2012), 9.

[3] Howe, *World of Our Fathers: The Journey of the Eastern European Jews to America and the Life They Found and Made*, 5.

[4] "The Pale of Settlement," Jewish Virtual Library, accessed July 7, 2022, https://www.jewishvirtuallibrary.org/the-pale-of-settlement; Jewish Virtual Library, "Vital Statistics: Jewish Population of the World," Jewish Virtual Library, n.d., https://www.jewishvirtuallibrary.org/jewish-population-of-the-world#europe; Jewish Virtual Library, "Russia," Jewish Virtual Library, accessed July 5, 2022, https://www.jewishvirtuallibrary.org/russia-virtual-jewish-history-tour; Michael Lipka, "The Continuing Decline of Europe's Jewish Population," *Pew Research Center* (blog), accessed July 7, 2022, https://www.pewresearch.org/fact-tank/2015/02/09/europes-jewish-population/.

[5] "Jewish Losses during the Holocaust: By Country," United States Holocaust Memorial Museum, accessed July 7, 2022, https://encyclopedia.ushmm.org/content/en/article/jewish-losses-during-the-holocaust-by-country.

[6] Howe, 26; "American Jewish Year Book: 1913-1914," American Jewish Yearbook (American Jewish Committee, 1913), https://ajcarchives.org/AJC_DATA/Files/1913_1914_8_Statistics.pdf.

⁷ Sergi Mikolaïovitch Plokhi, *The Gates of Europe: A History of Ukraine*, Revised edition (New York (N.Y.): Basic Books, 2021), 18; Israel Bartal, "The Establishment of East European Jewry," in *The Cambridge History of Judaism*, ed. Jonathan Karp and Adam Sutcliffe, 1st ed. (Cambridge University Press, 2017), 228, https://doi.org/10.1017/9781139017169.010; Jewish Virtual Library, "Russia."

⁸ See, for example: Doron M. Behar et al., "No Evidence from Genome-Wide Data of a Khazar Origin for the Ashkenazi Jews," *Human Biology* 85, no. 6 (December 2013): 859–900, https://doi.org/10.3378/027.085.0604; Gil Atzmon et al., "Abraham's Children in the Genome Era: Major Jewish Diaspora Populations Comprise Distinct Genetic Clusters with Shared Middle Eastern Ancestry," *The American Journal of Human Genetics* 86, no. 6 (June 2010): 850–59, https://doi.org/10.1016/j.ajhg.2010.04.015; Doron M. Behar et al., "Multiple Origins of Ashkenazi Levites: Y Chromosome Evidence for Both Near Eastern and European Ancestries," *The American Journal of Human Genetics* 73, no. 4 (October 2003): 768–79, https://doi.org/10.1086/378506.

⁹ Haim Hillel Ben-Sasson, "Expulsions of Jews," Jewish Virtual Library, 2008, https://www.jewishvirtuallibrary.org/expulsions.

¹⁰ Norman Davies, *God's Playground: A History of Poland: Volume I: The Origins to 1795*, Rev. ed, vol. 1 (New York: Columbia University Press, 2005), 78.

¹¹ Israel Bartal, *The Jews of Eastern Europe, 1772-1881*, Jewish Culture and Contexts (Philadelphia: University of Pennsylvania Press, 2005), 14–18; Davies, *God's Playground*, 2005, 1:66, 104; Shmuel Ettinger, "Jewish Participation in the Settlement of Ukraine," in *Ukrainian-Jewish Relations in Historical Perspective*, ed. Peter J. Potichnyj and Howard Aster, Second Edition (Edmonton: Canadian Institute of Ukrainian Studies, 1990); Bartal, "The Establishment of East European Jewry," 229.

¹² Bartal, "The Establishment of East European Jewry," 229–30; Gershon David Hundert, *Jews in Poland-Lithuania in the Eighteenth Century: A Genealogy of Modernity*, S. Mark Taper Foundation Imprint in Jewish Studies (Berkeley: University of California Press, 2004), 22–24.

¹³ Jewish Virtual Library, "Russia"; Ettinger, "Jewish Participation in the Settlement of Ukraine"; Research Directorate, Immigration and Refugee Board, Canada, "Jews in Russia and the Soviet Union: Chronology of Events:

1727 - 1 January 1992," November 1, 1994, https://www.refworld.org/docid/3ae6a865c.html.

[14] Nicholas V. Riasanovsky and Mark D. Steinberg, *A History of Russia*, Ninth edition (New York: Oxford University Press, 2019), 155, 235-39, 294; Plokhi, *The Gates of Europe*, 114-15; Timothy Snyder, *The Reconstruction of Nations: Poland, Ukraine, Lithuania, Belarus, 1569 - 1999* (New Haven, Conn.: Yale University Press, 2003); Orlando Figes, *The Story of Russia*, First edition (New York: Metropolitan Books/Henry Holt and Company, 2022), 125-26.

[15] Hundert, *Jews in Poland-Lithuania in the Eighteenth Century*, 22-24; Norman Davies, *God's Playground: A History of Poland: Volume II: 1795 to the Present*, Rev. ed, vol. 2 (New York: Columbia University Press, 2005), 176. Number takes Raphael Mahler's figure for the Jewish population in 1764-65 (750,000) and assumes a moderate 1.6% annual growth rate over the next 35 years.

[16] John Klier, "Pale of Settlement," YIVO Encyclopedia of Jews in Eastern Europe, September 14, 2010, https://yivoencyclopedia.org/article.aspx/Pale_of_Settlement.

Chapter 2

[17] Yohanan Petrovsky-Shtern, *The Golden Age Shtetl: A New History of Jewish Life in East Europe*, First paperback printing (Princeton Oxford: Princeton University Press, 2015), 32.

[18] Paul Robert Magocsi and Ĭokhanan Petrovskiĭ-Shtern, *Jews and Ukrainians: A Millennium of Co-Existence* (Toronto, Ontario: Distributed by the University of Toronto Press for the Chair of Ukrainian Studies, University of Toronto, 2016), 38.

[19] Benjamin Nathans, *Beyond the Pale: The Jewish Encounter with Late Imperial Russia*, Studies on the History of Society and Culture 45 (Berkeley; Los Angeles: University of California Press, 2002), 24-26.

[20] Nathans, 24-36.

[21] Plokhi, *The Gates of Europe*, 153-54; Nicholas V. Riasanovsky, *Russian Identities: A Historical Survey* (Oxford; New York: Oxford University Press, 2005), 132-34; Figes, *The Story of Russia*, 140-43.

[22] Yaffa Eliach, *There Once Was a World: A Nine-Hundred-Year Chronicle of the Shtetl of Eishyshok*, 1st ed (Boston: Little, Brown, 1998), 45.

[23] Michael Brenner, *A Short History of the Jews*, trans. Jeremiah Riemer, First paperback printing, 2012 (Princeton, N.J.: Princeton University Press, 2012), 225–28; Riasanovsky, *Russian Identities*, 164, 185; Riasanovsky and Steinberg, *A History of Russia*, 238–39.

[24] Riasanovsky, *Russian Identities*, chap. 7.

[25] Petrovsky-Shtern, *The Golden Age Shtetl*; Riasanovsky, *Russian Identities*, chap. 7; Figes, *The Story of Russia*, 125–26, 165–66.

[26] Petrovsky-Shtern, *The Golden Age Shtetl*, 51–59, 110–12, 343–47; Davies, *God's Playground*, 2005, 2:177, 185; Figes, *The Story of Russia*, 125–26; Howe, *World of Our Fathers: The Journey of the Eastern European Jews to America and the Life They Found and Made*, 6–7; Eliach, *There Once Was a World*, 45; John D. Klier, "The Ambiguous Legal Status of Russian Jewry in the Reign of Catherine II," *Slavic Review* 35, no. 3 (1976): 504–17, https://doi.org/10.2307/2495122.

[27] Petrovsky-Shtern, *The Golden Age Shtetl*, 48.

[28] Petrovsky-Shtern, 44–52.

[29] Eliach, *There Once Was a World*, 45–49; Jewish Virtual Library, "Cantonists," Jewish Virtual Library, accessed July 5, 2022, https://www.jewishvirtuallibrary.org/cantonists; Oleksandr Nayman, "Jews in the Russian Army," *The Journal of Slavic Military Studies* 11, no. 4 (December 1, 1998): 133–45, https://doi.org/10.1080/13518049808430363.

[30] Petrovsky-Shtern, *The Golden Age Shtetl*, 48–52; Davies, *God's Playground*, 2005, 2:66–75, 176–85; Antony Polonsky, *The Jews in Poland and Russia*, The Littman Library of Jewish Civilization (Oxford ; Portland, Or: Littman Library of Jewish Civilization, 2010), vol. 2, pp. 5–17; Figes, *The Story of Russia*, 165–66.

[31] "The Pale of Settlement"; "The Pale of Settlement," Facing History and Ourselves, accessed July 5, 2022, https://www.facinghistory.org/resource-library/image/pale-settlement.

[32] Howe, *World of Our Fathers: The Journey of the Eastern European Jews to America and the Life They Found and Made*, 10.

[33] Petrovsky-Shtern, *The Golden Age Shtetl*, 23.

[34] Davies, *God's Playground*, 2005, vol. 2, chap. 9.

[35] "The Pale of Settlement."

[36] Petrovsky-Shtern, *The Golden Age Shtetl*, 220.

[37] Eliach, *There Once Was a World*, 334–37.

38 Howe, *World of Our Fathers: The Journey of the Eastern European Jews to America and the Life They Found and Made*, 9.
39 Jocelyn Cohen and Daniel Soyer, eds., *My Future Is in America: Autobiographies of Eastern European Jewish Immigrants* (New York University Press, 2006), 210.
40 Petrovsky-Shtern, *The Golden Age Shtetl*, 343–47; Davies, *God's Playground*, 2005, 2:184.
41 Neil M. Cowan and Ruth Schwartz Cowan, *Our Parents' Lives: Jewish Assimilation and Everyday Life*, Rev. pbk. ed (New Brunswick, N.J: Rutgers University Press, 1996), 36.
42 Irena Grosfeld, Seyhun Orcan Sakalli, and Ekaterina Zhuravskaya, "Middleman Minorities and Ethnic Violence: Anti-Jewish Pogroms in the Russian Empire," *The Review of Economic Studies* 87, no. 1 (January 1, 2020): 289–342, https://doi.org/10.1093/restud/rdz001.
43 Cowan and Cowan, *Our Parents' Lives*, 37.
44 Howe, *World of Our Fathers: The Journey of the Eastern European Jews to America and the Life They Found and Made*, 6–7; Eliach, *There Once Was a World*, 45; Petrovsky-Shtern, *The Golden Age Shtetl*, 343–47; Klier, "The Ambiguous Legal Status of Russian Jewry in the Reign of Catherine II"; Brenner, *A Short History of the Jews*, 238–40.
45 Petrovsky-Shtern, *The Golden Age Shtetl*, 27.
46 "The Staszow Book," 286.
47 Petrovsky-Shtern, chap. 1.
48 "The Staszow Book," accessed July 5, 2022, https://www.jewishgen.org/yizkor/staszow/staszow.html.
49 "The Staszow Book," 25.
50 "The Staszow Book," 63.
51 Herman Rosenthal, "Agricultural Colonies In Russia," JewishEncyclopedia, n.d., https://www.jewishencyclopedia.com/articles/908-agricultural-colonies-in-russia.
52 Jewish Records Indexing-Poland and Kielce Archive-Sandomierz Branch, "Marriage Record for Froim Knobel and Gitla Krandla (Brandla)," Jewish Records Indexing-Poland, n.d., https://legacy.jri-poland.org/imagedata/SANDOMIERZ_ARCHIVES/STASZOW_MOJ/1826/_ _01019.JPG.

53 "Staszow | Encyclopedia.Com," accessed July 5, 2022, https://www.encyclopedia.com/religion/encyclopedias-almanacs-transcripts-and-maps/staszow.
54 "Asiatic Cholera Pandemic of 1817," accessed July 7, 2022, https://www.ph.ucla.edu/epi/Snow/pandemic1846-63.html.
55 "Gombin, Poland (Pages 13 -27)," accessed July 24, 2022, https://www.jewishgen.org/yizkor/gombin/gom013.html.

Chapter 3
56 "The Staszow Book"; "Gombin, Poland (Pages 13 -27)."
57 John Klier, *Russians, Jews, and the Pogroms of 1881-1882* (Cambridge ; New York: Cambridge University Press, 2011), 265.
58 "The Staszow Book," 274.
59 "The Staszow Book," 274.
60 "The Staszow Book," 230.
61 "The Staszow Book," 286.
62 "The Staszow Book," 286.
63 "The Staszow Book."
64 "The Staszow Book," 274.
65 "The Staszow Book"; "Gombin, Poland (Pages 13 -27)."
66 Pomorska Biblioteka Cyfrowa, "Ulica Kościelna," fotopolska.eu, November 2, 2011, https://fotopolska.eu/254054,foto.html?o=u162443.
67 J. Slusarski and Nakł. J. Slusarski, "Staszów, Gub. Rad. : Młyn," polona.pl, 1910, https://polona.pl/preview/31301bfe-ff89-42a9-8062-d0ea3182c88b.
68 Petrovsky-Shtern, *The Golden Age Shtetl*, 24, 27.
69 Shaul Stampfer, "Maps of Jewish Settlement in Ukraine in 1648," *Jewish History* 17, no. 2 (2003): 107–14, https://doi.org/10.1023/A:1022301825196.
70 For further reading on the history of the Ukrainian national idea, see Plokhi, *The Gates of Europe*; Serhii Plokhy, *The Frontline: Essays on Ukraine's Past and Present*, Harvard Series in Ukrainian Studies 81 (Cambridge, Massachusetts: Harvard University Press for the Ukrainian Research Institute, 2021); Snyder, *The Reconstruction of Nations*.
71 Riasanovsky, *Russian Identities*, 155.
72 Plokhi, *The Gates of Europe*, 97–100; Zenon E. Kohut, "The Khmelnytsky Uprising, the Image of Jews, and the Shaping of Ukrainian Historical

Memory," *Jewish History* 17, no. 2 (2003): 141–63, https://doi.org/10.1023/A:1022300121820; Shaul Stampfer, "What Actually Happened to the Jews of Ukraine in 1648?," *Jewish History* 17, no. 2 (2003): 207–27, https://doi.org/10.1023/A:1022330717763.

[73] "Russia and Ukraine: Did They Reunite in 1654?," in *The Frontline: Essays on Ukraine's Past and Present*, by Serhii Plokhy, Harvard Series in Ukrainian Studies 81 (Cambridge, Massachusetts: Harvard University Press for the Ukrainian Research Institute, 2021), 37–54; Plokhi, *The Gates of Europe*, 97–118; Vladimir Putin, "On the Historical Unity of Russians and Ukrainians," Kremlin.ru, July 12, 2021, http://en.kremlin.ru/events/president/news/66181; E. Kohut, "The Khmelnytsky Uprising, the Image of Jews, and the Shaping of Ukrainian Historical Memory"; Riasanovsky and Steinberg, *A History of Russia*, 154–55.

[74] Research Directorate, Immigration and Refugee Board, Canada, "Jews in Russia and the Soviet Union: Chronology of Events: 1727 - 1 January 1992."

[75] Sergi Mikolaïovitch Plokhi, *The Gates of Europe: A History of Ukraine*, Revised edition (New York (N.Y.): Basic Books, 2021), 145–54; Yohanan Petrovsky-Shtern, *The Golden Age Shtetl: A New History of Jewish Life in East Europe*, First paperback printing (Princeton Oxford: Princeton University Press, 2015).

[76] Petrovsky-Shtern, *The Golden Age Shtetl*, 31–41; Riasanovsky, *Russian Identities*, chap. 8; Norman Davies, *God's Playground: A History of Poland: Volume II: 1795 to the Present*, Rev. ed, vol. 2 (New York: Columbia University Press, 2005), chap. 2.

[77] Petrovsky-Shtern, *The Golden Age Shtetl*, chap. 1.

[78] Petrovsky-Shtern, chap. 1.

[79] Petrovsky-Shtern, 41–52.

[80] Hans Rogger, *Jewish Policies and Right-Wing Politics in Imperial Russia* (Palgrave Macmillan, a division of Macmillan Publishers Limited, 1986), 25–39; I. Michael Aronson, "The Attitudes of Russian Officials in the 1880s Toward Jewish Assimilation and Emigration," *Slavic Review* 34, no. 1 (March 1975): 1–18, https://doi.org/10.2307/2495871; Antony Polonsky, *The Jews in Poland and Russia*, The Littman Library of Jewish Civilization (Oxford ; Portland, Or: Littman Library of Jewish Civilization, 2010), vol. 2, pp. 5–17.

[81] Plokhi, *The Gates of Europe*, 223.

[82] Petrovsky-Shtern, p. 55

83 "History of Bershad (ברשאד העיר של) (A20-5)," accessed July 5, 2022, https://jew.bershad.org.ua/article/a-20-5.html.
84 Jacob Soll, "The Making of an Anti-Semitic Myth," The New Republic, April 10, 2019, https://newrepublic.com/article/153538/making-anti-semitic-myth.
85 "Jewish Surnames Adopted in Various Regions of the Russian Empire," accessed July 5, 2022, https://avotaynuonline.com/2008/10/jewish-surnames-adopted-in-various-regions-of-the-russian-empire-by-alexander-beider-2/.
86 "History of Bershad (ברשאד העיר של) (A20-5)"; Jewish Virtual Library, "Bershad," accessed July 5, 2022, https://www.jewishvirtuallibrary.org/bershad; History of Jewish Communities in Ukraine, "Bershad Cemetery," History of Jewish Communities in Ukraine, accessed July 5, 2022, https://jew.bershad.org.ua/photos/r-24.html; My Shtetl, "Bershad, Ukraine," My Shtetl, accessed July 5, 2022, http://myshtetl.org/vinnitskaja/bershad_en.html.
87 Joseph Telushkin, *A Code of Jewish Ethics*, 1st ed (New York: Bell Tower, 2006), 238.
88 My Shtetl, "Bershad, Ukraine."
89 My Shtetl.
90 "Kyiv: History," Virtual Shtetl, n.d., https://sztetl.org.pl/en/towns/k/1531-kiev/99-history/138953-history-of-community.
91 Jewish Virtual Library, "Kyiv, Ukraine," Jewish Virtual Library, n.d., https://www.jewishvirtuallibrary.org/kiev.
92 "Kyiv: History."
93 Internet Encyclopedia of Ukraine, "Chernihiv," Internet Encyclopedia of Ukraine, n.d., http://www.encyclopediaofukraine.com/display.asp?linkpath=pages%5CC%5CH%5CChernihiv.htm; Jewish Virtual Library, "Chernigov, Ukraine," Jewish Virtual Library, n.d., https://www.jewishvirtuallibrary.org/chernigov; Virtual Shtetl, "Chernihiv: History," Virtual Shtetl, n.d., https://sztetl.org.pl/en/towns/c/1151-chernihiv/99-history/137205-history-of-community; History of Jewish Communities in Ukraine, "Chernihiv," History of Jewish Communities in Ukraine, n.d., https://jewua.org/chernigov/.
94 History of Jewish Communities in Ukraine, "Chernihiv."

⁹⁵ History of Jewish Communities in Ukraine.

Chapter 4

⁹⁶ History of Jewish Communities in Ukraine, "Novgorod-Seversky," History of Jewish Communities in Ukraine, August 3, 2014, https://jewua.org/novgorod-seversky/; Sergi Mikolaïovitch Plokhi, *The Gates of Europe: A History of Ukraine*, Revised edition (New York (N.Y.): Basic Books, 2021), 222.

⁹⁷ "Новгород-Северский (Novgorod-Seversky)," My Shtetl, n.d., https://myshtetl.org/vostok/novgorod.html.

⁹⁸ History of Jewish Communities in Ukraine, "Novgorod-Seversky."

⁹⁹ "Novhorod-Siverskyi," Internet Encyclopedia of Ukraine, n.d., https://www.encyclopediaofukraine.com/display.asp?linkpath=pages%5CN%5CO%5CNovhorod6Siverskyi.htm.

¹⁰⁰ "Novhorod-Siverskyi."

¹⁰¹ Irving Howe, *World of Our Fathers: The Journey of the Eastern European Jews to America and the Life They Found and Made*, 30th Anniversary Edition (New York University Press, 2005), 25.

¹⁰² Hans Rogger, *Jewish Policies and Right-Wing Politics in Imperial Russia* (Palgrave Macmillan, a division of Macmillan Publishers Limited, 1986), 113–75; Nicholas V. Riasanovsky and Mark D. Steinberg, *A History of Russia*, Ninth edition (New York: Oxford University Press, 2019), 330–31, 380–92; Eli Lederhendler, "Classless: On the Social Status of Jews in Russia and Eastern Europe in the Late Nineteenth Century," *Comparative Studies in Society and History* 50, no. 2 (2008): 509–34.

¹⁰³ William I. Brustein and Ryan D. King, "Anti-Semitism in Europe before the Holocaust," *International Political Science Review* 25, no. 1 (January 2004): 35–53, https://doi.org/10.1177/0192512104038166.

¹⁰⁴ Irving Howe and Kenneth Libo, eds., *How We Lived: A Documentary History of Immigrant Jews in America, 1880-1930*, A Plume Book (New York: New American Library, 1981), 17; George Washington, "From George Washington to the Hebrew Congregation in Newport, Rhode Island, 18 August 1790," Founders Online, National Archives, n.d., https://founders.archives.gov/documents/Washington/05-06-02-0135.

[105] Mary Antin and Werner Sollors, *The Promised Land*, Penguin Classics (New York: Peguin Books, 2012), 156.
[106] Jocelyn Cohen and Daniel Soyer, eds., *My Future Is in America: Autobiographies of Eastern European Jewish Immigrants* (New York University Press, 2006), 45.
[107] Irving Howe, *World of Our Fathers: The Journey of the Eastern European Jews to America and the Life They Found and Made*, 30th Anniversary Edition (New York University Press, 2005), 27.
[108] Howe, 30.
[109] Cohen and Soyer, *My Future Is in America: Autobiographies of Eastern European Jewish Immigrants*, 21.
[110] Susan A. Glenn, *Daughters of the Shtetl: Life and Labor in the Immigrant Generation* (Ithaca: Cornell Univ. Press, 1995), 44.
[111] Rose Cohen, *Out of the Shadow: A Russian Jewish Girlhood on the Lower East Side*, Documents in American Social History (Ithaca, N.Y: Cornell University Press, 1995), 23.
[112] Howe, *World of Our Fathers: The Journey of the Eastern European Jews to America and the Life They Found and Made*, 60.
[113] Howe, 60.
[114] Lederhendler, "Classless."
[115] Michael Brenner, *A Short History of the Jews*, trans. Jeremiah Riemer, First paperback printing, 2012 (Princeton, N.J.: Princeton University Press, 2012), 243-44; Michael A. Meyer, "Looking Back: American Jews' Relationships to Their Places of Origin," *Modern Judaism - A Journal of Jewish Ideas and Experience* 37, no. 2 (May 2017): 143-64, https://doi.org/10.1093/mj/kjx020.
[116] Howe, *World of Our Fathers: The Journey of the Eastern European Jews to America and the Life They Found and Made*, 27.
[117] Howe, 27.
[118] Antin and Sollors, *The Promised Land*, 146-48.
[119] Cohen and Soyer, *My Future Is in America: Autobiographies of Eastern European Jewish Immigrants*, 61.
[120] Cohen and Soyer, 198.
[121] Lederhendler, "Classless."
[122] Jewish Virtual Library, "United Kingdom: History," Jewish Virtual Library, n.d., https://www.jewishvirtuallibrary.org/united-kingdom-virtual-jewish-history-tour.

123 Disraeli was born into a Sephardic Jewish family, but his father converted himself and the family to Anglicanism when Disraeli was 13. As his father had predicted—in fact, it was why they converted—this wound up being very advantageous in Disraeli's future political career. Jewish Virtual Library, "London," Jewish Virtual Library, accessed July 5, 2022, https://www.jewishvirtuallibrary.org/london; Jewish Virtual Library, "Lionel Nathan de Rothschild," accessed July 5, 2022, https://www.jewishvirtuallibrary.org/lionel-nathan-de-rothschild; Jewish Virtual Library, "Benjamin Disraeli," Jewish Virtual Library, n.d., https://www.jewishvirtuallibrary.org/benjamin-disraeli.

124 "The Jewish Board of Guardians," The Rothschild Archive, n.d., https://guide-to-the-archive.rothschildarchive.org/rothschild-family-collection/depts/papers-of-institutions/the-jewish-board-of-guardians; "American Jewish Yearbook (1920-1921): Statistics of Jews," accessed July 24, 2022, https://www.hillel.org/docs/default-source/historical/american-jewish-year-book-(1920-1921).pdf?sfvrsn=ee191282_2.

125 "Jew's Free School Database 1856-1907 Introduction & Contents," accessed July 5, 2022, https://www.jewishgen.org/databases/uk/jfs/index.html.

126 Jewish Virtual Library, "London"; David Englander, "Policing the Ghetto Jewish East London, 1880-1920," *Crime, Histoire & Sociétés / Crime, History & Societies* 14, no. 1 (2010): 29–50; "The Jewish Community of London, UK," ANU Museum of the Jewish People, n.d., https://dbs.anumuseum.org.il/skn/en/c6/e129847/Place/London_UK.

127 Englander, "Policing the Ghetto Jewish East London, 1880-1920."

128 Englander.

129 Englander.

130 Englander.

131 Englander.

132 "Schools," accessed July 24, 2022, http://www.stgitehistory.org.uk/media/schools.html.

133 "Schools."

134 Lloyd P. Gartner, "Notes on the Statistics of Jewish Immigration to England 1870-1914," *Jewish Social Studies* 22, no. 2 (1960): 97–102; "The Jewish Community of London, UK."

135 Englander, "Policing the Ghetto Jewish East London, 1880-1920."

136 Englander.
137 Richard Jones, "The Whitechapel Murders and the Jewish Community," Jack the Ripper 1888, n.d.
138 Englander, "Policing the Ghetto Jewish East London, 1880-1920."
139 Richard Jones, "The Jewish East End," Jack the Ripper 1888, n.d., https://www.jack-the-ripper.org/jewish-east-end.htm.

Chapter 5

140 Howe, *World of Our Fathers: The Journey of the Eastern European Jews to America and the Life They Found and Made*, 25.
141 Anastasiia Strakhova, "Unexpected Allies: Imperial Russian Support of Jewish Emigration at the Time of Its Legal Ban, 1881-1914," *QUEST Issues in Contemporary Jewish History*, no. 20 (December 1, 2021), https://doi.org/10.48248/issn.2037-741X/13064.
142 I. Michael Aronson, "The Attitudes of Russian Officials in the 1880s Toward Jewish Assimilation and Emigration," *Slavic Review* 34, no. 1 (March 1975): 1–18, https://doi.org/10.2307/2495871. Alternatively quoted as "They have already taken ample advantage of this right and their emigration has in no way been hindered" in Antony, *The Jews of Poland and Russia*, vol. 2, p. 19.
143 Rogger, *Jewish Policies and Right-Wing Politics in Imperial Russia*, 180.
144 Aronson, "The Attitudes of Russian Officials in the 1880s Toward Jewish Assimilation and Emigration"; Rogger, *Jewish Policies and Right-Wing Politics in Imperial Russia*, 176–86; Anastasiia Strakhova, "Unexpected Allies."
145 Howe, *World of Our Fathers: The Journey of the Eastern European Jews to America and the Life They Found and Made*, 30; Lloyd P. Gartner, "Jewish Migrants En Route from Europe to North America: Traditions and Realities," *Jewish History* 1, no. 2 (September 1986): 49–66, https://doi.org/10.1007/BF01680291.
146 Hoerder, "The Traffic of Emigration via Bremen/Bremerhaven: Merchants' Interests, Protective Legislation, and Migrants' Experiences," *Journal of American Ethnic History* 13, no. 1 (1993): 68–101.
147 Hoerder; Rogger, *Jewish Policies and Right-Wing Politics in Imperial Russia*, 176–86.
148 Cohen, *Out of the Shadow*, 32.
149 Hoerder, "The Traffic of Emigration via Bremen/Bremerhaven: Merchants' Interests, Protective Legislation, and Migrants' Experiences"; Gartner, "Jewish Migrants En Route from Europe to North America."

150 Meyer, "Looking Back."
151 Howe, *World of Our Fathers: The Journey of the Eastern European Jews to America and the Life They Found and Made*, 34.
152 Howe, 35.
153 Cohen, *Out of the Shadow*, 14–18.
154 Gartner, "Jewish Migrants En Route from Europe to North America"; Hoerder, "The Traffic of Emigration via Bremen/Bremerhaven: Merchants' Interests, Protective Legislation, and Migrants' Experiences."
155 Howe, *World of Our Fathers: The Journey of the Eastern European Jews to America and the Life They Found and Made*, 36.
156 Hoerder, "The Traffic of Emigration via Bremen/Bremerhaven: Merchants' Interests, Protective Legislation, and Migrants' Experiences."
157 Hoerder.
158 Howe, *World of Our Fathers: The Journey of the Eastern European Jews to America and the Life They Found and Made*, 37.
159 Cohen, *Out of the Shadow*, 57.
160 Gartner, "Jewish Migrants En Route from Europe to North America"; Hoerder, "The Traffic of Emigration via Bremen/Bremerhaven: Merchants' Interests, Protective Legislation, and Migrants' Experiences."
161 Antin and Sollors, *The Promised Land*, 176.
162 Cohen, *Out of the Shadow*, 60.
163 Cohen, 61.
164 Cohen, 62.
165 Cohen, 62.
166 Howe, *World of Our Fathers: The Journey of the Eastern European Jews to America and the Life They Found and Made*, 40.
167 Howe, 41.
168 Howe, 42.
169 Howe, 40.
170 Howe, 40.
171 Antin and Sollors, *The Promised Land*, 141.
172 Cohen and Soyer, *My Future Is in America: Autobiographies of Eastern European Jewish Immigrants*, 189.

[173] Jewish Virtual Library, "Kyiv, Ukraine"; John Klier, *Russians, Jews, and the Pogroms of 1881-1882* (Cambridge ; New York: Cambridge University Press, 2011), 56–58.

[174] Sydney Stahl Weinberg, *The World of Our Mothers: The Lives of Jewish Immigrant Women* (Chapel Hill: University of North Carolina Press, 1988), 60.

[175] Weinberg, 61.

[176] Weinberg, 61–74.

[177] Weinberg, 61–64.

[178] "Глава из книги Н. и М. Улановских История одной семьи," August 30, 2010, https://jew.bershad.org.ua/article/a-23.html.

[179] History of Jewish Communities in Ukraine, "History of Bershad (ברשאד העיר של) (A45-2)," History of Jewish Communities in Ukraine, accessed July 5, 2022, https://jew.bershad.org.ua/article/a-45-2.html.

[180] "History of Bershad (ברשאד העיר של) (A20-5)."

[181] "Глава из книги Н. и М. Улановских История одной семьи."

[182] Englander, "Policing the Ghetto Jewish East London, 1880-1920."

[183] Englander.

[184] Antony Polonsky, *The Jews in Poland and Russia*, The Littman Library of Jewish Civilization (Oxford ; Portland, Or: Littman Library of Jewish Civilization, 2010), vol. 2, p. 18.

[185] Klier, *Russians, Jews, and the Pogroms of 1881-1882*, 17–43, 58.

[186] Raphael G Bouchnik-Chen, "The Kishinev Pogrom as a Catalyst to the Russo-Japanese War," The Begin-Sadat Center for Strategic Studies, September 23, 2020, https://besacenter.org/kishinev-pogrom-russia-japan/; Shlomo Lambroza, "The Tsarist Government and the Pogroms of 1903-1906," *Modern Judaism* 7, no. 3 (1987): 287–96, https://doi.org/10.1093/mj/7.3.287.

[187] M. N. Penkower, "The Kishinev Pogrom of 1903: A Turning Point in Jewish History," *Modern Judaism* 24, no. 3 (October 1, 2004): 187–225, https://doi.org/10.1093/mj/kjh017.

[188] Bouchnik-Chen, "The Kishinev Pogrom as a Catalyst to the Russo-Japanese War."

[189] Jewish Virtual Library, "Cantonists," Jewish Virtual Library, accessed July 5, 2022, https://www.jewishvirtuallibrary.org/cantonists; Oleksandr Nayman, "Jews in the Russian Army," *The Journal of Slavic Military Studies* 11, no. 4 (December 1, 1998): 133–45, https://doi.org/10.1080/13518049808430363.

[190] Nayman, "Jews in the Russian Army."
[191] "ГЛАВА IX. Пути Примыкающие к Киеву, и Линии Северной Части Области," DaliZovut, n.d., http://dalizovut.narod.ru/semenov/semen_9.htm; Hoerder, "The Traffic of Emigration via Bremen/Bremerhaven: Merchants' Interests, Protective Legislation, and Migrants' Experiences"; Gartner, "Jewish Migrants En Route from Europe to North America."
[192] Ancestry.com, "Baltimore, Passenger Lists, 1820-1964," Online database (Provo, UT, USA: Ancestry.com Operations, Inc., 2006).
[193] Temple University Libraries Digital Collections, "Steamship Ticket Purchase Ledgers," accessed July 5, 2022, https://digital.library.temple.edu/digital/collection/p16002coll16.
[194] Temple University Libraries Digital Collections.
[195] Howe, *World of Our Fathers: The Journey of the Eastern European Jews to America and the Life They Found and Made*, 58–59.
[196] Howe, 58.
[197] Howe, 59.
[198] Howe, 61.
[199] Howe, 61.
[200] Howe, 63.

Chapter 6

[201] Adam Mickiewicz, *Forefather's Eve*, trans. Charles S. Kraszewski (London: Glagoslav Publications, 2016). 193
[202] For further details, see Timothy Snyder, *The Reconstruction of Nations: Poland, Ukraine, Lithuania, Belarus, 1569 - 1999* (New Haven, Conn.: Yale University Press, 2003).
[203] "The Immigration Act of 1924 (The Johnson-Reed Act)," Office of the Historian of the United States Department of State, n.d., https://history.state.gov/milestones/1921-1936/immigration-act.
[204] Howe, *World of Our Fathers: The Journey of the Eastern European Jews to America and the Life They Found and Made*, 53–55; "The Immigration Act of 1924 (The Johnson-Reed Act)"; Harry D. Boonin, *The Jewish quarter of Philadelphia: A History and Guide, 1881-1930*, 1st ed (Philadelphia, PA: Jewish Walking Tours of Philadelphia, 1999), 6–16.

205 Howe, *World of Our Fathers: The Journey of the Eastern European Jews to America and the Life They Found and Made*, 55–56.
206 Howe, 56.
207 "The Immigration Act of 1924 (The Johnson-Reed Act)."
208 Boonin, *The Jewish quarter of Philadelphia*, 1999, 30–31; "Table of the Quota System Targeting Specific Immigrant Groups," American Social History Project, n.d., https://shec.ashp.cuny.edu/items/show/1230; "The Immigration Act of 1924 (The Johnson-Reed Act)."
209 Plokhi, *The Gates of Europe*, 179; Plokhi, 185.
210 Plokhi, *The Gates of Europe*, 187–89.
211 Plokhi, 189–90.
212 History of Jewish Communities in Ukraine, "Chernihiv"; Yad Vashem, "Novgorod Severskiy," Yad Vashem, accessed July 5, 2022, https://collections.yadvashem.org/en/untold-stories/community/14621733-Novgorod-Severskiy.
213 Snyder, *The Reconstruction of Nations*, 137–39; Plokhi, *The Gates of Europe*, 215–24; Eli Lederhendler, *Jewish Immigrants and American Capitalism, 1880-1920: From Caste to Class* (Cambridge [England] ; New York: Cambridge University Press, 2009), 111.
214 Plokhi, *The Gates of Europe*, 223.
215 Snyder, *The Reconstruction of Nations*, 138; Plokhi, *The Gates of Europe*, 223–24.
216 "Holodomor: The Ukrainian Genocide," University of Minnesota College of Liberal Arts: Holocaust and Genocide Studies, n.d., https://cla.umn.edu/chgs/holocaust-genocide-education/resource-guides/holodomor.
217 Plokhi, *The Gates of Europe*, 245–53; Snyder, *The Reconstruction of Nations*, 148–53.
218 "Jewish Losses during the Holocaust: By Country," United States Holocaust Memorial Museum, accessed July 7, 2022, https://encyclopedia.ushmm.org/content/en/article/jewish-losses-during-the-holocaust-by-country; "Jewish Population of Europe in 1933: Population Data by Country," United States Holocaust Memorial Museum, n.d., https://encyclopedia.ushmm.org/content/en/article/jewish-population-of-europe-in-1933-population-data-by-country.

219 "Gombin: The Life and Destruction of a Jewish Town in Poland," accessed July 24, 2022, https://www.jewishgen.org/yizkor/gombin/gombin.html#TOC0; "Gabin: Mazovia," International Jewish Cemetery Project, n.d.; "Historia i Zabytki Gąbina," n.d., https://www.gabin.pl/miasto-i-gmina/historia-i-zabytki.
220 "The Staszow Book," 406–16, accessed July 5, 2022, https://www.jewishgen.org/yizkor/staszow/staszow.html.
221 "STASZOW: Świętokrzyskie | Poland | International Jewish Cemetery Project," IAJGS Cemetery Project, accessed July 8, 2022, http://iajgscemetery.org/eastern-europe/poland/staszow.
222 Jennifer Popowycz, "The 'Holocaust by Bullets' in Ukraine," The National WWII Museum, January 24, 2022, https://www.nationalww2museum.org/war/articles/ukraine-holocaust; "The Holocaust in Ukraine," United States Holocaust Memorial Museum, n.d., https://www.ushmm.org/information/exhibitions/online-exhibitions/ukraine.
223 "Mass Shootings at Babyn Yar (Babi Yar)," Holocaust Encyclopedia, September 29, 2021, https://encyclopedia.ushmm.org/content/en/article/kiev-and-babi-yar.
224 Jewish Virtual Library, "Chernigov, Ukraine," Jewish Virtual Library, n.d., https://www.jewishvirtuallibrary.org/chernigov; History of Jewish Communities in Ukraine, "Chernihiv," History of Jewish Communities in Ukraine, n.d., https://jewua.org/chernigov/.
225 Yahad in Unum, "Execution of Jews from Novgorod-Siverskyi in Ostroushky," Yahad in Unum | The Map of Holocaust by Bullets, n.d., https://yahadmap.org/?fbclid=IwAR0WgQ1Dad4Ib7tS36Tm0H0w8fNXqtGCe1AgVPIAc0AetTZNJjwA66rRlAY#village/ostroushky-novgorod-siverskyi-sumy-ukraine.1201.
226 History of Jewish Communities in Ukraine, "Novgorod-Seversky," History of Jewish Communities in Ukraine, August 3, 2014, https://jewua.org/novgorod-seversky/.
227 Cnaan Liphshiz, "Passed over by Nazis and Communists, Remnants of Ukraine's Last Shtetl Prepare to Celebrate," The Times of Israel, March 28, 2017, https://www.timesofisrael.com/passed-over-by-nazis-and-communists-remnants-of-ukraines-last-shtetl-prepare-to-celebrate/.

[228] Liphshiz.

Chapter 7
[229] Petrovsky-Shtern, p. 21
[230] Lederhendler, p. 54
[231] Mary Antin and Werner Sollors, *The Promised Land*, Penguin Classics (New York: Peguin Books, 2012), 182.
[232] Irving Howe and Kenneth Libo, eds., *How We Lived: A Documentary History of Immigrant Jews in America, 1880-1930*, A Plume Book (New York: New American Library, 1981), 16.
[233] Irving Howe, *World of Our Fathers: The Journey of the Eastern European Jews to America and the Life They Found and Made*, 30th Anniversary Edition (New York University Press, 2005), 42–46.
[234] Jocelyn Cohen and Daniel Soyer, eds., *My Future Is in America: Autobiographies of Eastern European Jewish Immigrants* (New York University Press, 2006), 138.
[235] Howe, *World of Our Fathers: The Journey of the Eastern European Jews to America and the Life They Found and Made*, 46–50.
[236] Howe, 44.
[237] Howe, 67–74.
[238] Cohen and Soyer, *My Future Is in America: Autobiographies of Eastern European Jewish Immigrants*, 66.
[239] Susan A. Glenn, *Daughters of the Shtetl: Life and Labor in the Immigrant Generation* (Ithaca: Cornell Univ. Press, 1995), 54–55.
[240] Howe, *World of Our Fathers: The Journey of the Eastern European Jews to America and the Life They Found and Made*, 67.
[241] Howe, 68–69.
[242] Howe, 71.
[243] Howe, 70.
[244] Howe and Libo, *How We Lived*, 21.
[245] "American Jewish Year Book: 1914-1915," American Jewish Yearbook (American Jewish Committee, 1914), https://www.jstor.org/stable/23600932?seq=19.
[246] Harry D. Boonin, *The Jewish quarter of Philadelphia: A History and Guide, 1881-1930*, 1st ed (Philadelphia, PA: Jewish Walking Tours of Philadelphia, 1999), 10.

247 Boonin, 18.
248 Murray Friedman, ed., *Jewish Life in Philadelphia, 1830-1940* (Philadelphia: Institute for the Study of Human Issues, 1983), 5; Boonin, *The Jewish quarter of Philadelphia*, 1999, 12, 17–18, 27.
249 Boonin, *The Jewish quarter of Philadelphia*, 1999, 11.
250 Friedman, *Jewish Life in Philadelphia, 1830-1940*, 138; "American Jewish Yearbook (1920-1921): Statistics of Jews," accessed July 24, 2022, https://www.hillel.org/docs/default-source/historical/american-jewish-yearbook-(1920-1921).pdf?sfvrsn=ee191282_2.
251 Boonin, *The Jewish quarter of Philadelphia*, 1999, 13, 16–19.
252 Friedman, *Jewish Life in Philadelphia, 1830-1940*, 129–36; Eli Lederhendler, *Jewish Immigrants and American Capitalism, 1880-1920: From Caste to Class* (Cambridge [England]; New York: Cambridge University Press, 2009), 103–7.
253 Friedman, *Jewish Life in Philadelphia, 1830-1940*, 133.
254 Friedman, 131–32; Boonin, *The Jewish quarter of Philadelphia*, 1999, 13–17.
255 Boonin, *The Jewish quarter of Philadelphia*, 1999, 16.
256 Friedman, *Jewish Life in Philadelphia, 1830-1940*, 132.
257 Friedman, 134–35. The United Hebrew Charities would later be incorporated into HIAS.
258 Friedman, 136.
259 Harry Boonin, "The Jewish quarter of Philadelphia," The PhillyHistory Blog, March 5, 2008, https://blog.phillyhistory.org/index.php/2008/03/the-jewish-quarter-of-philadelphia/.
260 Boonin, *The Jewish quarter of Philadelphia*, 1999, 27.
261 Boonin, 39.
262 Lederhendler, *Jewish Immigrants and American Capitalism, 1880-1920*, 54.
263 Eli Lederhendler, "Classless: On the Social Status of Jews in Russia and Eastern Europe in the Late Nineteenth Century," *Comparative Studies in Society and History* 50, no. 2 (2008): 509–34.
264 Glenn, *Daughters of the Shtetl*, 71.
265 Howe and Libo, *How We Lived*, 28.
266 Howe and Libo, 30.
267 Glenn, *Daughters of the Shtetl*, 74.

[268] Neil M. Cowan and Ruth Schwartz Cowan, *Our Parents' Lives: Jewish Assimilation and Everyday Life*, Rev. pbk. ed (New Brunswick, N.J: Rutgers University Press, 1996), 44.
[269] Cowan and Cowan, 48.
[270] Cowan and Cowan, 49.
[271] Jonathan D. Sarna, "The Myth of No Return: Jewish Return Migration to Eastern Europe, 1881–1914.," *American Jewish History* 71, no. 2 (1981): 256–68.
[272] "702 South 2nd Street," September 4, 1914, Public Words 9246-0, Philadelphia Department of Records, https://www.phillyhistory.org/PhotoArchive/Detail.aspx?assetId=7226.

Chapter 8

[273] "Slums - 530 Lombard St.," March 4, 1914, Public Words 9244-0, Philadelphia Department of Records, https://www.phillyhistory.org/PhotoArchive/Detail.aspx?assetId=42052.
[274] Carollo R Battisti, "Various Houses - Bainbridge Street, Pemberton Street, Monroe Street," August 20, 1962, Department of Public Property 49160-0, Philadelphia Department of Records, https://www.phillyhistory.org/PhotoArchive/Detail.aspx?assetId=145591.
[275] Howe and Libo, *How We Lived*, 19.
[276] James Truslow Adams, *The Epic of America*, n.d., 414, https://archive.org/details/in.ernet.dli.2015.262385/page/n5/mode/2up.
[277] Cohen and Soyer, *My Future Is in America: Autobiographies of Eastern European Jewish Immigrants*, 204–5.
[278] Boonin, *The Jewish quarter of Philadelphia*, 1999, 37.
[279] Charles S. Bernheimer, "The Russian Jew in Philadelphia: Educational Influences," The Museum of Family History, 1907, https://www.museumoffamilyhistory.com/ija-philadelphia-ptVI.htm.
[280] Bernheimer; Friedman, *Jewish Life in Philadelphia, 1830-1940*, 132–35.
[281] Howe and Libo, *How We Lived*, 18–19.
[282] Lederhendler, *Jewish Immigrants and American Capitalism, 1880-1920*, 59.
[283] Lederhendler, 59–61.
[284] Lederhendler, 54–55.
[285] Lederhendler, 54–57.

[286] Jonathan D. Sarna, *American Judaism: A History*, Second edition (New Haven: Yale University Press, 2019), 170-75.
[287] Friedman, *Jewish Life in Philadelphia, 1830-1940*, 277.
[288] Friedman, 90.
[289] Friedman, 80-98; Alexander Kulik, "Jews and the Language of Eastern Slavs," *Jewish quarterly Review* 104, no. 1 (2014): 105-43, https://doi.org/10.1353/jqr.2014.0002.
[290] Jenna Weissman Joselit, *The Wonders of America: Reinventing Jewish Culture, 1880 - 1950*, 1st Owl Books ed (New York: H. Holt, 2002), 11; Sarna, *American Judaism*, 173-75.
[291] Joselit, *The Wonders of America*, 12.
[292] Joselit, 16-17.
[293] Joselit, 17.
[294] Joselit, 23.
[295] Joselit, 90-95.
[296] Jenna Weissman Joselit, *The Wonders of America: Reinventing Jewish Culture, 1880 - 1950*, 1st Owl Books ed (New York: H. Holt, 2002), 105-33; Michael Feldberg, "The First Bat Mitzvah in the United States," Jewish Virtual Library, n.d., https://www.jewishvirtuallibrary.org/the-first-bat-mitzvah-in-the-united-states.
[297] Joselit, *The Wonders of America*, 120.
[298] Joselit, 93.
[299] Joselit, 116.
[300] Joselit, 120.
[301] Joselit, 133.
[302] Jonathan D. Sarna, *American Judaism: A History*, Second edition (New Haven: Yale University Press, 2019), 287-89.
[303] Sarna, 247-49.
[304] Joselit, *The Wonders of America*, 84-85.
[305] Joselit, 70.
[306] Gail F. Stern, Balch Institute for Ethnic Studies, and Jewish Agencies of Greater Philadelphia, eds., *Traditions in Transition: Jewish Culture in Philadelphia, 1840-1940: An Exhibition in the Museum of the Balch Institute for Ethnic Studies, April 24-October 21, 1989* (Philadelphia, Pa. : Lanham, Md: The Institute ; Distributed by AASLH Library, 1989), 60.

307 Sarna, *American Judaism*, 161.
308 Sarna, 158–61.
309 Sarna, 161–64.

Chapter 9

310 Anatole Leroy-Beaulieu, *Jewish Immigrants in Early 1900s America: A Visitor's Account*, trans. Steven Capsuto (New York: Books & Translations Services, 2016).

311 Neil M. Cowan and Ruth Schwartz Cowan, *Our Parents' Lives: Jewish Assimilation and Everyday Life*, Rev. pbk. ed (New Brunswick, N.J: Rutgers University Press, 1996), 103.

312 Harry D. Boonin, *The Jewish quarter of Philadelphia: A History and Guide, 1881-1930*, 1st ed (Philadelphia, PA: Jewish Walking Tours of Philadelphia, 1999), 111.

313 Irving Howe and Kenneth Libo, eds., *How We Lived: A Documentary History of Immigrant Jews in America, 1880-1930*, A Plume Book (New York: New American Library, 1981), 30.

314 Cowan and Cowan, *Our Parents' Lives*, 56.

315 Cowan and Cowan, 55.

316 Cowan and Cowan, 55.

317 Lower Merion Conservancy and Preservation Alliance of Greater Philadelphia, "Beechwood, Brookline and Penfield: A Tour of the Historic Residential Neighborhoods along the Philadelphia & Western Railroad," Lower Merion Conservancy and Preservation Alliance of Greater Philadelphia, n.d., https://storymaps.arcgis.com/stories/996f9ba9adfa44fcbcaba0caf74d8d23.

318 Cowan and Cowan, *Our Parents' Lives*, 34.

319 Cowan and Cowan, 35.

320 "Legal Notices," *The Philadelphia Inquirer*, January 7, 1924, Volume 190, Number 7 edition, sec. Legal Notices, Newspapers.com.

321 "Jeweler Ends Life; Too Proud to Beg," *The Philadelphia Inquirer*, October 21, 1933, Volume 109, Number 113 edition, Newspapers.com.

322 "Suicide and Insurance," accessed July 5, 2022, https://www-jstor-org.proxy.libraries.rutgers.edu/stable/1332606?seq=2.

323 "Shiroff v. Weiner, 299 Pa. 176 (1930) | Caselaw Access Project," accessed July 5, 2022, https://cite.case.law/pa/299/176/.

324 "Man Kills Himself In Movie Theatre; Motive Not Known," *The Philadelphia Inquirer*, June 29, 1927, Newspapers.com.

325 Asa Cadwallader, "Philadelphia Was 'Wet as the Atlantic Ocean' in 1920s," The Temple News, February 24, 2020, https://temple-news.com/philadelphia-was-wet-as-the-atlantic-ocean-in-1920s/.

326 Lavner, Fred. *Izzy: The True Story of Philadelpia's Most Arrested Carer Racketeer.* Novelco Publishing Group, 2021. p, 54.

327 Lavner, p 69

328 "Adverse Childhood Experiences (ACEs)," Centers for Disease Control and Prevention, n.d., https://www.cdc.gov/violenceprevention/aces/index.html; Holly C. Wilcox et al., "Psychiatric Morbidity, Violent Crime, and Suicide Among Children and Adolescents Exposed to Parental Death," *Journal of the American Academy of Child & Adolescent Psychiatry* 49, no. 5 (May 2010): 514–23, https://doi.org/10.1016/j.jaac.2010.01.020.

329 See, for example, Julie Cerel, John R. Jordan, and Paul R. Duberstein, "The Impact of Suicide on the Family," *Crisis* 29, no. 1 (January 2008): 38–44, https://doi.org/10.1027/0227-5910.29.1.38; Elizabeth A. Cutrer-Párraga et al., "Three Sibling Survivors' Perspectives of Their Father's Suicide: Implications for Postvention Support," *Journal of Child and Family Studies* 31, no. 7 (July 2022): 1838–58, https://doi.org/10.1007/s10826-022-02308-y; Natalie C. Hung and Laura A. Rabin, "Comprehending Childhood Bereavement by Parental Suicide: A Critical Review of Research on Outcomes, Grief Processes, and Interventions," *Death Studies* 33, no. 9 (September 18, 2009): 781–814, https://doi.org/10.1080/07481180903142357; Wilcox et al., "Psychiatric Morbidity, Violent Crime, and Suicide Among Children and Adolescents Exposed to Parental Death"; Carl-Aksel Sveen and Fredrik A. Walby, "Suicide Survivors' Mental Health and Grief Reactions: A Systematic Review of Controlled Studies," *Suicide and Life-Threatening Behavior* 38, no. 1 (February 2008): 13–29, https://doi.org/10.1521/suli.2008.38.1.13.

330 "Our City's Workers and What They Do," *Evening Public Ledger*, October 13, 1921, Newspapers.com.

Chapter 10

[331] Howe and Libo, *How We Lived*, 29.
[332] Sarna, *American Judaism*, 223-24.
[333] Sarna, 223.
[334] Howe and Libo, *How We Lived*, 45.
[335] Sarna, *American Judaism*, 223.
[336] Sarna, 164-75, 225, 283-85.
[337] Sarna, 224-25.
[338] Sarna, 166-67.
[339] Charles S. Bernheimer, "The Russian Jew in Philadelphia: General Aspects of the Population," The Museum of Family History, 1907, https://www.museumoffamilyhistory.com/ija-philadelphia-ptII.htm.
[340] Charles S. Bernheimer, "The Russian Jew in Philadelphia: Educational Influences," The Museum of Family History, 1907, https://www.museumoffamilyhistory.com/ija-philadelphia-ptVI.htm.
[341] Cowan and Cowan, *Our Parents' Lives*, 99.
[342] Cowan and Cowan, 105.
[343] Bernheimer, "Educational Influences."
[344] Bernheimer.
[345] Kaplan's thinking was, of course, much more detailed and nuanced than this. For further reading, see (as a primary and secondary source, respectively) Mordecai Menahem Kaplan, *Judaism as a Civilization: Toward a Reconstruction of American-Jewish Life*, second paperback edition (Philadelphia, PA: Jewish Publication Society, 2010); Scult, *The Radical American Judaism of Mordecai M. Kaplan*.
[346] Murray Friedman, ed., *Jewish Life in Philadelphia, 1830-1940* (Philadelphia: Institute for the Study of Human Issues, 1983), 70-71, 286-88; Sarna, *American Judaism*, 259-61.
[347] Orlando Figes, *The Story of Russia*, First edition (New York: Metropolitan Books/Henry Holt and Company, 2022), 166.
[348] Friedman, *Jewish Life in Philadelphia, 1830-1940*, 288.
[349] Mike Szilagyi, "Philadelphia Trolley Beginnings," Philadelphia Trolley Tracks, n.d., http://www.phillytrolley.org/Phila_trolley_history_1924/Phila_trolley_history_1924.html.

350 Allen Meyers, *The Jewish Community Around North Broad Street*, Images of America (Charleston, S.C.: Arcadia Publishing, 2002), 7–8.

Chapter 11

351 Howard Morley Sachar, *The Course of Modern Jewish History*, 5th ed. (New York, New York: Dell Publishing Company, 1958).

352 Irving Howe, *World of Our Fathers: The Journey of the Eastern European Jews to America and the Life They Found and Made*, 30th Anniversary Edition (New York University Press, 2005), 618.

353 Mary Antin and Werner Sollors, *The Promised Land*, Penguin Classics (New York: Peguin Books, 2012), 186.

354 An article in the Jewish Exponent claims that he had been involved from the start, which is unlikely (but not entirely impossible.

355 Jerry Edelstein, "Black Business Is Good-But Only With Preparation," *The Jewish Exponent*, January 22, 1971.

356 David Englander, "Policing the Ghetto Jewish East London, 1880-1920," *Crime, Histoire & Sociétés / Crime, History & Societies* 14, no. 1 (2010): 29–50.

357 Sarna, *American Judaism*, 277–93.

Afterword

358 Pew Research Center, "Jewish Americans in 2020," May 11, 2021, https://www.pewresearch.org/religion/2021/05/11/jewish-americans-in-2020/#fnref-34764-15.

359 "Age Distribution among Jews by Religious Attendance," Pew Research Center, n.d., https://www.pewresearch.org/religion/religious-landscape-study/compare/age-distribution/by/attendance-at-religious-services/among/religious-tradition/jewish/; "Age Distribution among Christians by Religious Attendance," Pew Research Center, n.d., https://www.pewresearch.org/religion/religious-landscape-study/compare/age-distribution/by/attendance-at-religious-services/among/christians/christian/; Zach Dawes, "Many U.S. Synagogues Experiencing Membership Growth or Stability," Good Faith Media, May 23, 2022, https://goodfaithmedia.org/many-u-s-synagogues-experiencing-membership-growth-or-stability/.

360 Scult, *The Radical American Judaism of Mordecai M. Kaplan*, 50.

[361] Nicole Ward and Nicole Batalova, "Frequently Requested Statistics on Immigrants and Immigration in the United States," Migration Policy Institute, March 14, 2023, https://www.migrationpolicy.org/article/frequently-requested-statistics-immigrants-and-immigration-united-states#immigrants_now_historically.

Genealogical Sources

Ancestry.com. "1891 England Census." Online database. Provo, UT, USA: Ancestry.com Operations, Inc., 2005.

———. "1900 United States Federal Census." Online database. Lehi, UT, USA: Ancestry.com Operations, Inc., 2004.

———. "1920 United States Federal Census." Online database. Provo, UT, USA: Ancestry.com Operations, Inc., 2010.

———. "1930 United States Federal Census." Online database. Provo, UT, USA: Ancestry.com Operations, Inc., 2002.

———. "1940 United States Federal Census." Online database. Provo, UT, USA: Ancestry.com Operations, Inc., 2012.

———. "1950 United States Federal Census." Online database. Lehi, UT, USA: Ancestry.com Operations, Inc., 2022.

———. "Pennsylvania, U.S., Federal Naturalization Records, 1795-1931." Online database. Lehi, UT, USA: Ancestry.com Operations, Inc., 2011.

———. "U.S., City Directories, 1822-1995." Online database. Lehi, UT, USA: Ancestry.com Operations, Inc., 2011.

Ancestry.com and the Church of Jesus Christ of Latter-day Saints. "1881 England Census." Online database. Provo, UT, USA: Ancestry.com Operations, Inc., 2004.

"Jewish Records Indexing-Poland," n.d. www.jri-poland.org.

JewishGen: The Global Home for Jewish Genealogy. "JewishGen," n.d. www.jewishgen.org.

Temple University Libraries Digital Collections. "Steamship Ticket Purchase Ledgers." Accessed July 5, 2022. https://digital.library.temple.edu/digital/collection/p16002coll16

www.ingramcontent.com/pod-product-compliance
Lightning Source LLC
Chambersburg PA
CBHW040639100526
44585CB00039B/2792